BEHAVIOR AND ORGANIZATION:

O & M AND THE SMALL GROUP

BEHAVIOR AND ORGANIZATION:

O & M and the Small Group

ROBERT T. GOLEMBIEWSKI
University of Illinois

RAND McNALLY & COMPANY, CHICAGO

RAND MᶜNALLY POLITICAL SCIENCE SERIES

MORTON GRODZINS, *Advisory Editor*

To My Small Group:
Peg, Alice, Hope, and Geoffrey

PREFACE

THERE ARE MANY REASONS WHY BOOKS GET WRITTEN. A MAJOR factor in the writing of this book is an uncomplicated conviction: too little is being done to transmit to students, in usable form, the results of behavioral research which have implications for organization study and practice.

This profession of conviction is not uncommonly heard. Indeed, supporting the position that something must be done about getting the results of behavioral research to the student is much like being in favor of virtue. Everybody favors it, there is great disagreement about what it means, and few people have done much to attain it.

This may seem too strong. The position, however, is reasonable and accurate. Certainly, elements of the behavioral research have affected teaching about organization and administration. Thus the "participation hypothesis" has been a common one in business administration, although its impact upon public administration has been less marked. But such osmosis of behavioral research into disciplines concerned with organization and administration has been of a very general sort, without the specification of the complex conditions under which certain relations may be expected. Some of the literature on leadership styles, for example, takes on the spirit of an old-fashioned revival meeting, the spirit being necessary to carry one over the gaps in the research.[1] This approach is esthetically unpleasing. More practically, it is bound to be self-defeating, for things are just not as simple as the common generalized formulations, and the truth will come out soon enough. That very little was known

[1] See the review of this literature in Robert T. Golembiewski, "Three Styles of Leadership and Their Uses," *Personnel*, XXXVIII (July-August, 1961), 34–45.

vii

about such intervening conditions until recently certainly explains the general nature of the literature, but does not change the verdict.

In reviewing the vast body of literature in small-group analysis which has been energetically developed within the last few years, the author became convinced of the applicability of that literature to the needs of the less-advanced student of organization and administration. The very favorable reaction to a brief development of this conviction in the *Public Administration Review* cinched matters.[2] Hence this effort, which attempts to integrate small-group findings and a broad range of behavioral research in an organization context. Another book resulting from these explorations, *The Small Group: A Critical Analysis of Research Concepts and Operations*, will be published by the University of Chicago Press. The reader may well graduate from the present book to this second volume.

The attempt here, then, is to provide material intended primarily for instructional purposes. Hopefully, the treatment also helps to shape the emerging theory of the small group in an organization context. But the primary emphasis of the book binds the treatment in two ways which will be emphasized in turn.

First, methodology will be emphasized below. The methodological recitation may strike the sophisticated reader as somewhat stuffy, but it has its point. It is simply not possible to understand behavioral research without having some sympathy for the nature of the natural-science approach to phenomena. Moreover, traditional patterns of thinking about organization and administration, most often implicit, must be set in proper perspective if behavioral research is to have its maximum impact. The emphasis upon methodology does the job. Finally, this book hopes to provide the student a suitable framework for work (perhaps his own!) which is still undone. Only the emphasis upon methodology touches both of these bases.

Second, the emphasis upon instructional use urged placing the treatment within an organization context. The context chosen is a reorganization of the Patent Office in the United States Department of Commerce. This attempt to drive home the

[2] "O & M and the Small Group," *Public Administration Review,* XX (Autumn, 1960), 205–12.

practical applications of behavioral research was not made scot-free. A major cost is the non-uniqueness of the treatment. That is, many theories may explain the reorganization of the Patent Office, especially given the time gap between the reorganization and this analysis. Consequently, again, this treatment is not so much an evidence for a theory as it is an instructional tool. Something is lost because of the fact. The cost is bearable, however, given the intention to cater to the needs of the student who is interested in seeing how one carries out such an analysis in such a situation.

A book, of course, is never written by one person. This author, however, must be particularly conscious of his debts to others, especially to those dedicated scholars who have built the literature of the small group. Some of these scholars are singled out in footnotes; many others could have been cited. The cliché, then, applies in this case: this book could not have been written without the contributions of many scholars.

Some other debts can be acknowledged more specifically. Though their contributions varied in extent and kind, I am particularly grateful to Professor James W. Fesler of Yale University, Professor Morton Grodzins of the University of Chicago, and Professor James G. March of the Carnegie Institute of Technology. Participants in a sixteen-week seminar on organization theory at the Rock Island Arsenal during 1961, who pretested this book, will see the imprint of their influence at numerous points. The Princeton University Research Fund supported some of the research, while the intensive investigation of which this book is one product was begun while the author was a Falk Fellow at Yale University.

Robert T. Golembiewski

Urbana, Illinois
September, 1961

TABLE OF CONTENTS

BEHAVIOR AND ORGANIZATION:

O & M and the Small Group

AN INTRODUCTION
TO TEACHERS AND STUDENTS

KNOWLEDGE ABOUT ADMINISTRATION AND ORGANIZATION HAS accumulated at a ballistic rate in recent years. "Mathematical" and "behavioral" suffice as labels to classify much of the research which has thrust forward the boundaries of our knowledge at a dizzying pace on a bewildering variety of fronts.

The work labeled "mathematical" covers a number of esoterically-named approaches to the phenomena of organization. "Operations research," "linear programing," "queuing theory" —at best curiosities a few short years ago—have amply demonstrated their usefulness in coping with a wide variety of management problems. These and similar mathematical approaches, it is safe to say, will revolutionize the way in which organization phenomena will be observed and handled. Consider only one sign of the times. The Ford Foundation is sponsoring a series of Mathematics Institutes—in one of which the author participated during the summer of 1961—for teachers in schools of business. The cost of such Institutes is already in six figures. All this to encourage the mathematical sophistication required of students of administration by recent advances, the pace of development having been so rapid that most graduate programs have not been able to do the job even for recent graduates.

"Behavioral" research, similarly, also has been bullish. It is not news that behavior is important in organizations, of course. But, for the first time, it has become possible to describe and predict behavior with substantial confidence. Thus personality and group properties permit description of a clarity beyond that possible even a few years ago. We are beginning to know what really goes on in organizations, in short.

1

This rapid progress well serves research purposes. The excitement attendant on the opening of new areas of knowledge generates the atmosphere in which ever more sophisticated additions to knowledge will be made ever faster. Certainly this is desirable in any science.

It may seem like crying with a loaf of bread under one's arm, but the extension of knowledge about administration and organization implies substantial problems. One is of particular relevance here: the challenge posed to the teaching of courses in organization and administration, in whatever discipline, and especially at the introductory level. The pace of development, in sum, has intensified the always-present problem of transmitting new knowledge to students.

This is a problem of abundance, rather than of scarcity. Thus it is pleasant, as problems go. But more than a pleasant feeling is necessary to capitalize on the opportunities offered by the new research, for a satisfactory solution of the transmission problem will infect the student with the enthusiasm felt by his teacher. It will also give the student the best current information. This is, of course, the dual process by which teachers become more effective.

Given a less favorable solution, the best that can be hoped for is a kind of controlled schizophrenia on the part of the teacher. Thus his own strivings and interests in new research must be compartmentalized from what he is teaching. The teacher must be unsatisfied under these conditions, and—unless he is a fine actor—his students also will feel the anxiety which makes teaching more difficult. If the teacher combines the rare talents of a Pagliacci—if he can, figuratively, laugh on the outside and cry on the inside—his students may be satisfied. But they will have been deprived of a more intense learning experience. In either of these cases, the learning experience will have undesirable features.

An optimum solution of the transmission problem, however, is seldom attained. The reasons for this unfortunate state of affairs may be outlined, with only slight simplification, in terms of three alternatives which presently may be open to the teacher.

The teacher, first, may direct his students to the research literature. This alternative, however, is often unavailable even in advanced undergraduate courses because of the practical problems involved. Moreover, little ground can be covered in this way, for much time must be spent on problems which are tangential at best to the purposes of a course in organization or administration. Finally, such an approach is often unsuitable for undergraduate courses.

These difficulties do not license neglect of the research literature. Neglect is impractical, for it avoids materials which could involve the student more intimately with his subject matter. One cannot trifle with students' attitudes. In a real sense, the best foot must be thrust forward early, and kept there.

The teacher, second, may direct his students to specialized courses in other departments. This is often desirable for advanced students. Even in their case, however, the major problem is the effective stress upon the relevance of the specialized work for the extradepartmental students' major interest. The problem is not always neatly solved. Understandably, such courses must cater largely to the training of departmental students. Thus any such course is likely to be too specialized for the needs of students outside the department.

The degree of "overspecialization" varies, of course, among the several traditional disciplines. But historical differences between disciplines still tend to be strong, even though interdisciplinary work is given much lip service. Consequently, integrative difficulties of an intense degree may obtain, what with the attempted mixture of several types of training, several promotion ladders, and the like.

In any case, this second alternative is not suitable for the less mature student for many reasons, practical and pedagogic.

The teacher, third, may hope for the best reflection of the new research in existing texts. Indeed, this is the only reasonable alternative open to most teachers of courses in organization or administration. This is not necessarily a counsel of despair, but it has a nasty habit of ending up as such, for substantial reasons. Two major ones will be emphasized.

First, the inevitable time lag between research and text sets more or less strict limits on the reflection of new research in texts. The lag varies in relation with three conditions. The first is the pace of new developments. Physics is the classic example of a discipline whose fantastic advances of the last decade or so have left its texts trailing woefully behind. The

3

recent outbursts of research activity in the area of organization and administration, then, will lengthen the time lag between research and text.

The second condition related to the research-text time lag is the degree to which the new research differs from the fundamental approaches in existing texts. More will be made of this later. For the present, note only that the approach of "behavioral research" and the approach of most texts are basically—and to a great degree, irreconcilably—different. This, of course, will lengthen the lag between research and textbook availability.

The third condition affecting the lag is the tendency—characteristic of texts in both business and public administration—for one or a few "leading ladies" to set the tone of texts which appear in the area. This tendency has two major consequences. Writers and publishers, first, are influenced by the prevailing stereotype of the "successful text." There is no need to challenge the dictum that one backs a winner. Under many circumstances, this is apt counsel, but it just happens to be the case that this strategy implies a built-in lag in digesting new findings. This lag will be particularly great in periods (such as the present one in behavioral research) of vigorous research activities.

A second consequence of the "leading lady" effect is more important, reflecting the "law of the conservation of energy in textbook writing" and complementing the "leading lady" effect. This "law" provides that the probability is very high that new research findings will be crowded into subsequent editions of texts written some time before, which sell well, or will find their way into newly-written texts which, however, are patterned on the style of the "leading ladies."

The fit is not always comfortable. To illustrate, consider the case of one of the best-selling texts in public administration. The first edition of this text emphasized almost exclusively the "statics" of administration, that is, the formal organization, rules and regulations, and the like. A later edition contained a few brief references to the famous Hawthorne experiments—some of which by this time were a decade or more old—and their implications for administration as "dynamics," that is, as something more than formal organization and all the rest. Such material was fitted in between the paragraphs of the earlier edition, with whose emphasis it could not have been less at home. A subsequent edition released a decade later was only a little more successful in making peace between the native emphasis and the increasingly-prestigious but still-interloping emphasis.

This may be an extreme example. Certain disciplines have made a more marked reorientation of texts in organization and administration since World War II. But there is no need to argue the point. The general tendency is marked enough in existing texts in all relevant disciplines to validate the general position, despite sometimes substantial deviations.

This tendency in texts *is not* perverse. Such books do a good job, within their limits. And it is reasonable that they cannot presume to do everything. But the effect of such reasonable limits cannot be avoided. The new research—and especially the *different* new research—tends to be neglected.

A second major reason for the failure of texts to reflect the new behavioral research is more elemental. In brief, most texts do not provide a comfortable home for new research, for the basic assumptions underlying the text differ from those which guided the research.

The existing differences are basic ones. Thus most texts dealing with administrative and organization phenomena emphasize the formal organization and related considerations. This is a legitimate focus. But the emphasis does reflect a choice (often implicit) of two related factors: a theory of what is important in administration or organization; and a methodology—the "how to do"—for studying these important somethings.

Some limits are necessary in early work to define any problem area. One cannot observe everything in every way even if one wished to do so. The dilemma is this: the choice of such limits must be made *before* enough is known about the subject-matter area to permit a satisfactory choice! The dilemma is a dangerous one, but careful explicitness can prevent undesirable consequences. Much of the literature, however, does not meet this test. The early limits of the study of organization phenomena tended to rigidify. They became *the* limits of work rather than convenient and flexible boundaries to guide work as far as they will permit, and only that far.

Thus the recent behavioral research must fashion new theory and methods. It must also conquer the old. In the sharpest terms, the early theoretical and methodological commitments operate to exclude (or to encourage the milk-toast presentation of) a "behavioral approach." Some recent texts do evidence

5

a greater-than-usual concern with the basic questions of theory and methodology. Most texts avoid such questions, however. This helps to explain the heavily descriptive rather than analytical nature of the texts.

There is no monolithic explanation of the nature of texts, but several elements seem prominent. Thus a descriptive approach is patently important. Company X could hardly operate without a production-control unit, you see, and this is how it is organized. Moreover, the descriptive approach also implies less of a research burden, for it seems to avoid the problems of theory and method. That is, the "why" and the "how" of the description of production-control units appear to be quite straightforward. But they are not. Of course, most students are agreed on the "why" and "how." This only makes the matter seem straightforward, however. Indeed, this agreement is precisely what encourages the time lag between research and text.

Of course, it is interesting to know that the Green Company organizes Department Y into units a, b, and c. For some purposes, indeed, this information is crucial. But it has strict limits. Thus such information tells us little about why Department Y is an effective (or ineffective) department, or whether the actual patterns of behavior in the department are consistent with those prescribed by the formal organization. Behavioral research, in contrast, provides some of this information.

This second reason contributing to the time lag between research and text is a vital one which will receive explicit treatment in the body of this book. For the present, only the basic inhospitality between the methodological assumptions of most texts and the methodology underlying the new behavioral research need be stressed. This inhospitality is understandable, for the text tends to reflect the research yesterday and its guiding assumptions. But the effect remains.

Three alternative paths to the transmission of knowledge about recent research relevant to organization and administration, then, have been reviewed. This book provides a fourth alternative, which takes the form of a review of one line of behavioral study —the analysis of group properties and their consequences for performance in organization—in the context of the reorganization of low-level work processes in an organization.

The approach here has its plusses and its minuses. Thus, on the negative side, it considers only a sample of the work which is revolutionizing study and practice in organizations. But this fourth approach does have saving graces. Most broadly, the effort complements and supplements existing texts dealing with organization and administrative phenomena, whether of the "public" or the "business" variety, in a way presently unavailable in the literature. More specifically, the effort will have relevance for a broad spectrum of approaches to organization phenomena which includes courses in "human relations" (with their emphasis upon behavior), courses in organization (with their mixed emphasis on behavior and structure), and courses in production or Organization and Methods (with their emphasis upon formal and mechanical factors). In addition, the book is written on a level which should make it a serviceable introduction to the more complex problems of research. Its basic purpose, however, is to introduce students to the new behavioral research.

The shape of this fourth alternative can be blocked out more clearly in terms of the several emphases which it encompasses. First, the book deals with what is perhaps the most outstanding of all the new behavioral research areas, small-group analysis. A wide variety of behavioral research from other areas, in addition, is employed when appropriate to extend the group research in terms of things already known. Topics like "frustration" and "conflict," for example, frame the group research in a broad behavioral theory applicable to life in organizations.

The growth curve of small-group analysis is impressive, and its findings are of great theoretical and methodological—and thus practical—significance. There need be no anxiety, then, concerning the book's orientation to recent research. Nor need there be any reservations about the applicability of such research.

Second, the book deals with small-group analysis in the context of an approach—Organization and Methods or, briefly, O & M—common to many disciplines dealing with coordinated human behavior in organizations. Moreover, the book deals with a specific O & M application and attempts to isolate the inadequacies of theory and method which underlay the application. Thus the danger of a lack of relevance of small-group analysis to organization and administrative phenomena ought to be minimized.

Third, the book deals with small-group analysis treated so as to be most useful *and* least complex. There is, of course, a tension between these intentions. In general, however, the thornier problems of small-group analysis can be successfully avoided for all but research purposes. At the same time, albeit with some care, the substantial honesty of the treatment can be respected. This has disadvantages, to be sure. The more advanced student soon will have to be referred to more technical—and thus less simplified but more useful—treatments for further guidance of specific research interests. The heavy loading of illustrative material will serve to demonstrate the potency and nature of small-group forces to all students, however, and organization study should profit.

Fourth, the book attempts to provide an explicit theoretical and methodological base for small-group analysis *as it applies* to some of the problems encountered in O & M applications. This is not as sticky as it sounds, fortunately. It is well learned in any case. The present lack of miscibility of O & M and small-group analysis cannot be understood except through a comparison of their respective basic assumptions (and, thus, their respective limitations). This very practical consideration encourages the effort below. Moreover, some relatively simple, but basic, distinctions between types of theories and their related methods will accomplish two purposes. These distinctions will provide a satisfactory analytical home for existing small-group studies, and they will provide a useful framework for interpreting or carrying forward future behavioral studies in an organization context.

Fifth, the book is conceived of as contributing to the great problem of the study of organization and administration: the reconciliation of the formal emphasis and the behavioral emphasis. These emphases have tended to be isolated. They are, however, two approaches to a single subject matter. Thus their isolation is unfortunate and, in the long run, cannot be tolerated.

As one student remarked, it is inadequate to study the "organizations without people" implied by the formal emphasis. Nor is it adequate to study the "people without organizations" sometimes reflected in what is called "human relations." This book, if nothing else, attempts to bring off some part of this reconciliation. And it does so in an area in which the formal emphasis has been dominant, but in which the behavioral emphasis has a patent application.

1

AN INTRODUCTION TO O & M

THIS SLIM VOLUME HAS EXPANSIVE AMBITIONS, WHICH MAY BE summarized briefly. The book proposes to contribute to the integration of two approaches to the study of organization which have been compartmentalized: the "formal approach" and the "behavioral approach." They will be distinguished in some detail below.

The motivation of this volume also is capable of simple summary. The separation of the two approaches has detracted from the study of, and teaching about, organization. This separation cannot long be endured, however. The existing commitment to organized effort is so pervasive that no less than full knowledge of the problems and the products of attempts to coordinate human behavior is acceptable.

The emphasis here on the isolation of the two approaches is not pious tongue-clucking about the failure of many students to make an obvious connection. There were ample reasons for the separation of what are two related approaches to the same phenomena. For example, the "formal approach" has a longish history. The behavioral study of organization, in contrast, has but fairly begun. This time lapse made difficult the integration of the two approaches. The point of this effort, then, is simply this: The last few years, especially, have seen the accumulation of a significant body of information relevant to behavior in organizations. Indeed, this is the Age of the Atom in a social as well as a physical sense. The recent growth of knowledge of the basic constituents of social organization—of the "atoms" of personality characteristics and of the "molecules" of group rela-tions—parallels that of the earlier growth of knowledge of the basic constituents of physical organization. Similarly, also, knowledge of social organization taps forces which rival the magnitude of those unleashed by atomic fission and fusion.

Simply, not enough has been made of the relevance of such behavioral study to the "formal approach" which has character-ized the study of productive organization. And time is a-wast-ing, especially in communicating existing knowledge to students of organization.

A PREVIEW:

LONG- AND SHORT-RANGE OBJECTIVES

The attainment of the expansive ambitions of this volume, to preview the long-range argument, involves four major steps. This and the following chapter, first, deal largely with the "formal approach" to organization. The specific focus of this analysis will be an Organization and Methods (O & M) appli-cation in a federal agency, the Copy-Pulling Section of the Patent Office. Both agencies lie within the mammoth United States Department of Commerce.

A second major step may be labeled "transitional." Chapters 3 and 4 carry the burden of this second step. They aim to indicate the points of connection between the formal and the behavioral approaches to organization within the specific con-text of organization theory.

Chapters 5 through 7, third, comprise a "behavioral" step, for they provide some of the building blocks—variables which describe important properties of small groups—of a sophisticated approach to organization as behavior *within* a formal framework.

The last three chapters take a fourth and final step. They are "integrational" in approach and reflect two emphases. These chapters argue for the usefulness of small-group variables in O & M applications, and they outline the costs of the failure to integrate a behavioral approach with the formal approach of O & M applications.

But the ambitions of this volume cannot be achieved with an outline. The immediate contribution to these ambitions in this chapter, to preview short-range aims, is the brief description of the genus "formal approach" to organization. The basic underlying question, then, will be: What does the "formal approach" consider important in organizations? A following chapter will be more specific. It will illustrate the answer to this underlying question through an analysis of a 1946 O & M application to the Copy-Pulling Section of the Patent Office. O & M is, in effect, one of the species of work within the broader genus "formal approach" to organization. The genus "behavioral approach" also will be described and contrasted with the "formal approach" to organization.

The Formal Approach to Organization

The "formal approach" to organization can be outlined accurately in terms of the shadow cast by the work of one man, Frederick W. Taylor. This focus is admittedly arbitary. The contributions of many others are required to etch in the details of the genus "formal approach." Indeed, Taylor was not the first to take this approach to organization. And, most relevantly, Taylor in many respects provided an extreme example of work in the tradition. But the focus does have its point. An analysis of Taylor's efforts, with only a little simplification, provides a workable outline of the "formal approach" to organization.

"Shadow" is, from one point of view, an inappropriate figure of speech to apply to work in the "formal tradition." It is as substantial as the proverbial broad side of a barn. Thus the manipulation of formal or mechanical elements in organization often has been spectacularly successful. As a result, work in the "formal tradition" is enormously influential in the study and practice of organization.

This success is illustrated by the first application of Taylor's "workshop management" to the loading of ingots of pig iron for shipment by rail. Prevailing work patterns among handlers of the ingots yielded an average daily work load of less than thirteen tons per man. Taylor's analysis, however, led him to conclude that a first-class workman should be able to handle forty-seven tons per day. Four basic changes, however, were required:

1. that only husky men be selected for the work;

2. that the work pattern be prescribed in detail;
3. that premium rates be paid to workmen; and
4. that rest periods be utilized to permit the more efficient distribution of energy.

Taylor's predictions proved accurate. The changes increased production more than threefold, while the unit cost of handling pig iron dropped sharply; and the work force was reduced substantially, although wages rose 60 per cent.

No wonder, then, that Taylor's precise studies of the "time and motion" of workmen often were accorded enthusiastic receptions. "Taylorism," or the "Taylorian system," included a bewildering variety of techniques and methods, but the common emphasis was upon the primacy of planning and supervision, based upon the minute observation of work. For example, Taylor's observation of men and materials—with stop watch, scale, and tape—led him to the conclusion that upwards of 50 per cent of labor and materials might be wasted due to improper planning and supervision. He often was successful in achieving substantial reductions in these losses, again by precise observation and often brilliant technological insight. These economies, expressed "in specific terms of minutes, cents and ounces," drew favorable attention, if not adulation.[1] Even labor unions were numbered among the enthusiasts for Taylorism.

Taylor looked at organized behavior in what was then a unique way. His basic approach was the catalyst for a complex revolution in the study and practice of organization. Thus it is important to know how Taylor conceived his work. The analysis of his conceptions will not apply with equal force to all who have worked with the "formal approach" to organization, for the approach has its heroes and its heretics. Taylor's "system," however, does provide a useful block outline of this related work.

Taylor distinguished three main levels of concern, running the gamut from specific tools to quite vague notions about the normative limits of their applications. These three levels are: (1) "mechanisms," or techniques; (2) "underlying principles"; and (3) "essence," or "fundamental philosophy."[2] Each of these levels of concern deserves brief description.

[1] A. Shaw, " 'Scientific Management' in Business," *Review of Reviews,* XLIII (March, 1911), 327.

[2] See, especially, Frederick W. Taylor, *The Principles of Scientific Management* (New York: Harper, 1911), pp. 128–30; and Dwight Waldo, *The Administrative State* (New York: Ronald, 1948), pp. 48–51.

The "mechanisms" of Taylor's "system," first, seem to imply no difficulties. They are techniques for physical measurement. Thus Taylor emphasized "Time study, with implements and methods for properly making it . . ." such as a stop watch, a scale, a tape.[3]

These "mechanisms," as they reflect what Taylor thought was significant in organizations, must be evaluated in these terms: "Yes, but. . . ." The reason for the "yes" part of the evaluation is straightforward, for there can be no argument with the position (for example) that reducing the distance a worker must walk in performing a task often will make him more efficient. And the Taylorian "mechanisms" certainly sparked a useful revolution in the way in which work was looked at.

But such "mechanisms" cannot be dismissed so lightly. The "but" part of the evaluation of the "mechanisms" concerns the assumptions which underlay them. Three related assumptions suffice to suggest the bases of Taylor's work.[4] First, he emphasized the *mechanical aspects* of work. Commonly, for example, Taylor and his followers referred to organization as "a complex and delicate machine." Indeed, his followers went so far as to see this logical implication of their work: a set of nicely-meshing relations in society as a whole, which brave new world was significantly called (with all seriousness) "The New Machine." This curious case of the tail of work wagging the dog of society was an outgrowth of the frenetic desire to control the work situation. In brief, it was realized that an individual's social experience—his loves and hates and the meanings he gave to things—affected the individual's behavior in organizations.[5] Hence his social experience required control. But this position also implies this revealing assumption of work in the "formal approach": when reality did not fit the "mechanisms" of stop watch, scale, and tape, the attempt was made to change reality rather than to accommodate the "mechanisms" to it. This is a harmless game, as long as one does not coax himself into acting as if a *desire to change* people to think and act consistently with the dictates of the "mechanisms" were the same as *an actual change*. The delusion—as will be documented later—was not

[3] Taylor, *The Principles of Scientific Management*, p. 128.

[4] Relatedly, see the insightful analysis in James C. Worthy, *Big Business and Free Men* (New York: Harper, 1959), pp. 62–79.

[5] Leon P. Alford, *Henry Lawrence Gantt* (New York: Harper, 1934), pp. 264–77.

13

avoided in the "formal approach." Society was, or should be, mechanical. It was all the same in the "formal approach."

Second, consistent with this emphasis upon mechanics, Taylor was interested only in what may be called "partial man," or "physiological man." That is, he was not interested in "real people," in "whole men" as they exist in an emotional, social, physiological altogetherness. He was interested in only those characteristics of man which served the limited purposes of his "complex and delicate machine." Or to put it another way, Taylor was interested in *abstract functions* which he organized in "the one best way." Man was of interest only so far as he performed such functions; he was a cog in Taylor's mechanical system. Whatever else the individual brought to his work in addition to his physiological properties was, as far as Taylor was concerned, largely irrelevant. The flavor of Taylor's orientation in this regard is clearly reflected in this dictum, which he never tired of repeating: "In the past man has been first; in the future the system must be first."[6]

Third, and relatedly, Taylor assumed the necessity of *minute specialization*. This is in keeping with the two assumptions outlined above, that of work as mechanics, and that of man as a performer of a particular simple function rather than as a complex entity. To illustrate the point, Taylor consistently attempted to separate "thinking" and "doing." As he instructed his workers: "You are not supposed to think. There are other people paid for thinking around here."[7] The aim, then, was to break jobs into component specialties, to integrate these specialties as the wheels and levers of a watch, and to control men in the consistent performance of their simple function.

Taylor's assumptions of what was significant in organizations, and the "mechanisms" developed to observe and record these significant factors, hindered as well as aided the study of organization; for the "mechanisms" of physical measurement, in effect, cut off the "formal approach" from many of the behavioral phenomena associated with work. Thus the application of Tay-

6 Frederick W. Taylor, *Scientific Management* (New York: Harper, 1947), p. 7.
7 Frank B. Copley, *Frederick W. Taylor, Father of Scientific Management* (New York: Harper, 1932), I, 189.

lor's "mechanisms" will be of limited usefulness if behavior *is not changed* as physical measurements indicate it *ought to be*. Indeed, just such a case of limited usefulness will be analyzed in subsequent chapters. This analysis has a patent conclusion: the integration of the "formal approach" and the "behavioral approach" is compelling. The study of the physical and behavioral aspects of work will each be more complete to the degree that each makes provision for the other.

But such techniques did not exhaust the content of Taylor's system. He realized that, in themselves, the techniques provided no direction for his work. The techniques were neutral. Two other major concerns in Taylor's system, then, centered on the normative question: What ought to be done with the techniques and the results to which they led? Taylor's handling of this question is often unclear, but he thought an answer was required.

The "underlying principles of management" reflect, in part, Taylor's concern with the purposes to which the techniques of "scientific management" were to be put. He isolated four "great underlying principles." They are:

First. The development of a true science.
Second. The scientific selection of workmen.
Third. His scientific education and development.
Fourth. Intimate friendly cooperation between management and the men.[8]

These "principles" raise more problems than they answer, however. On the most general level, they are patently meant to be directions for, and limits on, the use of the Taylorian techniques. Thus the "development of a true science" is the goal of the application of Taylorian techniques. Similarly, "intimate friendly cooperation" seems to have been a limit precluding the use of the Taylorian techniques to coerce effort, as by a "speed-up." But Taylor's "principles" are weak on specifics. Thus, given the goal of a "true science," Taylor did not develop what this meant in any precise sense. Nor did he give specific content to "intimate

[8] Taylor, *The Principles of Scientific Management*, pp. 36–37.

friendly cooperation." Indeed, in practice, Taylor's applications of his own techniques (to put it mildly) often were met by violent resistance.

The "essence" of the Taylorian system also implied a general set of limits on the use of the techniques of scientific management. Thus, in some contexts, the "essence" of Taylor's approach simply (as above) consisted of "a certain philosophy [that is, in Taylor's meaning, a set of normative values to be attained], which results . . . in a combination of the four great underlying principles of management." In a second sense, the "essence" of the system was an intended combination of two elements: the end of class conflict between worker and management, and the objective study of productive relations.[9]

This second meaning of the Taylorian "essence" requires analysis. Patently, of course, the two elements of this "essence" might be at cross-purposes. But Taylor's apparent goal was the use of his techniques in a double-barreled way. Thus the "objective" study of productive relations should make work easier and more remunerative for the worker, and more profitable for the employer. Taylor realized his techniques might increase class conflict if the time-and-motion experts approached their task "subjectively," that is, if they kept only the interest of management, or of the workers, in mind. He was, however, apparently sanguine about this possibility, even though he knew that applications of his technique would invariably be paid for by management. Such applications, reasonably, would tend to be more solicitous of management's short-run interests.

In sum, then, Taylor conceived of "scientific management" as involving two general classes of factors, one empirical, the other normative. The empirical factors concerned the objective study of the work situation. The normative factors set limits for the development of models of more efficient productive systems. Illustratively, Taylorian engineers were not free to prescribe a forced-labor system, no matter what its efficiencies of cost, for such a system was precluded by the general normative limits Taylor sketched. That is, it would heighten rather than reduce labor-management conflict.

The development of Taylor's general system, however, has

[9] *Ibid.*, p. 130.

not been a balanced one. Thus, on the empirical side, Taylor and others did develop tools for the observation and analysis of organization phenomena. On the normative side, however, he was less successful in the development and explanation of the value limits on the use of his techniques. Indeed, Taylor himself often gave the impression that the more efficient system simply sprang from the data describing any work situation. But, in his better moments, he dissociated himself from such sleight-of-hand. He realized that his techniques, and the results to which they led, were neutral. That worker x shoveled y pounds of material z, for example, may be an important observation. But these data do not answer such normative questions as: How many pounds should a worker shovel per hour? and Which techniques may be utilized to encourage or force him to do so?

Despite (or, more probably, because of) the failure to spell out the normative limits of applications of the Taylorian system, however, its applications often yielded "favorable" results. And since nothing succeeds like success, the Taylorian approach to organization spread far and wide. Indeed, early practitioners were so taken by their success that they attributed it to a mystical "vital element" which "compels extension of the area of its influence after a nucleus has been established at any point."[10]

"Vital element" aside, the quotation describes with reasonable accuracy the fate of Taylor's work. The quotation refers only to work processes at more or less the same organization level, and to how the improvements derived from the Taylorian approach at one work station force similar "horizontal" improvements in related work stations.

But the quotation also applies to distinct lines of development of Taylor's approach. To explain, the "nucleus" was, of course, work such as that of Taylor with pig-iron handlers. Early work was applied to only the "lower," more routine aspects of organization. Thus one student concluded that "Taylor did not go beyond the foreman. . . ."[11] Taylor himself implied a similar emphasis when he defined the "art of management" as "know-

[10] H. S. Person, "The Development and Influence of Scientific Management," *Advanced Management*, V (October-December, 1940), 189.

[11] Norman M. Pearson, "Fayolism as a Necessary Complement to Taylorism," *American Political Science Review*, XXXIX (February, 1945), 69.

17

ing exactly what you want men to do, and seeing that they do it in the best and cheapest way."[12] This "nucleus" supported a number of lines of development which took two major tacks. One line concentrated upon more minute analysis of the job than Taylor employed. A second line of development extended the approach to "higher" organization levels. As with Taylor's work, both lines of development emphasized empirical areas (e.g., the use of the slow-motion picture camera for observation). Normative factors have been understressed.

In job analysis, first, Taylor's work inspired a large volume of research on work motions. Early pioneers, for example, thought it possible to develop a set of "basic movements" for which "standard performance times" could be determined. This was a more precise approach than that of Taylor, but it was in the same tradition. Hopefully, these basic movements could be arranged so as to result in the "one best" pattern for the performance of any task. The eighteen "therbligs," or basic movements, developed by the Gilbreth husband-wife team constitute the best-known system of this kind.[13]

Recent research has demonstrated that the therbligs are not the interchangeable units the Gilbreths assumed they were. The performance time for any therblig depends upon a number of unknown and complex conditions, especially on relatively difficult tasks. But some industrial applications of various "basic movement" systems have been developed. Thus one such system provides sets of time data for these therbligs: reach, move, turn, grasp, position, disengage, and release. Each therblig, however, has several standard times. Thus the standard time required to "reach" depends upon whether the hand was previously in motion or at rest, the accuracy required to "reach" the desired object, and so on. The use of such "basic movement" systems, however, has been limited. Thus two students conclude that

At present, time standards for industrial jobs are still usually estimated directly, and only in a minority of cases are they synthesized from standard data on component units. The

12 Frederick W. Taylor, *Shop Management* (New York: Harper, 1912), p. 21.
13 F. B. and L. M. Gilbreth, *Applied Motion Study* (New York: Sturgis and Walton, 1917).

human organism, even when it is regarded as a neurophysiological "machine," has proved far more complex than pioneers like Gilbreth hoped and expected when they undertook to analyze human work into its component therbligs.[14]

Second, Taylor's work encouraged the close observation of various work movements which led to the development of the "principles of motion economy." This was a less demanding approach than the determination of therbligs and their associated standard times, for the principles provided general guide lines for the design of jobs rather than specific time standards. Many sets of such principles have been developed. However, a few illustrations from the twenty-two principles offered by Barnes suggest their nature:

1. The two hands should begin as well as complete their motion at the same time.
2. The two hands should not be idle at the same time except during rest periods.
3. Motions of the arms should be made in opposite and asymmetrical directions and should be made simultaneously.[15]

Third, the "nucleus" of Taylor's work also encouraged extensions from the factory into administrative work. Thus "office management" and "Organization and Methods" (O & M) must be reckoned among the progeny of Taylor's pathfinding studies. Both of these approaches to organization deal with the planning of routine administrative work. In a nutshell, they extend the Taylorian approach from pig iron to papers (the processing of which is a major burden in routine administrative work).

The focus below will be upon one O & M application. Thus it will suffice here to distinguish briefly such planning of routine administrative work from the other types which derived from Taylor's early work. The essential distinction is one of degree,

[14] Reprinted with permission from James G. March and Herbert A. Simon, *Organizations* (New York: Wiley, 1958), p. 16.
[15] R. M. Barnes, *Motion and Time Study* (New York: Wiley, 1949), pp. 556–57.

sometimes sharp, sometimes blurred. The distinction is this: "Office management" and O & M are more concerned with the problems of work flow, that is, of the *interrelation of tasks*. The types of related work discussed above, in contrast, stress the analysis of *specific tasks*.

These several types of work stemming from Taylor's contributions patently have their differences of focus and method. But this diversity derives from elements common to Taylor's work and the three offshoots reviewed above. That agreement hinges upon the major implicit premise that the prescribed pattern of work, or the formal organization, is the essence—if not the entirety—of the study of man's attempts at coordinated human behavior. The aim is the construction of a model whose properties mesh nicely with one another. This is a legitimate aim, but its pursuit encourages the neglect of the diversity of behavior which is likely to exist in the actual performance of any task. This neglect is significant. As a very practical consequence, for example, it becomes impossible to account for such common facts of organization life as this: two work units, with identical formal structures and similar staff, may differ widely in output.

Thus, in greater or less degree, the types of work reviewed above neglect man's behavioral diversity. They assume that individuals are essentially physiological beings for all practical purposes. Illustratively, little explicit provision is made for the properties of individuals which do not seem directly relevant to a task. For example, Barnes's interest in the individual (in the three rules cited above) is restricted to such questions as whether or not individuals have the physical coordination to perform the required movements. Thus such work is characterized in this volume as the "formal approach" to organization.

Several preliminary conclusions, then, are in order. Primarily, some foundation upon which to build has been established, but several following chapters will be necessary to understand fully the "formal approach." Moreover, the "formal approach" to organization need not be denigrated, for it has great value. But, finally, the "formal approach" has distinct limits. Two will be stressed. Individuals often do not behave as the "formal approach" intends. Moreover, and perhaps more striking, increased output does not necessarily result when individuals do behave as the theory of the "formal approach" intends.

20

The burden of the following three chapters will be the more specific description of these two limits. Chapter 2 will describe an O & M application as a case study of the "formal approach" in action. Chapter 3 will present a set of guide lines for evaluating the adequacy of the "formal approach" and, more specifically, of the O & M application. And Chapter 4, using these guide lines, will evaluate the O & M application as it represents the "formal approach."

The Behavioral Approach to Organization

Such an effort in subsequent chapters must be based upon at least preliminary evidence that the assumptions of the "formal approach" in fact do limit its usefulness. This section will provide this preliminary evidence.

The success of the formal approach to organization must not be overvalued, for, to set the record right, the influence of the Taylorian tradition has been extended beyond its competence. The spectacular failures of the approach which have been reported from time to time establish the point. Parenthetically, it is no easy matter to determine the precise degree to which an application of the Taylorian "system" really pays its way. A full-fledged application of the "system" in its early days, to explain, would include a wide variety of changes which would have more or less easily measurable effects on output. For example, the use of the so-called high-speed steel for machining purposes or of improved belts to drive machines might have easily demonstrable effects on the flow of work. Other elements of the "system," however, might make cost comparisons difficult. Thus new cost accounting methods might lower costs in the sense that they provided more precise estimates of costs which also happened to be lower than the rough guesses which they replaced; and the increases in the indirect labor which usually accompanied applications of Taylorism might be charged to "overhead" rather than to "production," and/or might be concealed in more accurate and sometimes lower estimates of "overhead."

A simple example, the "Case of the Raincoats," will serve the present purpose of illustrating the limits of the "formal ap-

21

proach."[16] A total-assembly-by-individual-operator system had been used on the job for some time. A stable level of production under this "total" system, however, was interpreted as meaning that the operators were producing at the physical peak for that system. Consequently, the job was reorganized. The changes made reflect the Taylorian tradition. The operation was broken up into a number of suboperations, each of which was assigned to one or more operators. The emphasis was upon changes in the physical characteristics of the job and the adjustment of operations in the "delicate system" characteristic of the "formal approach." No attention, in contrast, was paid to the meaning of the changes to the employees and how such meaning might affect behavior.

Changes in the work system were to yield productivity increases. The bias toward formal features, however, did not prove adequate. After a generous learning period, output had decreased appreciably rather than increased! In addition, operator dissatisfaction grew. Management reverted to the "total" pattern. The results of this change-back also dramatically reflect the limits of the assumptions underlying the reorganization. Productivity sharply increased when the "total" system was reinstituted, and increased significantly beyond the level which had been assumed to be the maximum for the "total" pattern. Moreover, operator satisfaction also markedly increased.

In a nutshell, the "formal approach" is indispensable for engineering a task, that is, for breaking a task down into its components, determining how each component might be performed most effectively, and so on. But the "formal approach" is not always adequate when it comes to *organizing* the results of such *engineering*.[17] That is, this core question faces the "formal ap-

[16] Burleigh B. Gardner and David G. Moore, *Human Relations in Industry* (Homewood, Ill.: Irwin, 1950), p. 202. The interested reader may consult with profit the account of the biggest "failure" of the Taylorian approach, in Hugh G. J. Aitken, *Taylorism at Watertown Arsenal* (Cambridge, Mass.: Harvard, 1960). A strike in 1916 stemmed from an attempted time-and-motion analysis and, as a result, stop watches were banned in government facilities until August, 1949!

[17] The analysis is spelled out in detail in Robert T. Golembiewski, "Organizing Work: Techniques and Theories," *Advanced Management*, XXVI (January, 1961). The argument takes this general form: the general practice has been to assume that the "formal approach" applies to organizing as well as engineering of tasks. Much evidence is presented which shows this is simply not the case. Organizing is a distinct process,

proach": How are the bits and pieces which are engineered to be put together? For, as in the "Case of the Raincoats," different patterns of organizing work will be evaluated differently by different people.

This is not the place for a full-dress development of the position that the "formal approach" has been insensitive to such questions about organizing work, especially since the point will be amply demonstrated. A general conclusion serves present purposes. Failures of the "formal approach" often result from the attempt to make a mechanics do where a psychology is also necessary. Sometimes, in sum, an awareness of physiological or technical characteristics is sufficient to permit successful prescription of patterns of organizing work; often, however, this awareness is far from adequate empirically.

Such findings should not be surprising. Indeed, the importance of behavioral factors was implicit in the earliest stages of the development of the "formal approach" to organization phenomena. Taylor's stress on the "principle" of "intimate friendly cooperation," in fact, is the general emphasis for which a comprehensive behavioral approach is required. Taylor's observation was a practical one, of course, for it revealed that he learned early—as did the workers—that one could "beat the system." Thus it is too much to claim, as some students have done, that Taylor's "principle" foresaw today's advanced behavioral knowledge.[18] But the development of behavioral knowledge does square with Taylor's goal of a "true science" of organization. No "true science," indeed, could exist without a sophisticated behavioral underpinning.

Work based directly upon Taylor's efforts demonstrated the limits of his approach. Three lines of development from Taylor's time-and-motion work were reviewed in the previous section. A fourth line of development—the research beginning with the famous Hawthorne experiments—had the unintended consequence of showing that the basic assumptions of Taylor's work were inadequate. This research is the mother lode, as it were, of

with its own unique rules. Such factors as the grouping of component operations, span of control, type of supervision, and form of formal organization were analyzed to suggest the nature of these handy rules for organizing.

[18] H. S. Person, "The Genius of Frederick W. Taylor," *Advanced Management*, X (January-March, 1945), 7.

the "behavioral approach" to organization. Paradoxically, the integration of such work with the "formal approach" has been made only incompletely.

In brief, then, this fourth line of development evolved from the "formal approach." But it has been, so to speak, a black sheep. Both features may be illustrated in a brief review of some of the work at Hawthorne.

The Hawthorne experiments were a blend of the formal and behavioral approaches. They reflected their Taylorian pedigree in their design. Early study designs, to illustrate, concentrated upon the relation of physiologically-based factors (e.g., illumination and humidity) and output. But design had to give way to results. These experiments turned into pathfinding, if preliminary, demonstrations of the marked effects of behavioral factors in the work situation. Thus one guiding prediction held that output varies directly with illumination. As a matter of fact, however, output increased continuously in the test group while illumination was varied widely. Indeed, production did not drop until illumination was reduced to the level of ordinary moonlight. As one commentator summarized these unexpected results:

> In the illumination experiments, therefore, we have a classic example of trying to deal with a human situation in non-human terms. The experimenters had obtained no human data; they had been handling electric-light bulbs and plotting average output curves. Hence their results had no human significance. That is why they seemed screwy . . . the results were not screwy, but the experimenters were [in their] notion of a simple cause-and-effect, direct relationship between physical changes in the workers' environment and the responses of the workers to these changes.[19]

The weight of such findings has not yet forced the mating of the "formal approach" and the "behavioral approach." But both approaches are necessary, for either approach in isolation neglects important organization phenomena. Behavioral and formal factors exist together, complexly interwoven.

[19] Fritz J. Roethlisberger, *Management and Morale* (Cambridge, Mass.: Harvard, 1950), pp. 10–11.

The Normative Approach to Organization:

Organization Theory and Values

Work in the Taylorian tradition also has been criticized—when applied to humans—because of its insensitivity to value elements. That is, the "formal approach" to organization inadequately handles questions of *what ought to be the case*. Such questions will be called "normative," or "value," questions. The difficulties of the "formal approach" with empirical problems, of course, were sketched immediately above.

Despite the possible unfamiliarity of the terms "normative" or "value," the concept to which they refer ought not to prove too troublesome. The distinction between the empirical and normative aspects of organization can be illustrated by an out-of-field example. Assume that fifty murders per year are committed in city X. This is an empirical datum, an *is*. Such a datum may be useful. But its utility does not extend to questions like: How many murders *ought* there to be in city X? A normative choice must precede answers to such questions. Thus in the Judaeo-Christian tradition, the normative prescription "Thou shalt not kill" would supply the necessary answer.

Taylor sometimes acknowledged that a similar problem plagued his own efforts, as recounted above. But many exponents of the "formal approach" have attempted to duck the issue. Thus it often has been argued that there is a "one best way" to organize a particular job efficiently. Such arguments often imply a dollars-and-cents definition of "efficiency." But the choice of a dollars-and-cents definition of "best," or any other definition, implies a normative choice.

This analysis poses some of the normative problems of the "formal approach," albeit few answers. The persevering reader will find a similar pattern in the following pages. This it not to say, however, that the reader may let his values go to sleep on him. Indeed, he must be alert to weigh the values implicit in two contrasting approaches to organization phenomena, for the emphasis below will be upon an alternative to the "formal approach" which achieves at least similar results. This contrast of alternatives, of course, sharply poses this normative question which cannot be avoided: Which of the alternatives *ought* to be chosen? The lack of such a practical alternative has in the past encouraged the neglect of this question, but the present reader will not be able to take this convenient, if inadequate, approach.

An Introduction to the Proposed Synthesis

Long-current practice in the "formal approach" to organization reflects the empirical and normative inadequacies stressed above. But these inadequacies are not inherent in such work, which can be oriented—both empirically and normatively—around the important fact that organizations are composed of human beings. This conviction underlies the following reanalysis of an O & M application to low-level work processes in a federal agency.

This reanalysis, in sum, will have two focal points. Major attention will be centered upon two empirical factors: the inadequacy of the behavioral assumptions of the theory underlying O & M, and the usefulness of small-group theory in partially remedying this inadequacy. A normative problem—the value preferences implied by O & M—will receive less extensive attention. Thus it will be shown that knowledge of small-group behavioral uniformities could have been used to attain the goals of the O & M application, and this with different (and to this writer, more desirable) value consequences.

2

O & M AND THE PATENT OFFICE

THE USEFULNESS OF SMALL-GROUP THEORY FOR O & M WORK WILL be framed in the context of the case study "Production Planning in the Patent Office."[1] This illustration should serve three purposes. First, it should demonstrate the value of the integration of the "behavioral approach" and the "formal approach" in a type of situation which is often encountered in organization.

Second, the illustration does not deal with a straw man: indeed, it concerns an apparently successful O & M application. This skeletal history makes the point. In July, 1945, the Patent Copy Sales Branch of the parent Patent Office had built up a three-month backlog of work. The O & M study and reorganization of the agency's formal work process took place over the next few months. These efforts bore apparently ample fruit. Thus, by mid-1946, the time for processing an order had dropped to approximately three days. Moreover, unit costs were substantially lower. In addition, although requests for patent copies increased by approximately 20 per cent, a reduction in force was made in the agency's Copy-Pulling Section in the first half of 1946 from fifty-four to forty-four employees.[2]

Third, the illustration also has the virtue of demonstrating the

[1] Harold Stein (ed.), *Public Administration and Policy Development: A Case Book* (New York: Harcourt, 1952), pp. 1–13. Arch Dotson is the author of the case. The O & M application also is analyzed in Executive Office of the President, Bureau of the Budget, *Production Planning and Control in Office Operations* (Washington, D.C.: Government Printing Office, 1949).

[2] "Production Planning in the Patent Office," p. 13.

27

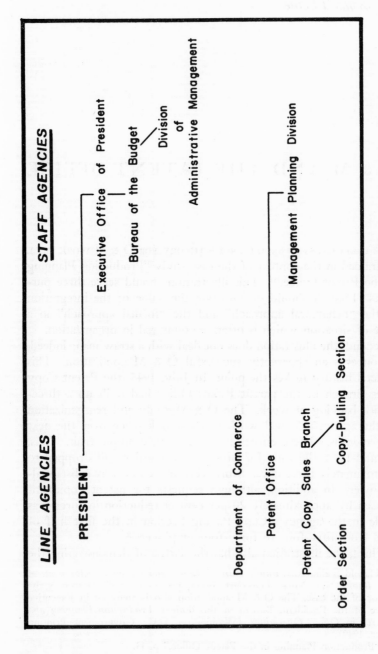

FIGURE 1. *Agencies Involved in the Reorganization of the Patent Office, 1945-46*

TABLE I

Copies of Patents Sold, Patent Copy Sales Branch
1939–46

	Fiscal Year	Copies of Patents Sold
Ending June 30,	1939	4,041,895
	1940	3,961,541
	1941	4,021,821
	1942	3,407,088
	1943	less than 3,000,000
	1944	less than 3,000,000
	1945	4,202,423
	1946	4,540,625

Source: Data are from the *Annual Reports* of the Commerce Department for the fiscal years 1939–47.

importance of such situations. The end of the European phase of World War II precipitated a flood of requests for patent copies. Table I suggests the sharp upturn in orders after a major wartime slump. But the table tells only a partial story, for output did not rise as sharply as demand. A backlog, therefore, quickly grew to alarming proportions. This was reason enough for management concern. In addition, the delayed processing of patent requests would have a significant impact on the economic recovery to a peacetime footing, which would be hectic even under the best of circumstances. This impact was heightened, of course, by the fantastic technological progress of the wartime period. Patent copies were thus all the more important. The backlog in filling patent orders, then, was of some consequence.

THE AGENCIES INVOLVED

The reorganization of the Patent Office involved several agencies of the federal government. Figure 1 conveniently depicts the agencies concerned with the reorganization.

As might be expected, most of the agencies involved were in the Commerce Department. The backlog in the Patent Copy Sales Branch, indeed, was considered serious enough to be one of the first orders of business, in late 1945, for Caspar Ooms, the new head of the Patent Office, who quickly organized a Management Planning Division as an executive staff to aid in the reduction of the backlog.

Extradepartmental aid came from representatives of the Bureau of the Budget's Division of Administrative Management. The Bureau is a staff agency of the President. The Division, in the immediate postwar period, actively promoted the introduction of "business methods" in government operations. The campaign took many forms, one of which was the direct involvement of the Division in such reorganizations as that of the Patent Office. Thus it was that the Division supplied much of the impetus toward, and direction for, the changes which were made in the work processes of the Patent Copy Sales Branch.

The dynamics of the reorganization worked themselves out in the general organization context outlined in Figure 1. However, only a portion of this broad context will be emphasized below. Indeed, an analytical microscope will be focused on only a single agency, the Copy-Pulling Section of the Sales Branch.

This approach cuts two ways. The advantages and disadvantages stem from the attempt to know more and more about less and less. But the disadvantages are minimized in this case, for emphasis here is upon the evaluation of the organization changes prescribed by the O & M application, which were credited with the sharp increase in production during 1946 in the Sales Branch. The Copy-Pulling Section was the major obstacle to increased productivity in the Branch. Thus the focus will be narrowed below, but the narrowing has more support than convenience.

THE ORIGINAL WORK FLOW:

A "PARALLEL" ORGANIZATION

The problem in the Copy-Pulling Section perceived by the O & M teams centered on the pattern of work flow. This work flow, and the changes prescribed to increase production, are detailed in this and the following section. For convenience, January, 1946, will be considered the transition point. Pre-January, 1946, will be referred to as the "before condition," or BC. Post-January, 1946, will be referred to as the "after condition," or AC.

The BC organization of the Copy-Pulling Section was based upon the source of orders handled. There were fifteen types of orders classified by sources, although six types accounted for the bulk of the work. Each type was handled by different personnel in parallel lines. The report of the Budget Bureau's Division of Administrative Management characterized this work process in these terms:

> [The work process was] built around the various types of requests for patent copies (work items) received. Copies of patents are furnished to the public, for 25 cents each, in response to various types of orders. Small coupons (3″ x 5″), sold in books by the Patent Office, may be exchanged for copies of patents and used as order forms as well. On the other hand, some customers order by letter and send cash. Others maintain open accounts. Some have standing orders for copies of all patents issued in specified classes. Orders are distinguished also by origin (e.g., lawyers who rent windows for delivery of patent copies, patent examiners, and government agencies). . . . A different group of workers handled each order. The over-all flow of work was divided in parallel on that basis.[3]

Although the work process was organized in parallel lines according to types of sources of orders, however, common work steps were performed *within* each of the parallel work lines. These several common work steps were: coding and batching of orders, sorting of orders, pulling of copies of patents, and assembling (on the basis of the coding step) and mailing of orders. Figure 2 depicts the parallel work lines for the six major types of sources of orders, as well as the work steps which were common to all work lines. Cash and account orders, it should be noted, were processed through two additional accounting steps.

The Reorganized Work Flow:

A "Series" Organization

The collaborative research resulted in two kinds of action. One type concerned housekeeping matters: the storage areas were

[3] *Production Planning and Control in Office Operations,* pp. 21–22.

31

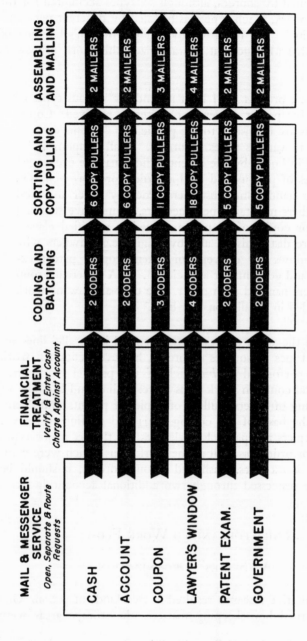

FIGURE 2. *Original "Parallel" Work Flow, Patent Copy Sales Branch*

Source: Executive Office of the President, Bureau of the Budget, *Production Planning and Control in Office Operations* (Washington, D.C.: Government Printing Office, 1949), p. 22.

policed (their BC state was poor); long-accumulated back copies were filed; and a concerted effort was made to reduce the backlog of the duplication of out-of-stock copies.

A second type of derivative action—to which a lion's share of the productivity increase was attributed in the case report— dealt with a fundamental change of organization. Operations were channeled, wherever possible, into a single flow. Thus coding and batching, sorting, copy pulling, and assembling and mailing no longer were done in separate channels for each type of order. The key to this channeling was the development of a "line item" slip. As the report of the Budget Bureau's Division of Administrative Management put it:

> By identifying the work item as a single "line item" (the number of copies of any one patent requested in a single order), it was possible to make *all work items essentially the same.* Each 3" x 5" coupon already represented a single line item: letters and lists could be converted to similar units by making out a 3" x 5" card for each patent listed, showing the copies ordered and an order number. It was then possible to combine the separate flows into one, to process all orders through common work steps, and to specialize the copy pullers by file-floor area (numerical segment).[4]

Two points require emphasis. First, such "line item" slips would permit a change in the organization, which had been based upon the different sources of orders. AC orders would be undistinguishable according to source. Second, making a "line item" slip for orders would mean an increase in work. The cost was expected to be far outweighed by the economics it would permit. Figure 3 graphically presents the new serial work flow.

A number of favorable consequences were expected to result from the channeling of work into four work stations. These consequences, it should be noted, often would occur only after the backlog had been reduced to control proportions.

1. The channeling was designed to reduce work-load fluctuations. The resulting daily "rhythm" was expected to induce

[4] *Ibid.,* pp. 22–23. Italics supplied.

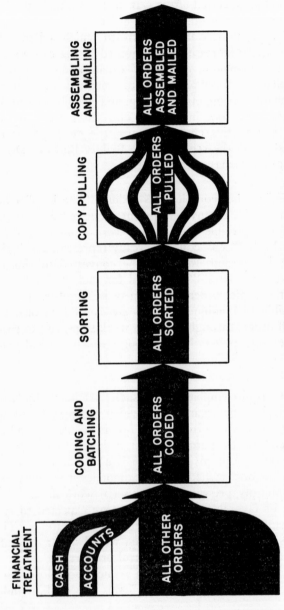

FIGURE 3. *The Reorganized "Serial" Work Flow, Patent Copy Sales Branch*

Source: Executive Office of the President, Bureau of the Budget, *Production Planning and Control in Office Operations* (Washington, D.C.: Government Printing Office, 1949), p. 23.

greater productivity. In any case, an uneven work flow through the parallel stations had characterized the BC work process. Operating statistics were not kept adequately before Ooms's management. These statistics, when gathered, explained the unevenness of flow: regular and violent daily fluctuations in the types of sources of incoming orders occurred, although the average daily volume of all orders was fairly stable. Channeling would require adjustment only to the limited daily variation of total orders. Patently, also, the more constant work flow would reduce the problems of gearing operations to a fluctuating volume of orders. For, with a fluctuating load, management would face such unattractive alternatives as gearing operations toward the high side of fluctuations, with potential unused capacity on slack days; and gearing operations toward the low side of fluctuations, with likely increases in backlog.

Figure 4 suggests the reduced fluctuations in orders which channeling would encourage. Thus BC fluctuations in individual lines were high. For example, the number of "Other Type Orders" received per day varied between approximately 225 per cent of its weekly average (on Tuesdays) to approximately 20 per cent of its weekly average (on Thursdays). In contrast, the daily variation in total orders (traced by the heavy black line in Figure 4) had a more restricted range: from a high of approximately 115 per cent of the daily average (on Fridays) to a low of approximately 80 per cent of the daily average (on Thursdays).

2. The channeling would permit efficiencies of scale through the mass sorting of coupons, forms, and letters containing orders. In the BC process, individual copy pullers had done their own sorting. Pulling and sorting in the AC process were functional specialties.

3. Combined operations would permit greater control of work flow. As one student explained:

With a large volume of orders moving regularly through a single channel, work could be dispatched according to a predetermined time schedule, thus establishing a rhythmic beat or tempo of work. The resulting even flow would make it possible to determine staff needs at each work station with greater certainty than before, to plan and check

35

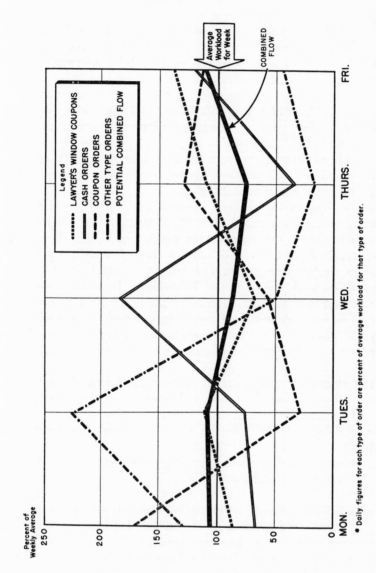

FIGURE 4. *Daily Fluctuations by Source of Orders versus Daily Fluctuations in Total Volume of Orders, Patent Copy Sales Branch, January 7-11, 1946*

SOURCE: Executive Office of the President, Bureau of the Budget, *Production Planning and Control in Office Operations* (Washington, D.C.: Government Printing Office, 1949), p. 25.

the progress of current work, and to provide a psychological stimulus to worker production.[5]

4. The combination of channels was expected, after the backlog was pared to manageable levels, to reduce the possible "fractional loss" encouraged by parallel lines of operations. "Fractional loss" occurs, for example, when a line has too much load for one worker and not enough for two. The more lines, the more possible fractional loss.

Table II illustrates the differences in fractional losses between a parallel and a serial organization of operations. The illustration is, of course, hypothetical, but parallel organization does tend to increase the probability of fractional loss.

There is an alternative to such greater fractional loss in a parallel system. It is possible to "save" on fractional loss by allowing a backlog to accumulate. Such an approach, of course, merely puts off the day of final reckoning unless such provisions are made as the periodic transfer of personnel from process to process in order to wipe out the backlog. The Copy-Pulling Section "saved" on fractional loss by allowing a backlog to develop, but no provisions were made for periodic reduction of the backlog to control levels.

These general changes affected the entire Patent Copy Sales Branch, but the special interest here is in the Copy-Pulling Section. The reorganization there fundamentally changed the copy-pulling task. Of course, copy pullers were deprived of the sorting of orders for copies by the channeling. Moreover, the AC basis of specialization for copy pullers was the area of the files. In contrast, the BC basis of specialization had been the source of orders. The BC work area of copy pullers was not specialized. Any copy puller might work in any area of the files.

The new areal basis of organization in the Section permitted the development of five *units* in the files. The units had roughly the same expected work load, as estimated by a sample taken from one week's orders. The areas covered by the units, however, varied considerably. *Segments*, in turn, were carved from each of these units. The segments had similar estimated frequencies of demand, but unequal areas. *Each segment* had one

---

[5] "Production Planning in the Patent Office," pp. 8–9.

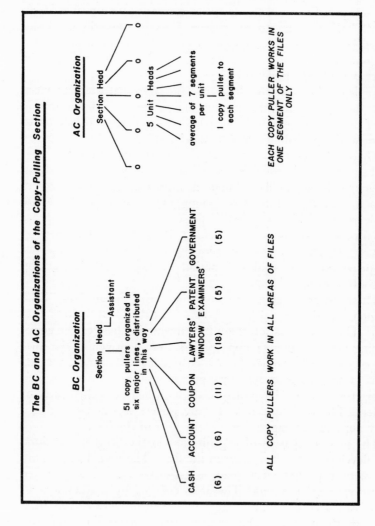

FIGURE 5. *The Copy-Pulling Section, Before and After the Reorganization*

TABLE II

An Illustration of "Fractional Loss" in Parallel and Serial Operations

(Per Work Day)	Parallel Operations							Serial Operations
	A	B	C	D	E	F	Totals	
Work Capacity per man	50	50	50	50	50	50		50
Work Load	70	80	85	85	60	80	460	460
Men Required	2	2	2	2	2	2	12	10
Fractional Loss, Parallel Operations								140 units, or 2.8 men per day
Fractional Loss, Serial Operations								40 units, or .8 of a man per day

permanently-assigned puller. The copy pullers also had responsibility for the maintenance of their segments.

This reorganization was expected to increase productivity by permitting a higher density of copy-pulling assignments. There had been much walking BC. The files covered approximately two and one-half acres of space, over all of which copy pullers might range in filling orders. The reorganization restricted any copy puller to one segment of one unit of the files.

This reorganization of the Copy-Pulling Section also opened a number of positions to be filled by promotion. The six most productive copy pullers prior to the reorganization were promoted to supervisory positions. Five of these onetime copy pullers were made Unit Heads. They supervised the copy pullers within each of the five units of the files. The Unit Heads, in turn, reported to a newly-promoted Section Head, who was another BC high producer in the Section. Figure 5 compares the BC and AC organization of the Copy-Pulling Section.

THE SHORT-TERM RESULT: FAILURE

The channeling of work into four stations and the area specialization of copy pulling—the two major characteristics of the reorganization described above—did not have the predicted consequences. Thus O & M personnel "living with" the agency after the changeover circumspectly noted the "persistence of a certain fluctuation in work loads after the channeling." This officialese may be translated simply: One of the four work stations was dragging its productive feet.

This "fluctuation" posed a difficult problem. Not that the solution was unclear. Elimination of the fluctuation, simply, would permit the work to flow evenly from one station to another. Moreover, the recalcitrant group was pinpointed: the Copy-Pulling Section. The problem was behavioral, as opposed to mechanical. As was explained:

> To achieve better staff distribution it was first necessary to know how many patent copies a copy puller could normally be expected to handle. Here, past experience actually proved to be an obstacle to proper orientation of the new procedure: it was a tradition in the Copy-Pulling Section that 300 copies were "a day's work." In spite of the fact that under the new system copy pullers worked in restricted areas where requests occurred at closer intervals, it appeared that custom and group opinion were restraining them from pulling more than 300 daily.[6]

SOME ADJUSTMENTS OF THE REORGANIZATION

Three "adjustments" were made in the face of this unexpected failure of the reorganization. First, a period of "experimentation" with varying work loads was begun to determine copy-puller capacity. That the assigned work loads were "to be done before a given deadline" suggests the coercive nature of this "experimentation." "Optimum capacity" was determined in this way.

The term "optimum capacity," however, is presumptuous. Practically, "optimum capacity" was the point at which the O & M teams were satisfied with output and/or the copy pullers could not be urged on to even greater output without the use of techniques which the O & M teams were unwilling or unable to apply. Thus a "satisfactory capacity" was attained, rather than an optimum.

[6] *Ibid.*, p. 11.

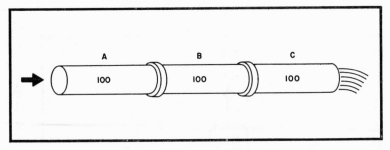

FIGURE 6. *Balanced Pipe Line*

In any case, the point reached was far above the informal limit of 300 copies per day. Sources differ as to the precise level of this "optimum capacity," but it was at least twice as great as the informal limit.[7]

A second "adjustment" made by the O & M teams was intended as a capstone of the determination of "optimum capacity." This was the inauguration in March, 1946, of a system for controlling the flow of work. By this time, production had increased substantially, but complaints that orders were not filled promptly were still being received. Two advantages were expected from the control of the flow of work. First, the processing of individual pieces of work could be monitored, and any stoppages could be readily identified and remedied. Second, work-flow controls (in the words of the author of the case study) "maintained production (a) by making certain that the work was brought to the worker when he was ready for it and (b) by establishing a rhythmic tempo to which the worker found it physically and psychologically easy to respond."[8]

The procedure developed for this control was not complicated. Batches of work were accumulated and mass-sorted twice daily, sent to the Copy-Pulling Section in two batches, and finally reached the Mailing Section in the same two batches. The batches, of course, had to be divided in each unit of the Copy-Pulling Section for assignment to pullers in the several segments

[7] *Ibid.* states that "as many as 800 or 900 copies a day were a reasonable pulling load under the new system." The Budget Bureau report (cited in note 1, above), however, notes that "the [initial] production rate [was] 300 copies per man per day . . . a reasonable load under the new system was nearly double the earlier figure." (P. 63.)

[8] "Production Planning in the Patent Office," p. 12.

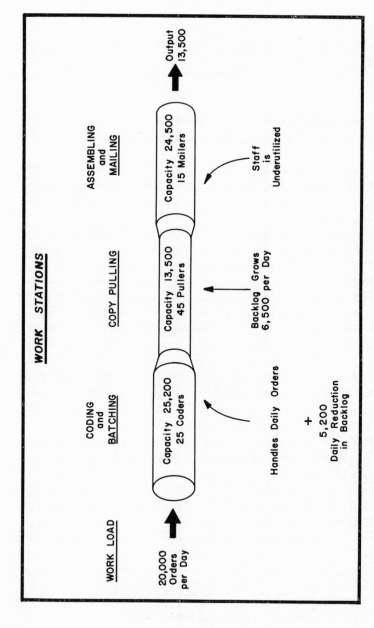

FIGURE 7. *Unbalanced Pipe Line, The Condition in the Patent Office, Early AC Stage*

of the files. But each *total batch* was handled as a unit for control purposes. A simple control sheet was used to check each batch of orders in and out of the several work stations.

The "balancing" of personnel at the several work stations, third, was a final adjustment. It complemented the reduced work-load fluctuation achieved by the AC reorganization. The combination of "balance" plus reduced fluctuation would yield greater control. This, in the starkest possible outline, was the equation which underlay production planning in the Patent Office. As the report of the Budget Bureau's Division of Administrative Management explained:

> A second major necessity for controlling the flow of work is balancing—provision, on a planned basis, for the proper number of personnel along the pipe line, so that each work station can economically handle a volume of work that is correct in relation to the capacity of other work stations. Only if the volume of work and the number of staff at each work station are related on a planned basis can there be assurance that work will flow without creating bottlenecks, without putting undue pressure on some workers while leaving other workers idle. Balancing also simplifies the job of scheduling by providing information on the capacity of the system and of each work station in it. [9]

In terms of a "pipe line," then, the objective of balancing can be illustrated by Figure 6, in which segments A, B, and C are staffed to handle 100 units of work per day.

This "pipe line" analogy underlying the Patent Office reorganization can be used to illustrate the nature of the work-process changeover. For purposes of illustration, only three of the work stations will be considered: Coding and Batching, Copy Pulling, and Assembling and Mailing. The early AC situation, roughly, can be characterized as in Figure 7. The figures are approximate, but, in essence, they reflect the actual condition.

Interpretatively, then, the early AC work process was an "unbalanced pipe line." The bottleneck was the Copy-Pulling Section. The 300-copy norm still limited productivity, despite

[9] *Production Planning and Control in Office Operations*, p. 55.

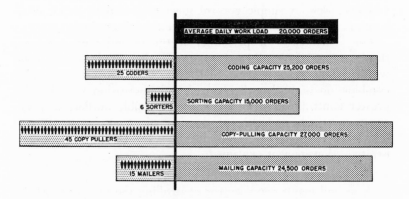

FIGURE 8A. *The Four Work Stations, Patent Copy Sales Branch, Before Balancing*

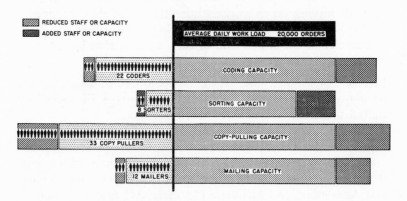

FIGURE 8B. *The Four Work Stations, Patent Copy Sales Branch, After Balancing*

Source: Executive Office of the President, Bureau of the Budget, *Production Planning and Control in Office Operations* (Washington, D.C.: Government Printing Office, 1949), p. 56.

the work-process change. As a result, the full capacity of the Assembling and Mailing station could not be utilized. Moreover, because the Coding and Batching station was not limited by the 300-copy norm, a backlog of partially-processed orders of patent copies grew.

The early AC "pipe line" could have been balanced by the addition of some twenty-two copy pullers, of course. The later AC "experimentation," however, sought the balance by increasing output. The goal was attained: output rose to at least 600 copies per day per puller. Thus the capacity of the Copy-Pulling station was raised to at least 27,000 copies per day, that is, 20,000 copies to meet daily demand and a 7,000-copy reduction of the backlog. All three work stations were producing at levels above daily demand.

With the backlog reduced to control levels, each of the work stations had excess capacity. Figure 8A graphically depicts this excess capacity, and Figure 8B reflects the staff reductions and additions necessary to balance the work stations. (Notice that the figures include the Sorting station which, for reasons of convenience, was not considered above.)

The Reasons for a Reanalysis:

Apparent Success and Long-Run Failure

The reorganization of the Patent Office illustrates a typical "formal approach" to a common problem in organization. If one follows the theory that one always backs a winner, there may seem ample reason to let well enough do in the Patent Office. The practical reader must respect the substantial increases in output resulting from the reorganization in what may be called the intermediate run. Tinkering with the theory underlying the reorganization, then, may seem dilettantish, if not dangerous.

But one cannot be satisfied with the predictive performance of the O & M application. Two factors, especially, demand a reanalysis. Thus the early AC failure of the reorganization to "take" underscores this position. Moreover, in the long run, a reorganization was necessary in 1948.

Both of these predictive failures can be traced, in some detail, to the neglect of behavioral factors in the O & M application, but it will be necessary to move slowly toward the analysis of such factors. Thus the following two chapters comprise a "transitional theme." They will outline some of the major dimensions of the complex analysis required. The prime purpose is the development of an analytical yardstick which will be put to two uses. First, it will be used as a standard to evaluate the "formal approach" of the O & M application. Second, it will be used as the foundation for demonstrating the relevance of small-group analysis for O & M and organization study in general.

3

ORGANIZATION THEORY AND PRACTICE: SOME PRELIMINARY DISTINCTIONS

Sometimes repetition of even the most elementary sort is useful, if only because it prevents the neglect of those things which are important. Such repetition is particularly useful here, for this chapter may seem somewhat beside the point of the analysis of an O & M application. But it most certainly is not; hence some repetition is in order to fix it firmly in the scheme of things.

This and the following chapter comprise a "transitional theme," linking the "formal approach," so prominent earlier, with the "behavioral approach." The latter will become an increasingly prominent emphasis in the chapters to come. These transitional chapters are, in a real sense, a linchpin. They will help in understanding a large number of important things about the "formal approach," and they also are a general sketch of the nature of a satisfactory approach to organization phenomena. In this sense, the "transitional theme" will do two basic jobs. Its constituent chapters will explain the predictive inadequacy of the O & M "formal approach" and they will outline the place of the "behavioral approach" in organization study.

These things can be done with an economy of words and with an almost painful simplicity. The plain fact, however, is that these few and simple words are uncommon, and thus tend to elude full comprehension. The uncommon, without care, often runs a poor second to the familiar but less useful. Fortunately, this chapter does not stand alone. It should draw support from, as well as contribute content to, the chapters which surround it.

Theory and Organization

The theme of this chapter is simple, if sometimes subtle: A satisfactory approach to organization study and practice requires a theory which combines the "formal approach" and the "behavioral approach." Perhaps "simple" overstates the case, for common usage conceives of organization as a bustling, a doing, a practice, which is down to earth and realistic. And "theory" is thought of as a direct opposite, as speculative, impractical, unrealistic.

This distinction is unfortunate, for theory is the very substance of our lives. We continuously predict the consequences of our actions, with more or less accuracy, whether the point at issue is stepping through a fifth-story window or studying for an examination. Moreover, we continually attempt to modify our working theories—that is, unless our original theory was bad enough to advise stepping out of the fifth-story window—so that they will permit more accurate prediction. The task is not an easy one. Note an obvious problem: the difficulty of tracing the consequences of our actions. That is, our working theories often cannot be tested easily to determine whether they have the results we expect them to have. But the practice of living as we intend is not a simple matter.

The same may be said of organization. It too depends upon a theory of how various purposes may be attained. The more adequately tested the underlying theory of organization, the more effective the derivative practice in organization. Thus the attempt to separate theory and practice in organization can have only unfortunate consequences.

This chapter, then, stresses the importance of theory to practice. This stress will be applied via the sketch of the senses in which the following proposition is an apt one: There is nothing so practical as a good theory. To balance matters, there is nothing so pernicious as an ill-conceived theory. Indeed, the bad reputation of theory stems from just this source. But it is bad practice and confused logic to toss out the baby with the bath water, to neglect theory because some theories have proved inadequate. The path of sanity is to become more sophisticated about which theories to accept provisionally, and which to resist. This chapter follows the path of sanity, and pays the price of an explicitness not required by the simple rejection of all theory out of hand.

Establishing the usefulness of theory will require some straightforward distinctions between three types of theories and the methods associated with them. These distinctions will help the reader to understand the character of the organization theory which underlay the reorganization of the Patent Office. They also are indispensable to understanding the nature of the more useful theory which must supplant the traditional theory of organization.

THREE TYPES OF THEORIES

The proposition that there is nothing so practical as a good theory lacks specificity, for there are several types of theories, each of which has its own usefulness and limits. Three types of theory will receive attention here. The purpose is the more precise specification of the boundaries of the practicality of each type.

The first type may be called *empirical theory*. Empirical theory has as its purpose the statement of the relations which exist in the physical or social worlds, that is, the statement of what is related to what. Thus an example of a proposition from an empirical theory is: The earth revolves around the sun.

This proposition is a commonplace. But it was not very long ago—an instant, measured in terms of man's history—when men were called fools (and worse) for supporting this proposition. The nature of empirical theory, then, can be illuminated by describing how man made this journey from ignorance to knowledge.

Empirical theory contrasts sharply with early beliefs of the relation of sun to earth. Thus it was believed that the earth *must be* the center of the universe. The rationale is straightforward and, granted certain assumptions, plausible. Man was made in God's image; thus man had to be the focal point of creation; and therefore earth, man's home, had to be the focal body of the universe. Eclipses were explained simply as unpredictable acts of God. Empirical theory started from quite a different base. Much information on eclipses, phases of the moon, and the like, had convinced a few early scientists that the earth revolved about the sun, rather than vice versa. This implied quite a different explanation of eclipses.

But the choice between theories was not straightforward, for the early scientists could not be certain that their conviction was correct, although it was consistent with available information. Logically, their theory had no firmer footing than the theory they challenged. Indeed, both theories were of this form: "If A, then B." More fully:

1. If (A) God wills, then (B) an eclipse will occur; and
2. If (A) the moon is in a certain position with respect to the earth as the earth revolves about the sun, then (B) an eclipse with predictable characteristics will occur at a predictable time.

Good enough. But only the B's of the argument can be observed, for God's will cannot be observed directly, and only space travel will permit the direct observation of the movement of the moon around the earth and the earth around the sun. Thus propositions of the type "If A, then B," must be handled gingerly. Moreover, it is illogical to argue that, because B is the case, A also must be the case. This unacceptable style of argument is known as the "fallacy of affirming the consequent." A homely example illustrates the point. Consider the statement: "If mother is cruel, baby will cry." Whenever baby cries, however, it does not follow that mother has been cruel.

Empirical theory often faces such a proof. The problem is the determination of which of many possible explanations for a particular event is appropriate. Sometimes both A's and B's may be observed, as in a controlled experiment in which an attempt is made to see that other factors do not affect the relations. But it is very difficult to control such factors, especially in the study of behavior. Unlike the atom, man can change his behavior when (for example) he reads the results of a previous study about it.

All is not chaos, however. Theories may predict accurately for the wrong reasons, and there may be many explanations of a particular event. But there is a way of choosing between theoretical propositions. Essentially, the utility of any empirical theory depends upon the ability to predict accurately the outcomes of similar events, and the continued extension of the theory to cover related phenomena. Thus any empirical theory is held tentatively, and only so long as it meets these two tests. Failing this, the theory must be modified or discarded. The early theory about eclipses, for example, could not predict the time of eclipses. It did "explain" eclipses, of course. Thus this theory was inferior to that based upon the earth's rotation about the sun. This is the case in the senses that the latter theory permitted the precise prediction of the time of eclipses, and it also explained and predicted related prenomena.

A good empirical theory, then, would benefit the practice of organization enormously, for organization implies the physical and social knowledge of what is related to what.

This an accurate position, but it is simplistic. Organization practice cannot wait until the world is explained scientifically. Organization practice always has faced the pressure of *now*. It gains but little solace from the research promises of tomorrow. This characteristic of organization practice implies a major problem. Given the pressure of *now*, accepted patterns of organization are likely to be based on (at best) a partially-tested empirical theory. Consequently, the task of empirical theory in organization study is twofold. First, work toward an increasingly comprehensive organization theory must be pushed forward despite pressures to leave well enough alone or (more usually) despite pressures to "watch the store." Second, organization practice must be continually shaken loose from the inadequate theory of yesterday.

Many practitioners, of course, are effective in spite of their suspicion of theory. (They have developed an empirical theory of their own, but prefer to call it "experience.") Even the effective practitioners, however, would profit from a comprehensive empirical theory, for it sums up the insights of many observers of organization behavior. Ineffective practitioners, of course, need well-tested empirical theory.

The second type of theory may be called *goal-based, empirical theory*. It is built upon empirical theory, but it is quite distinct from it. The point of distinction may seem minor, but it is crucial: empirical theory describes *what is;* goal-based, empirical theory prescribes *what must be done in order to attain what is desired*, based upon knowledge of reality. In contrast to empirical theory, then, goal-based, empirical theory takes a conditional form. Thus such a proposition would state: If you want to accomplish these purposes, then you must do A, B, and C. Patently, there can be many goal-based, empirical theories, one for each of the innumerable sets of goals or values which can be imagined. In contrast, there will be but one general empirical theory for any problem area.

This second type of theory has a crucial relevance for present purposes, for any application of an organization theory must be a goal-based, empirical theory. That is, assume that a complete empirical theory has been developed: we know what is related to what under which conditions in organizations. Such a theory does not directly prescribe, let us say, a pattern of organization. Only a goal-based, empirical theory can fill this bill, and such a theory develops in two stages. First, decisions must be made concerning what is desired. Normative or value choices, in short, are the foundation of goal-based, empirical theory. Then, second, empirical theory must be surveyed in order to determine which conditions must exist if the normative choices are to be achieved in practice. One of these stages alone cannot do the job of goal-based, empirical theory. For example, it is one thing to desire that men were angels. It is quite another to determine those empirical conditions under which men can (and will) be angels.

Goal-based, empirical theory, then, must have a prominent place in our attention. A good theory of this second type will be very practical indeed for organization purposes.

But this practicality of goal-based, empirical theory must be tempered by several substantial limitations. First, there cannot be *a* theory of organization. There are many possible theories of organization, deriving from the many possible goal bases of this type of theory. Thus an organization theory can be developed from the normative choice of "forced labor" as the technique which may be utilized to achieve organization purposes. This goal-based, empirical theory of organization would have wide normative limits: anything goes. Similarly, other theories could be developed around more restricted goal bases. For example, a goal-based, empirical theory of organization could be developed around such goal bases as the facilitation of friendly contact on the job. This character of organization theory, however, has not been acknowledged consistently. Most students present their version of *the* organization theory as applicable universally. This is understandable, if unfortunate. The early tendency in all areas of study is to presume a greater simplicity than exists.

Second, common notions about desirable behavior in organization may change. Organization theory, in short, must be dynamic rather than static. Illustratively, even a satisfactory goal-based, empirical theory of organization might obsolesce quickly. Traditional organization theory, in fact, has experienced just such a change: its implied normative preferences conflict rather sharply with more recently-developed preferences. This change in two fundamental normative notions—what organization ought to be like and what techniques may be utilized to support organization purposes—may be demonstrated briefly. Let the reader develop a mental picture of what he thinks organization ought to be like. This picture should contrast vividly with these excerpts from a list of work rules drawn by Zachary U. Geiger, dated April 5, 1872:

> 5. This office will open at 7 A.M. and close at 8:00 P.M. daily except on the Sabbath, on which day it will remain closed. Each employee is expected to spend the Sabbath by attending Church and contributing liberally to the cause of the Lord. . . .
> 9. Any employee who smokes Spanish cigars, uses liquor in any form, gets shaved at a barber shop, or frequents pool and public halls, will give me good reason to suspect his worth, intentions, integrity, and honesty.
> 10. The employee who has performed his labors faithfully and without fault for a period of five years . . . and who has been thrifty and attentive to his religious duties, and is looked upon by his fellowmen as a substantial and law abiding citizen, will be given an increase of five cents per day in his pay, providing a just return in profits from the business permits it.[1]

[1] These (and other) work rules were reprinted in the *Acme Steel News*, Acme Steel Co., Chicago, Illinois. They are reproduced in the *Journal of the Academy of Management*, I (August, 1958), 50.

Third, any application of organization theory—that is, any goal-based, empirical theory—must be evaluated in terms of affirmative answers to two questions: Are the goal bases of any organization theory normatively acceptable? and Does the theory reflect a knowledge of the empirical world sufficient to warrant a reasonable expectation that following the theory will achieve organization purposes? The first question, of course, poses a host of difficult judgments about which sincere men may differ, but which they cannot avoid. This feature does not make the development of a goal-based, empirical theory a simple matter. In addition, a "yes" answer to the second question presumes an empirical theory. The problems of the development of empirical theory have been outlined above. Goal-based, empirical theory falls heir to them. On two counts, then, this second type of theory is an analytical bearcat to handle.

A third type of theory will be called "utopian theory." This type must be distinguished carefully, for it is, at the same time, similar to and very unlike the two types of empirical theory. The failure to respect the senses in which utopian theory is very unlike the two types of empirical theories, in addition, has caused much grief in the study of social organization. There are, then, substantial reasons for emphasizing the character and role of utopian theory.

Two properties suffice to distinguish utopian theory from the two empirical types. First, utopian theory deals with (or is applicable to) aspects of the empirical world. Thus it is not ethical, or value, theory. Ethical theory deals only with desirable relations which ought to exist between man and man and between man and his Maker, rather than with the actual relations which do exist. The Ten Commandments, for example, are an ethical theory. Nor is utopian theory the same as logical theories, such as some mathematical structures, which are not testable because their properties have no empirical referents. Such differences, however, should not be interpreted in too strict a way, for a utopian theory may—and often does—imply or state some ethical preferences. And utopian theories can be tight logical structures.

In this first sense, then, utopian theory is like the two types of empirical theories, for all three types of theories deal with the empirical world. And they may be characterized by a high degree of logical rigor in their development. In addition, utopian theory and goal-based, empirical theory are alike in the respect that both may be based upon a set of ethical preferences-to-be-attained.

Second, and paradoxically, utopian theory is insensitive to empirical data at the same time that it deals with, or is applicable to, empirical relations. This is the case in two possible senses. Either the properties of a utopian theory will not have been tested, even though it is possible to do so. Or the properties of a utopian theory will not be changed, even when evidence demonstrates their inadequacy. Organization theory fell victim to both of these possibilities, but there is no need to get ahead of the story. The general characteristics of utopian theory will be applied to the analysis of organization theory in due time.

In this second sense, utopian theory is very unlike the two types of empirical theories. Indeed, they could not be two more different kinds of animals. The major dimensions of this difference may be touched upon. The properties of a utopian theory are fixed and unchanging. The properties of an empirical theory are provisional and subject to continuous challenge. Relatedly, propositions of both empirical types of theory depend upon their development from, and their test against, physical or social reality. But the propositions of a utopian theory are constructs of the imagination *which do not require empirical counterparts*. Thus a utopian theory might be developed from these two properties: that people have three hands, and that they obey orders instantly.

Utopian theories do not just grow, willy-nilly. The choice of propositions for a utopian theory, to be sure, is limited only by the imagination of the developer. But the treatment of these propositions is governed by the rules of logic, on the basis of which the propositions are developed into a comprehensive and consistent system. Thus utopian theory plays a wide field in its choice of basic propositions, but it treats these propositions very strictly.

If utopian theory seems uncommon, a few examples will serve to dispel the illusion. The early theory of eclipses, for example, was a utopian theory. Plane geometry also is. That is, both systems are based upon certain assumptions which are taken as given (e.g., a straight line is the shortest distance between two points). Logically consistent systems are then developed from these propositions. Illustratively, there are many possible geometries. Indeed, their number is limited only by man's ingenuity in developing sets of properties which are taken as the basic givens. Thus plane geometry conceives of space with two dimensions, length and width. Solid geometry builds upon three dimensions; other geometries endow space with four, five, and more dimensions. With it all, the properties of space (whatever number there are) are incompletely known.

It might seem strange to argue that utopian theory is practical, but it has its uses. First, utopian theory (e.g., plane geometry) serves the function of developing reasoning skills.

Second, utopian theorizing permits the development of models of the nature of things were certain conditions to exist, whether or not these conditions ever have existed or ever will exist. Such models are useful in suggesting the end results of what appear to be developmental trends, in isolating possible problems, and the like.

Third, utopian theory may aid the development of empirical theory. Thus it may suggest certain relations which may be tested empirically, although these relations were derived from propositions which were originally only convenient or interesting.

Fourth, the properties of a utopian theory may approximate reality closely enough to be useful for certain purposes. For example, there is no "space" corresponding to that assumed by plane geometry. "Space" in the real world, whatever its complete properties, is not restricted to length and width; nor is the shortest distance between two points necessarily a straight line. But plane geometry is useful for certain purposes, such as making a picture frame.

The use of any utopian theory must be monitored carefully, however. Two types of tests should be applied to theories of this type before they are used as patterns after which to model empirical relations. These are an empirical test, and a normative test. Empirically, the use of plane geometry to plan a transoceanic flight would be ill advised. Events would sharply demonstrate that the shortest distance between two points is not always a straight line, no matter how convincing the logical argument of plane geometry. Moreover, the propositions of any theory should be checked normatively before an attempt is made to pattern relations after the utopian system. That is, are the propositions of the utopian theory desirable? This question would be appropriate, for example, to the application of a utopian theory one of whose properties held that "efficient administration" required that all individuals should obey *all orders* from formal superiors without question.

Utopian theory and its characteristics must be noted carefully, for traditional organization theory, as will be shown, is essentially a utopian theory. This is understandable. The problems of development of the two types of empirical theory, plus the coercion of *now* in the practice of organization, forced the choice of the more convenient utopian approach. The application of this utopian theory of organization, however, has not been restricted by posing the empirical and normative questions outlined above. In large measure, the lack of knowledge of the properties of types of theories, and of their uses and limits, explains this convenient oversight.

The Stuff of Empirical Theory:

Concepts and Operations

The basic difference between the two empirical types of theory and utopian theory may be established more firmly. Unlike utopian theory, the two types of empirical theory cannot simply assume certain propositions and let it go at that. The more demanding process of deriving the stuff of empirical theory can be outlined broadly. The process further details the differences between empirical and utopian work.

Basically, the problem of empirical work is the isolation of the important "somethings" which describe the empirical world. That is, scientists do not go about counting the leaves on trees. They concentrate on less obvious, but more important, "somethings" such as "temperature," "humidity," "length," and "gravity." The tendency is to think of these "somethings" as somehow immutable, as being obvious always and ever. They were and are not, however. They are mere conventions for describing reality. Once unknown, they are convenient now, but may not always be useful.

The demonstration of the fragile nature of the stuff of the two empirical types of theory illustrates the problems of empirical work and further differentiates it from utopian theory.[2]

Consider "time," for example. What is it? Most people think they know, but most people are wrong, for "time" is not universal or unalterable. It has had many faces, and no doubt will have many more as prediction requires ever finer discriminations. Table III summarizes some major features of the development of our present notions of "time."

"Time," however, does have a general universal definition. It is defined in terms of two related elements: a *nominal* definition of "time," that is, a statement of what "time" is conceived to be; and an *operational* definition of "time," that is, a technique for the measurement of the "something" which has been defined as "time" and which is thought to be important in describing reality. But these related elements have changed, and probably will continue to change.

Thus there is no simple or constant answer to the question: What is "time"? The following table, for example, presents only a partial list of the combinatory answers to this leading question which were applicable at one point or another.

The progression, then, is from gross to fine nominal definition. Thus Conception I encouraged operational measures which are useful for rather limited, if sometimes important, purposes. Illustratively, it is useful to know that it is "the growing season," but it is of little help in catching the 8:15. Conception III, in contrast, encouraged the development of far more precise operational measures which (for example) may measure intervals as brief as one-thousandth of a second or less. Such accuracy is necessary only for scientific purposes, of course, but this greater specificity is the way of empirical theory.

Operationally, also, the movement is from less reliable to more reliable measurements. Measures of time based on the rotation of the earth around the sun cannot be constant, for the earth is slowing down due to friction. Thus the day is getting longer, although one would have to live a long time to notice any great difference. The operational definition of "time" in terms of

[2] The interested reader also may consult such sources as Carl G. Hempel, *Fundamentals of Concept Formation in Empirical Science*, Vol. II, No. 7 of the *International Encyclopedia of Unified Science* (Chicago: Chicago, 1952).

TABLE III

Elements in an Answer to the Question:
What is "Time"?

Nominal Definition	Operational Definition
I. "Time" conceived as: *macroscopic,* or covering long periods; and *discontinuous.*	I. "Time" measured by: "the growing season" or "the harvesting season," which are based upon the earth's longish movement around the sun.
II. "Time" conceived as: *microscopic,* or covering relatively short periods; and *discontinuous.*	II. "Time" measured by: a "moon," which is based on the moon's rotation about the earth.
III. "Time" conceived as: *microscopic;* and *continuous.*	III. "Time" measured by: A. the passage of grains of sand between the chambers of an hour glass, based upon the earth's rotation around the sun, as subdivided into convenient but approximate intervals. B. the movement of the gears and levers of a watch, based upon the earth's rotation around the sun, as subdivided into relatively uniform intervals. C. the radioactive decay of ammonia, which is independent of the earth's rotation and whose intervals are very uniform.

radioactive decay, in contrast, is independent of this slowing down. For many purposes, this development is hardly of pressing significance. But the accuracy is there if it is needed, and many sophisticated uses require it.

All this is to say, in addition, that one cannot become overconfident about an answer to the question: What is "time"? For the usefulness of any concept and its operation is determined only by consistent prediction and extension into increasingly broader areas. There is no sign that the process for "time" is at an end. Thus space travel may force major conceptual and operational changes in "time." Einstein has predicted, for example, that passengers in a space ship will age less quickly than if they had remained on earth for the same period! "Relative time" is no child's plaything. One bard, however, contrasted "relative time" with our common conception of "time" in this light way:

> There was a young man, they say,
> Who traveled faster than light,
> He left one day, in a relative way,
> And returned the previous night.

In brief, "time" may require still newer conceptual and operational definitions to permit us to cope with the finer predictions required (for example, in space flight) as our knowledge of the universe increases.

The subtlety of the problems of conceptual and operational definition, however, should not obscure the basic point of this analysis. In sum, the two types of empirical theory are tentative and cumulative; utopian work is definite and final. This is the case whether the empirical work deals with physical or social phenomena. Parenthetically, the development of concepts and operations in the social area has lagged behind such developments in the physical area. Einstein was near the mark when he explained that study in the physical area is simply easier. The control of the physical environment is also patently more pressing *at first*.

A Note on the Usefulness

of the Distinctions

The above analysis, in brief, has a substantial usefulness, which will be more evident in the following chapters. By way of brief preview here, however, the theory underlying the O & M application is essentially a utopian theory. This position will be supported fully below. The neglect of the "behavioral approach," detailed in Chapter 1, suffices here to suggest the validity of the position, for this neglect reflects the use of propositions which *assume* how people behave *under all conditions*. These take the place of propositions which describe how people *do behave under specified conditions*. There is a difference. Moreover, this neglect reflects (and depends upon) the lack of testing of traditional organization theory. Similarly, traditional organization theory is often held as dogma. In double-barreled contrast, the watchwords of empirical work are tentativeness and testing.

The difference between utopian theory and the two empirical types of theory is not a quibble. Indeed, the chapters below will demonstrate that such neglect can have very practical consequences, as when predictions derived from traditional organization theory lead to unexpected results.

In addition, to continue the thumbnail preview of the following chapters, a review of small-group analysis will demonstrate the specific changes necessary to develop any theory of organization which is grounded more solidly in empirical reality. The brief description of the stuff of empirical research—concepts and operations—also will be useful in understanding the problems of small-group analysis and the limits of such research.

There need be no amazement that traditional organization theory is utopian in spite of all the kind things which have been said about the two empirical types of theory, for the practice of organization could not (and did not) wait on the scientific explanation of the world. Things had to be done, if crudely. The existing theory was a necessary stopgap. Nor should traditional organization theory be overly disparaged, for, in some cases, the properties of this utopian theory will coincide quite closely with the real world (often because threatening techniques encourage individuals to behave as the theory assumes they ought). In such cases, the theory would permit accurate prediction of "what leads to what."

But clashes of a utopian theory of organization with the properties of the empirical world are inevitable (if only because individuals are often adamant even in the face of threat). Thus predictive failures also spot the record of traditional organization theory. Fortunately, recent research points a way out. It permits empirical advances far beyond the limits built into traditional organization theory by students who did not have this research at their disposal.

4

O & M AND ORGANIZATION THEORY: SOME MAJOR INADEQUACIES

IT IS NOT ALWAYS ACKNOWLEDGED, BUT DESCRIPTION AND prescription both presume an underlying theory, of whatever degree of refinement. Description depends upon, and contributes to, an empirical theory (that is, a set of statements of what is related to what). Prescription depends upon a goal-based, empirical theory (that is, a set of statements of how specific goals may be achieved through knowledge of what is related to what).

Bluntly, then, description would be wasteful, non-cumulative, and not particularly useful without a theoretical base. Similarly, prescription presumes a theory of how desired results can be obtained. There simply can be no prescription without such a theoretical base, whether explicit or implicit, whether rigorously tested or naively assumed. Even picking suggestions out of a hat implies a theory, if it is only that such a method is as good as any.

This chapter focuses upon the theory underlying the prescription and description of the reorganization of the Patent Office. Four questions, particularly, will interest this analysis. They are:

1. What are the major propositions of the theory underlying the prescription and description of the reorganization?
2. What type of theory underlies the prescription and description of the reorganization?
3. How adequate is the theory underlying the prescription and description of the reorganization? and
4. What steps, if any, are necessary to increase the adequacy of the theory underlying the prescription and description of the reorganization?

THE THEORY UNDERLYING THE REORGANIZATION

The O & M practitioners who handled the Patent Office reorganization faced two main tasks. First, they had to decide upon a set of goals. These, in effect, would be the answers to this compound question: What were the objectives of the reorganization and what techniques could be used to achieve them? Second, the O & M teams also had to solve an empirical problem: How could the desired goals be accomplished in the on-going administrative situation? In terms of the analysis of the previous chapter, then, the O & M specialists faced a goal-based, empirical task.

The O & M (Organization and Methods) application reviewed in Chapter 2 is based upon a theory which will be analyzed below. It will be referred to, for brevity, either as "the O & M theory" or as "traditional organization theory." This is no mere convenience, for the generally-accepted theory of organization and the O & M theory are identical.

Whatever its designation, however, it is clear what the O & M theory is not. Patently, traditional organization theory does not fit the guide lines of either of the two empirical types of theory, for the O & M theory is largely implicit. And it did not permit consistent prediction, but was not therefore altered. In contrast, both empirical types of theory must be painfully explicit, to permit retesting. Moreover, both types must be convincing and unique, or they must be modified or scrapped.

The conclusion by elimination—that traditional organization theory is utopian—happens to be correct. The point, however, may be established usefully in a complete fashion. A first step requires the isolation of the major propositions underlying the O & M theory. These propositions hold that administrative efficiency is increased as:

1. authority is a formal, one-way relation from organization superiors to organization subordinates;
2. supervision is close and constant;
3. for practical job-relevant purposes, the individual is considered a physiological organism who is socially isolated; and
4. specialization and routinization are increased.

Prescriptions derived from these propositions are assumed to be necessary and sufficient to induce high productivity. That is, whenever they exist, productivity is high. When they do not exist, it is implied, productivity is low. This claim will be examined closely in subsequent chapters.

The immediate task is threefold. First, each of the propositions will be introduced. This will involve tracing the logical relatedness of the propositions, substantiating their common use in the literature of public and business administration, and illustrating the ways in which they were reflected in the reorganization of the Patent Office. Second, some of the empirical evidence which has been offered to support the propositions will be analyzed. Third, the theory underlying the reorganization will be shown to be essentially utopian.

The first order of business, then, is the introduction of the four theoretical propositions which underlay the O & M application in the Copy-Pulling Section. These propositions, more broadly, also characterize work in the "formal approach."

The first underlying theoretical proposition assumes that high productivity depends upon the existence of authority as a formal, one-way relation. Thus, to illustrate, the work-process changes in the Patent Office were made unilaterally. The proposed changes were made known to employees only at the last minute, and then only in bits and pieces to those employees directly concerned. The gradually-expanding knowledge of the O & M specialists about the inadequacy of their theory, of course, in part explains this fitful trickle down of information about organization changes. But there is a consistent rationale underlying the way in which the changes were introduced. It may be briefly sketched in these terms. Employees have only one job-relevant source of authority. They will accept management directives, then, without question. Consequently, the way in which job-relevant directives are issued is irrelevant.

The proposition that authority is a one-way relation is reflected prominently in the "formal approach." To illustrate, one perceptive student has characterized traditional organization theory in this way:

> Thus the assumption is made that administrative and organization efficiency is increased by arranging the parts in a determinate hierarchy of authority where the part on top [of the organization] can direct and control the part on the bottom. [1]

Thus authority flows downward, and responsibility flows upward. In addition, authority and responsibility flow in single streams. The assumed necessity of this single flow has been explained in terms such as these: "a workman subject to orders from several superiors will be confused, inefficient, and *irresponsible;* a workman subject to orders from but one superior may be methodical, efficient, and *responsible.*" [2]

The second theoretical proposition underlying the O & M application in the Patent Office is: The exertion of authority is most effective under conditions of close supervision. This proposition is often referred to as the "three and seven rule," and is perhaps the feature of the traditional theory which is the most firmly held. The "rule" is intended to govern the process of division in an organization so that, wherever possible, no fewer than three and no more than seven subordinates should report to any one superior. Very often, it is also urged that the lower limit of the "span of control" be approached as the peak of the organization is approached, and that the higher number of subordinates be approached at low organization levels. The rationale for the "three and seven rule" (or for any limited "span of control") may be outlined briefly. Where division results in more

[1] Chris Argyris, *Personality and Organization* (New York: Harper, 1957), p. 60.

[2] Luther Gulick, "Notes on the Theory of Organization," in Luther Gulick and Lyndall Urwick (eds.), *Papers on the Science of Administration* (New York: Institute of Public Administration, 1927), p. 7. Italics supplied.

than seven units, inspection and control are held to be overly difficult. And when fewer than three units result from the process of division in an organization, it is argued that the supervisor will be tempted to intrude too directly in operations and that there are too few units to encourage a "friendly competition." [3]

The narrow "spans of control" of the new Section Head (with five supervisees) and of the new Unit Heads (with approximately seven copy pullers each to supervise) fit nicely within the "three and seven" rule. In contrast, there were fifteen parallel work flows with which the BC head of the Copy-Pulling Section had to contend. Moreover, there had been (to illustrate) eighteen copy pullers in the Lawyer's Window line of work flow alone.

These first two theoretical propositions are intimately related. Close supervision, permitted by the limited "span of control," is consistent with the one-way conception of authority, for if authority has such a characteristic, then it must be directly and continuously applied. A narrow span of control, reasonably, fills this bill.

The third theoretical proposition underlying the O & M application logically complements the first two. This third proposition is that, on the job, man is a physiological organism without binding social ties. This may seem the most curious of the three, but curious or not, such a proposition consistently underlies work in the "formal approach." Waldo's characterization of traditional organization theory expresses the point succinctly. "Perhaps the most striking aspect of the 'theory of organization,'" he wrote, "is its rationalism. People are conceived as fundamentally rational, society as a fundamentally rational institution. People and organization parts are . . . more or less . . . interchangeable parts of modern machinery." [4] Chapter 1, of course, also supports the present interpretation of the bias of the "formal approach."

This emphasis in traditional organization theory on the physiological individual is not simply "theoretical": it has an enormous

---

[3] E. G. Hart, "The Art and Science of Organization, I," *The Human Factor*, VII (October, 1933), especially 337–38.

[4] Waldo, *The Administrative State*, pp. 173–74. Copyright 1948 The Ronald Press Company.

bread-and-butter importance. Thus one distinguished student reflected the influence of this proposition in describing how a formal organization should be planned. He described this very practical undertaking as:

> Manifestly that is a drawing office job. It is a designing process. And it may be objected with a great deal of . . . support . . . that organization is never done that way . . . [and that] it is impossible to start with a clean sheet. . . . [It also may be argued that the] organizer has to make the best possible use of the human material that already is available. . . . [And it may be contended that the organizer] can't sit down in a cold-blooded, detached spirit and draw an ideal structure, an optimum distribution of duties and responsibilities and relationships, and then expect the infinite variety of human nature to fit into it. . . . To which the reply is that [the organizer] can and should. If he has not got a clean sheet, that is no earthly reason why he should not make the *slight effort of imagination required to assume* that he has a clean sheet. [5]

The Patent Office reorganization also indicates the practical importance of the proposition of the physiological individual. The proposition was one of the products, in effect, of the O & M specialists' "slight effort of the imagination" required to assume they had a clean slate. Disregarding his other characteristics, the O & M teams emphasized a physiological caricature of the copy puller. The emphases upon "rhythm," walking distance, time, and "even flow," to cite but a few evidences, patently reflect an underlying model of man which more than anything resembles a machine. The "effort of the imagination" of the O & M specialists, then, amounted to this: they were concerned with organizations without people as they exist, with mere shadows of individuals performing limited functions.

The interdependence of these first three propositions must be stressed. Thus one-line authority and close supervision are the necessary complements of the physiological model of man. Take a more complex model of man, to demonstrate the point. Thus

[5] Lyndall Urwick, *The Elements of Administration* (New York: Harper, 1953), pp. 36–39. Italics supplied.

consider man as a social as well as physiological entity, as a participant in a social system as well as a contributor to a mechanical system. This model implies a "cross-pressure" condition, that is, the possible conflict of job-relevant directives intended to control behavior; for the individual's behavior is affected by two factors—the authority of the formal organization and the power of the individual's social ties—which often will vie for the control of his behavior. Similarly, close supervision becomes more uncertain, the greater the complexity of man. Thus, if man is social as well as physiological, his broad social experience as well as his narrow task contributions must be controlled. Not strangely, then, exponents of the "formal approach" began with the control of the job and ended up envisioning the creation of a machinelike society. Prediction in the cross-pressure condition, in short, is very iffy. But such is life. Traditional organization theory prefers simplicity to validity.

A fourth proposition serves as a linchpin for the O & M theory: Specialization and routinization are the keys to increased efficiency. Despite its centrality, however, the proposition is grossly unspecific. Thus it is not clear what is to be specialized or how. Indeed, four bases of specialization normally are offered: purpose, process, clientele, and area. The type of specialization, or the combination of specialties, to be chosen in a specific case, however, *is* the significant problem. But the theory is mute on this crucial matter of choice. Thus the emphasis upon "specialization" begs more questions than it answers.

The 1776 view of Adam Smith is a general one among students of organization. "The greatest improvement in the productive powers of labor," he wrote in that year, "and the greater part of the skill, dexterity and judgment with which it is anywhere directed or applied, seem to have been the effects of the division of labor." Writing especially of the serial organization form, Smith enumerated these advantages of division of work:

1. *Increased dexterity of each workman.* ". . . the division of labor, reducing each man's business to some one simple operation and . . . making this operation the sole employment . . . ," permits the worker to concentrate his efforts toward a high degree of skill in a limited action rather than a lesser skill in a variety of actions.

2. *Decreased change-over time.* "It is impossible to pass very quickly from one kind of work to another that is carried on in a different place and with different tools. . . . A man commonly saunters a little in turning his hand from one sort of employment to another."

3. *Increased use of machinery.* ". . . the invention of all those machines by which labor is so much facilitated and abridged seems to have been originally owing to the division of labor." [6]

That "specialization" is the key element of the O & M theory may be demonstrated easily. For example, one-way authority and close supervision, credibly, apply most appropriately in cases in which the unit of work to be monitored is discrete and simple. Moreover, specialization patently emphasizes physiological considerations, for routinization implies the perfection by practice of a few relatively simple actions. And simplification also implies that operator skills, planning, intelligence, and so on—that is, the characteristics which sharply differentiate individuals—are less important.

True to the "formal approach," the Patent Office reorganization emphasized specialization and routinization. Thus individual copy pullers became AC area specialists in one segment of one unit of the files. In addition, the copy-pulling task was routinized by developing a new work station for sorting orders. BC, copy pullers had performed the sorting task.

O & M THEORY AS EMPIRICAL THEORY

The previous section has introduced four basic propositions of the theory underlying the Patent Office reorganization. The purpose of this section is twofold: to analyze the underlying theory in order to determine the degree to which its propositions are consistent with the empirical state of affairs; and, relatedly, to determine the nature of the theory underlying the reorganization.

On the first count, the system derived from the underlying

[6] As quoted in *Production Planning and Control in Office Operations,* p. 21.

theory did not have the predicted results. The early AC failure of the system in the Copy-Pulling Section evidences this. Moreover, the necessity of re-reorganizing the Patent Office in 1948 also suggests that the O & M theory did not lead to the desired consequences in the long run.

In sum, the O & M theory was not a satisfactory example of goal-based, empirical theory.

But there is no excuse for claiming a cheap victory over the O & M theory. A more extended analysis, indeed, will serve a very useful purpose. The immediate concern is with the O & M theory as an example of one of the two types of empirical effort —empirical theory or goal-based, empirical theory. A following section will consider it as an example of utopian theory.

The O & M theory, first, does not respect the two T's of empirical work: testing and tentativeness. The "three and seven" rule, for example, seems to depend more upon a mystical faith in the numbers than upon supporting evidence. The evidence presented by Graicunas in support of a limited span of control illustrates this point. Thus he noted that most individuals can remember only six consecutive digits. Further evidence—which is more complex but no more convincing—was provided by his demonstration that, as the number of interacting individuals increases, the number of possible pair-relations increases very sharply after four. Thus three individuals (a, b, c,) have only three possible pair-relations (a, b; b, c; and a, c). When five individuals are involved, the number of pair-relations rises to ten; and with six individuals, fifteen pair-relations are involved; and so on.[7]

There may be, of course, *some limit* on the number of persons who may be supervised by any one individual. But even these limits will vary widely with different conditions. For example, if the purpose is close supervision of subordinates, patently a narrow span of control is in order. But close control is but a single condition, and (as will be shown) general supervision often yields more favorable results. If the purpose is general supervision, or control by objectives rather than by minute direction, a very wide span of control is indicated. In any case, the evidence offered does not establish that the most desirable

[7] V. A. Graicunas, "Relationship in Organization," in Gulick and Urwick, *Papers on the Science of Administration*, pp. 183–87.

limits of the span of control are defined by the "three and seven" rule. Indeed, the evidence—intended to support one-line authority—assumes that one-line authority does not exist! That is, Graicunas' evidence implies a cross-pressure condition. A single-pressure condition would add one pair-relation for each individual added, that is, the pair-relation between supervisor and subordinate.

The lack of empirical verification also can be demonstrated by testing predictions drawn from the theory underlying the "formal approach." This theory was a monumental step forward in the scientific study of productive organization, but the theory did not reach that goal. To develop some of its major inadequacies as specifically as possible, in the interest of building upon the work of others, the emphasis here is upon Taylor's "scientific management." The conclusions, however, apply to all work in the same tradition.

The empirical limitations of Taylor's contributions are reflected in the organization theory—the second major facet of his work—which he developed from his time-and-motion studies. The organization implications which Taylor drew from his work may be summarized in this way: "The theory was, then, that if each operating process was studied and designed for optimum mechanical and physiological efficiency, the productive association itself would thereby operate at maximum efficiency." [8] Consequently, Taylor supplemented the administrative and disciplinary functions of management. He provided for a "technical expert" who had complete control of production processes. [9]

A valid theory should permit accurate prediction. A test of Taylor's theory, then, is appropriate. Consider an experiment concerning the effects of varying degrees of illumination on output. The experimental design is simple. Experienced workers who perform the same task in roughly the same mechanical way are to be observed as illumination is varied. To support Taylor's theory, observations must support these two predictions:

    I. Variable Condition: all other things being equal, output will increase with increasing illumina-

---

[8] David B. Hertz and Robert T. Livingston, "Contemporary Organization Theory: A Review of Current Concepts and Methods," *Human Relations*, III (November, 1950), 374.

[9] Frederick W. Taylor, *The Principles of Scientific Management*, p. 11.

tion, until the worker reaches his physical capacity and/or his optimum illumination level; and

II. Control Condition: all other things being equal, output will remain constant with constant illumination.

The test of these hypotheses, already mentioned in Chapter 1, proved negative. Both variable and control conditions showed *increases* in production, whether illumination levels *were varied up or down or were held constant.* [10]

In sum, then, Taylor's theory requires modification or rejection. And the phenomena with which the theory does not square are behavioral factors. These were not "controlled" in the experiment. That is, "all other things" were not equal as illumination varied. There were a number of these unequal "other things." A group developed and harnessed the efforts of operators to the task. The operators also felt "closer" to various levels of management, for many higher-ups had a deep interest in the experiment. This interest encouraged an unprecedentedly intimate relation between management and the experimental subjects.

The effects of these unequal "other things" could not be predicted from Taylor's theory of organization. Indeed, there was no place for these "other things" in the theory. The experiment, in short, had a meaning for participants which transcended the physiological impact of illumination levels and Taylor's theory.

The experiment also demonstrates that the propositions underlying the reorganization of the Patent Office, save that of routinization, were inadequate. That is, authority was not exclusively a one-way, formal relation; the operators had characteristics other than physiological ones which were job-relevant; and

---

[10] No serious student of organization can neglect the very marked limits of the "formal approach" even in a country in which individual behavior is subject to arbitrary control in a high degree. Even under these "favorable" conditions, the applications of various techniques of work saving in the Soviet Union amply demonstrated the influence of what we have called "behavioral organization." A summary of the history of such attempts is available conveniently in David Granick, *The Red Executive* (Garden City: Doubleday, 1960).

management at several levels was "closer" to the work unit than the limited span of control permits. Yet productivity increased.

O & M Theory as Utopian Theory

The empirical considerations above, in a real sense, are beside the point of the O & M theory, for Taylor's "scientific management" and work in the "formal approach" is basically utopian. And if one is engaged in utopian (rather than empirical) work, empirical factors need not be considered in building a model.

Curiously, many students of organization have taken a utopian tack. True, few have done so explicitly and carefully followed the methodological requirements of utopian theorizing. Stene is one of the exceptions, having developed a set of propositions about organization derived from an explicit set of goals and definitions. [11] Weber was similarly concerned in his "The Monocratic Type of Bureaucracy." [12] Many more students of organization have been less rigorous and explicit, but they followed a similar path. The O & M teams in the Patent Office, for example, took this tack.

Urwick characteristically explained this utopian concern with "rational organization." "It is impossible," he wrote, "to advance . . . knowledge of organization, *unless* the factor of structure is isolated from other considerations, however artificial such an isolation may appear." [13] Urwick had a point, for the short run. Over the long haul, however, knowledge of organization cannot advance if the factor of structure *is* considered in isolation.

The critic must be careful to distinguish two features of such work. The temptation is to stress exclusively the fact that important phenomena are overlooked in what Taylor called the

[11] Edwin O. Stene provided this exception in his "Public Administration: An Approach to a Science of Administration," *American Political Science Review*, XXXIV (December, 1940), 1124–37.

[12] Max Weber, "The Essentials of Bureaucratic Organization: An Ideal-Type Construction," in Robert K. Merton, *et al.* (eds.), *Reader in Bureaucracy* (Glencoe, Ill.: Free Press, 1952), p. 24.

[13] L. Urwick, "The Function of Administration: With Special Reference to the Work of Henry Fayol," in Gulick and Urwick, *Papers on the Science of Administration*, p. 122.

study of "every factor in the managerial situation." This temptation must be resisted, even though the judgment is accurate, for the emphasis of "scientific management" is essentially mechanical. The unrelieved stress upon such factors as the physical capacity of man or machine, of floor space, and the like, massively supports this judgment. [14] The neglect of behavior factors limits the usefulness of "scientific management," but this neglect is not damning.

The critic, however, must stress a less obvious and more crucial feature of "scientific management." That certain phenomena are overlooked is significant. Far more important, however, is the fact that "scientific management" cuts itself off from the possibility of improving its theory. To explain, the neglect of significant factors is not crucial, if the ground rules of empirical theory are followed, for the modification or rejection of any inadequate theoretical proposition will be forced soon enough. Unsuccessful attempts to retest the proposition, or to extend it to related phenomena, would do the job.

Proponents of "scientific management," however, typically reject the ground rules for empirical work, and thus must draw the critic's fire. In effect, the rejection precludes the improvement of the theory of the "formal approach." Urwick illustrates this "scientific intellectual method" (as opposed to the "scientific empirical method") in organization study. [15] What this means in practice is the exercise of a "slight effort of imagination" necessary to assume that such theoretical propositions as the four above are empirically adequate. Simply, the safeguards of empirical theory-making are disregarded by an effort of the will. This is the significant liability of work in the "formal approach."

Thus important empirical factors are neglected in "scientific management." But, in addition, this neglect is raised to the level of a method, if not a virtue. Such theory-making, of course, would tend strongly toward self-fulfillment rather than self-correction. Put simply, this is the death of empirical theory.

One need not wonder, then, at the moderate impact of recent

[14] This characteristic of "scientific management" has been cited often. See, for example, Herbert Emmerich, "Some Folklore of Executive Management," *Public Management*, XX (September, 1938), especially 265.

[15] L. Urwick, "Rational Organization," in International Industrial Relations Association, *Rational Organization and Industrial Organization* (The Hague, Holland, 1929), p. 37.

behavioral research upon the "formal approach" to organization. The two approaches are based upon conflicting methods. Consequently, no matter how impressive the evidence, the integration of the two approaches faces the resistance caused by unrecognized, but basic, differences in methods. A finding which is of great importance in the "behavioral approach," in short, is methodologically of no concern to the "formal approach."

Utopian analysis can play an important role. This should not be overlooked, but its usefulness is limited by severe ground rules.

Ground Rule 1: Goals and theoretical propositions must be stated clearly. The O & M theory rests upon four major propositions. Let us neglect the point that the meaning of some of them is less than clear. These propositions, even given this enormous benefit of a doubt, do not pass muster. The propositions of traditional organization theory, as McGregor demonstrated brilliantly, depend upon an *implicit* world view. This world view, at first glance, seems to describe *how things are*. But, on closer investigation, it dissolves into a mélange of wishes about *how the world ought to be*.

This world view—which McGregor calls "Theory X"—includes such elements as these:

1. work is inherently distasteful to most people;
2. most people prefer to be directed, and have little desire for responsibility and little ambition;
3. most people have little capacity for creativity in solving organization problems;
4. motivation occurs only (or most often) as a response to threat to the physiological and safety needs of the individual; and
5. therefore, most people must be closely directed and controlled, and often coerced, in the achievement of organization objectives. [16]

It requires only a little imagination to see how the four propositions of traditional organization theory must rest on this implicit "Theory X." Elements 2 and 3 in "Theory X," for example, support specialization and routinization; and elements

[16] These propositions of "Theory X" were inspired by Douglas McGregor, but do not coincide with his development in all respects. See *The Human Side of Enterprise* (New York: McGraw, 1960), pp. 33–58.

2, 4, and 5, especially, support a limited span of control. The reader can easily carry through a similar analysis of the ways in which "Theory X" supports the other propositions of O & M theory.

This lack of explicitness in traditional organization theory is significant for two major reasons. First, the assumptions of "Theory X" determine the nature of traditional organization theory. Different assumptions would give rise to different organization theories. Any such underlying assumptions, then, should have substantial support.

Second, however, "Theory X" does not rest very firmly on empirical evidence. Indeed, "Theory X" patently is an outrageous caricature, but this should not be surprising. If you do not spell out your assumptions, you cannot test them. And if you do not test your assumptions, outrageous caricatures are likely. This point was missed by those who accepted traditional organization theory and thus accepted "Theory X," whether they knew it or not.

Ground Rule 2: The usefulness of utopian theory lies in its independence of the empirical world. A utopian theory cannot purport to represent the empirical world. Rather, it demonstrates the properties of an organization embodying certain characteristics, whether or not such characteristics are likely to exist. A utopian theory does not bestow reality on the theorist's assumptions underlying the theory. The point has been neglected by many utopian theorists.

The utopian theorist, in brief, may tuck the proverbial ace up his sleeve by basing his theory on any assumptions he desires. But he may not argue, when he develops a logical structure from these assumptions, that he has discovered anything about the empirical world. He simply displays his own handiwork.

Ground Rule 3: There is all the difference in the world between developing a utopian theory and using it as a pattern for empirical relations. Even the wildest flight of imagination provides fit meat for developing a utopian theory. The use of such a theory as a pattern for relations of man to man is quite another matter.

What must be done prior to the application of a utopian model is clear enough: empirical and normative tests must be applied to the model to determine whether it can, and should, be achieved.

What has been done by utopian theorists of organization also is clear. Such checks seldom have been applied. Thus prescriptions derived from utopian theories of organization should be phrased in humble terms: If these goals are to be achieved, and if these propositions approximate reality closely enough, then the organization should have such-and-such characteristics. But prescriptions for organization are typically presented more pretentiously as statements of absolute and universal necessity.

This seems a blanket condemnation, but it is generally accurate. Illustratively, on the empirical level, one student developed an allegedly universal theory of organization. The author did note that "the organization of the British city violates most of [these] principles," yet works admirably.[17] But he went no further. The empirical evidence he cited should have forced him on, but his utopian method did not encourage the continual re-examination of theory required by an empirical approach.

Similarly, such checks usually have been avoided on the normative level. Indeed, the following capsule characterization of "scientific management" reflects the common assumption that no normative checks are applicable to utopian systems: ". . . 'in the past man has been first, in the future the system will be first'; the system emerges from, *is immanent in*, the 'facts' of existence and emerges from them when they are recorded and manipulated."[18]

This position is untenable. The most that may be squeezed from any set of data are statements of co-variation which might prove useful in an empirical theory. Any theory which prescribes a state of affairs, rather than describes reality, must be based upon value criteria. All goal-based, empirical theories are prescriptive. Utopian theories, *when they are applied*, are also prescriptive. These two types of theories, then, cannot "emerge" from any data "when they are recorded and manipulated." As it were, what emerges will depend upon the normative "magic words" that one utters.

Claims that the latter two types of theory are "immanent in" any set of empirical data, consequently, must be rejected.

[17] Harvey Walker, *Public Administration in the United States* (New York: Rinehart, 1927), p. 86.
[18] Waldo, *The Administrative State*, p. 178. Copyright 1948 The Ronald Press Company. Italics supplied.

These claims make light of a complex problem. This is reason enough for the emphasis here. More broadly, in addition, the general failure of work in the Taylorian tradition to make explicit and analyze its goal bases betrays a lack of respect for the properties of both goal-based, empirical and utopian theory as well.

Of course, the dominant value in "scientific management" has been a narrow, machinelike conception of efficiency. Such a goal is a legitimate one for utopian study, but there is nothing inevitable about its choice as the goal base for organization theory. Indeed, although the demonstration of the point is beyond the scope of this effort, the narrow concept of efficiency implies behaviors which are generally regarded as undesirable. Moreover, it is not clear that individuals can be conditioned so as to provide the required behaviors over long periods, even if extraordinary techniques (such as training from birth) are employed.

Whatever the case, this much may be stated bluntly: the assumptions in utopian theory of what things are like become presumptions of what things should be like when that theory is used as a model to be achieved. In organization theory, this illegitimate shell game would take this form: man must be treated as a physiological being because that is what he is. This form of argument cannot be dismissed lightly. For one thing, it is a kind of self-fulfilling prophecy. That is, if you treat an individual as a physiological being, you can often expect him to act as if he were. The experience in Nazi extermination camps during World War II provides a grisly example. A piece of raw meat, tossed among starving inmates, had precisely the expected effect of pitting man against man in a tragic struggle. The conclusion is not that man is antisocial. Rather the conclusion is that he will be antisocial, and blatantly so, if he must be. The attempt to achieve the utopian model of traditional organization theory often has a similar effect, if not often to the same degree.

The moral question, of course, cannot be avoided even if all men acted at all times in the ways implied by traditional organization theory. But the matter of moral evaluation need not be restricted to the high ground of moral necessity. The evaluation also makes sense in the catch-as-catch-can world of meeting today's production schedule. To explain, it is fortunate—but not crucial—that empirical findings add much impetus to such a moral evaluation of traditional organization theory. Thus most men often do not act in the simplistic way the theory assumes. This adds practical force to the moral judgment against considering man as a physiological being. A further piece of information supplies a practical clincher. As will be demonstrated, even when men act in the ways that traditional organization theory requires, output and efficiency are not affected as the theory says they should be.

There is no reason, in sum, to avoid the moral issues posed by traditional organization theory. Indeed, quite the opposite is the case: there is every practical reason to attempt to meet them.

The Theory Underlying

the Description of the Reorganization

The case study describing the reorganization of the Patent Office cannot be neglected in the analysis of the O & M theory. The case treatment does imply theoretical notions of the important "somethings" in the reorganization which are the same as those reviewed above. But it is not enough to make this section a long string of ditto marks, whose meaning would be that everything said about the O & M theory applies to the writing of the case study. The case technique has been a research fashion in a wide variety of disciplines. Thus, of necessity, the present argument must be applied specifically to the case technique.

It is convenient to begin by outlining the way in which the case literature interprets its analytical task. To sharpen the discussion, the focus will be specifically upon the Inter-University Case Program, under whose auspices the study of the Patent Office reorganization was published. This emphasis, however, has a patent narrowness, for the Inter-University Case Program is in the throes of methodological developments which may change its approach sharply. Moreover, some users of the technique, such as the Harvard Business School faculty, have evidenced a methodological sophistication beyond that normally encountered.[19] Thus the effort proceeds at the expense of saying too much, but

[19] There are notable exceptions to the usually unreflective considerations of the case approach. A prime example is provided in Kenneth R. Andrews (ed.), *The Case Method of Teaching Human Relations and Administration: An Interim Statement* (Cambridge, Mass.: Harvard, 1953).

the analysis below will have historical validity, at the very least.

The very acceptance of the case approach tends to obscure an important point. The approach, per se, is not an analytical be-all and end-all. It is simply a general orientation to action sequences, such as the illness of a human or the reorganization of a government agency. The *content* of the approach—concepts and operations and their theoretical relations—determines the usefulness of any application of the technique. Thus the research question is not case study or no case study. Rather the question is: What is to be observed and how are those observations to be reported? The "what" and the "how"—usually called the problems of nominal and operational definition—are the vitals of the scientifically useful effort.

This description of the case study as an orientation toward action, whose usefulness is determined only by the concepts and operations utilized, is not a common one. Thus, more or less typically, one student wrote of the "case study *technique* as defined."[20] A less ambiguous designation would be the "case approach whose analytical content in this case includes such-and-such concepts and operations." Supporting this uncommon position will be the object below.

A sketch of the theoretical and methodological posture of the existing cases in the Inter-University Case Program roster will serve to point up these general observations. This writer's work appears in the ICP Series, and thus he is not simply throwing stones in the glass houses of his neighbors. The comments below apply to his contribution as well as to the contributions of others.

The history of the Inter-University Case Program can be written in terms of two themes: the accurate perception of the problems of filling in the content of the case approach, and the unfortunate neglect of these problems in the cases produced.[21] The request of the ICP to the Carnegie Foundation for financial assistance articulated the former theme. That request contained these scientific ambitions:

[20] Harold Stein, "Preparation of Case Studies: The Problem of Abundance," *American Political Science Review*, LI (June, 1951), especially 480–81. Italics supplied.

[21] The focus here is upon published work only. Thus this analysis will slight work which is in process, and judgments about such work must be reserved.

1. To provide the basis for realistic concepts, hypotheses, and generalizations about administrative organization, behavior and policy-making by utilizing a clinical approach . . . .
2. To explore the application and possibility of integration of the various social sciences and disciplines in administrative policy-making . . . .
3. To make generally available a body of case materials which will, it is hoped, be particularly useful for teaching purposes, for scholarly inquiry, and to practitioners in the field of Public Administration.[22]

Thus the drafter(s) realized that description requires and leads to a theory, that is, a statement of the purportedly existing relations which exist in the empirical world.

This perception of the importance of theory, however, had to be complemented by a new kind of historical research and writing, for the importance of empirical theory received little support from historians.[23] In fact, most have insulated themselves from the laborious development of theory and its component concepts and operations. Their insulating device is familiar, that is, many historians have assumed a utopian theory. The enormously influential Weber, to illustrate, advised the historian and social scientist to choose a "demon" or a "god"—that is, some theoretical frame of reference—and to interpret historical phenomena in terms of it.[24] The riot of historical "interpretations" of this or that massively evidences Weber's influence. These "interpretations" stand as mute testimony that if empirical data did not conform to the speculative frame of reference, so much the worse for the empirical data. The speculative theory, in effect, selected the data. This reverses the necessary procedure.

For Public Administration thus to surpass its parent discipline

[22] Stein, *Public Administration and Policy Development*, p. xlii.

[23] See the futile encouragement to historians offered by Carl G. Hempel, "The Function of General Laws in History," *Journal of Philosophy*, XXXIX (January, 1942), 35–48. The painful change process required of historians to act upon suggestions such as Hempel's is interestingly sketched in David M. Potter, *People of Plenty: Economic Abundance and the American Character* (Chicago: Chicago, 1954).

[24] Leo Strauss's discussion in *Natural Right and History* (Chicago: Chicago, 1953), especially Chapter I, helps one understand this orientation to empirical phenomena.

in study design was a great achievement. But ingrained patterns of thinking persisted. The case-study literature thus reflects little concern with the problems of empirical theory.

This vitality of traditional patterns of thought is illustrated in an article on case studies, provocatively subtitled "The Problem of Abundance."[25] Abundance, of course, bedevils any empirical investigation. That is, the fundamental research questions in any empirical research are: Which of the numberless data in any action sequence are important? and How are these important data to be reported? No action sequence can be described completely, and it is unnecessary to do so in any case. Thus the "problem of abundance" in empirical work requires the development of concepts and operations to isolate the significant and discard the trivial. The goal is a theoretical model which abstracts the important relations in any action sequence. The "problem of abundance" is not manageable in other terms.

"The Problem of Abundance," however, took a different tack when the author restricted the materials relevant for the "case method" to those used by any historian attempting to organize contemporary history. These materials were "government files, official documents, . . . interviews [etc.]." This diminished the "problem of abundance." For example, the approach of the psychologist was eschewed as lying "outside the effective scope of the . . . cases," although the importance of the approach was acknowledged. Diminishing the problem of abundance in this way, however, also limited the validity of the case reports based upon it. Curiously, in addition, this eating of one's research cake existed along with an expectation of having it as well, for the article also noted that among the major emphases "selected for highlighting are: informal organization [and] decision as a process. . . ."

Rather than theory-building, Item 3 in the application for support has been emphasized in effect, and apparently by intention. Thus, as Mosher noted: "The cases have probably been most valuable as teaching material and have served only secondarily to advance general knowledge in the field."[26]

The provision of teaching materials had an understandable

[25] Stein, "Preparation of Case Studies," pp. 480–81, 486.
[26] Frederick C. Mosher, "Research in Public Administration: Some Notes and Suggestions," *Public Administration Review*, XVI (Summer, 1956), 171.

short-run priority in the Program, but the long-run failure to pursue the development of relevant concepts and operations has had two unfortunate consequences. First, the usefulness of case studies as teaching material is limited sharply because description—whatever its purposes—depends upon concepts and operations which permit the isolation and reporting of relevant data. Following the spoor of memoranda, letters, and hearings normally associated with an administrative action sequence, to be sure, taps one level of relevant phenomena. But it is only one level. The relative immediacy of the spoor—having one's nose in it, so to speak—also may limit the "interpretation" either consciously or unconsciously made. But this is no guarantee that relevant phenomena will be observed and described, and without the development of concepts and operations, generalization from cases will be inhibited.

Second, the traditional historical approach of the ICP case studies was rationalized because a more rigorous approach "seems unrealizable in any proximate future." [27] This lowering of aims was convenient and, to a degree, necessary. But the particularistic thinking about the case approach has contributed to making the long-run goal unrealizable in fact. Thus the inadequacies of the analytical content of the case approach have tended to become the givens which circumscribe the research area, even when advances are attempted.[28] Moreover, the lowering of research aims reflected an overmodesty about then-existing insights into the description and explanation of behavior. In any case, the postwar explosion in the behavioral sciences has made the dominant rationale far more inconsistent with the state of existing knowledge. A more rigorous approach to cases, then, does seem far more realizable in the proximate future than it did only a few years ago.

Similar characterizations of other major attempts to exploit the case approach can also be made, although to differing degrees. These analytical shortcomings probably help to explain the lessening enthusiasm for teaching and research with the case approach. The approach seems to have reached its high-water mark

---

[27] Stein, *Public Administration and Policy Development*, p. xl.
[28] See the conclusions of Herbert Kaufman concerning the so-called cluster technique of the Inter-University Case Program in "The Next Step in Case Studies," *Public Administration Review*, XVIII (Winter, 1958), 59.

of influence, in short, unless methodological changes are made in what has become the normal way of observing and reporting case sequences.

Two major propositions concerning the case literature, then, constitute the foundation upon which the following redescription of the Patent Office reorganization will attempt to build. First, the case approach has contributed significantly to the early research and teaching progress in disciplines dealing with the study of public as well as business administration. But, second, the increased usefulness of the case approach requires improvement in its content of concepts and operations. That is, the point has been reached where the use of "everyday language" pays diminishing returns. This is not to say that existing cases are without underlying theory or methodology, for *any* reported observation requires them. The point is simply that the theory of cases has been implicit, particularistic, and taps only part of the rich empirical phenomena in any action sequence.

A note of caution should be read as if in bold-face type, in conclusion. Much of the traditional material of case analysis is not presently amenable to the kind of full-scale treatment which will be given to the Patent Office. This author, for example, is completing work on a case whose working title is "The Coroner and the Unburied Corpse." An analysis of certain obvious features (e.g., the jurisdiction of several agencies) carries one a long way in understanding the case. This leaves part of the job undone, of course. Except in a deep psychoanalytical sense, however, the case is not amenable to the type of analysis used here (or, at least, this author does not see the amenability). This level of analysis is not accessible, although what should be done ideally is clear. We simply must learn to live with incompleteness, then, if it is necessary to do so.

But there are degrees of incompleteness, and constant effort must be directed toward moving from greater to lesser incompleteness. Thus the position here is not the unreasonable one that there is no value in cases as presently conceived and that wholesale changes must be made now. Rather, it has two more reasonable emphases. Too little has been made in case writing of the research advances which have been made. Moreover, this disuse stems from the failure to consciously think through the methodology of the case approach. This consciousness about method must precede, and at the same time will grow from, the increased use of the products of the natural-science approach to behavior. The present analysis, in one of its most basic aims, attempts to encourage the acceptance of the natural-science method and its results in case analysis.

THEORY AND THE REORGANIZATION:

SOME DIRECTIONS FOR A REANALYSIS

This analysis demonstrates the rough-and-ready nature of the theory underlying the Patent Office reorganization. The emphasis below upon the small group thus will complement the contributions of Taylor and, more generally, of the "formal approach" to organization.

More specifically, the following reanalysis of the reorganization of the Patent Office must reflect three emphases in evaluating, and improving upon, the theory which underlies the prescription and description of the reorganization. The first two emphases are empirical, the third is normative.

First, the predictive failure of the theory in the Copy-Pulling Section implies a considerable margin for more precise specification of the conditions under which the O & M theory can be expected to hold. The following analysis must provide a convincing and unique explanation of any predictive failure of the O & M theory, and it must also provide a theory capable of more precise predictions.

Second, the theories underlying prescription and description—even in the most developed sciences—are self-corrective. That is, it is not unusual that a particular theory or theoretical proposition is found to be adequate for limited purposes only. This lesson is relevant for O & M theory, which has been unyielding even in the face of substantial evidence of its limited predictive power. This lesson also has relevance for the following analysis of small-group properties. This analysis must be accepted in a scientific sense, in the atmosphere that the last word in theory has not been uttered. But the words employed below should improve upon the O & M theory.

Third, the propositions of the O & M theory must be evaluated normatively. This point will be reflected, from time to time, in the isolation of alternative ways in which the productivity increase in the Copy-Pulling Section might have been achieved. These alternatives, of course, raise such questions of choice and normative valuation as: Is Method A preferable to Method B, as judged by their respective normative side effects? Work in the "formal approach," in contrast, often has attempted to side-step such questions by assuming that there is a "one best way" to organize work, but life is not so simple.

The complex questions involved cannot be settled here. Some tentative answers and their implications can be sketched below, however, for small-group theory has normative implications which contrast sharply with those of traditional organization theory. This analysis, at least, can direct attention to the normative choice implied in this contrast.

5

THE SMALL GROUP
AND ORGANIZATION THEORY:
SOME RELEVANT VARIABLES, I

THE EMPIRICAL AND NORMATIVE CRITICISMS OF THE O & M THEORY reviewed in the preceding chapters are not all novel. But existing criticisms do not meet their own challenge of providing specific directions to the analytical promised land. That is, these criticisms do not meet the scholarly equivalent of the pointed taunt "Put up, or shut up."

The following chapters will attempt to meet this challenge by providing a detailed demonstration of the directions in which the development of a sophisticated organization theory must proceed. The research in small-group analysis to be reviewed does not reflect a passing scholarly fancy. Studies have long demonstrated the small group's control of member behavior in striking, if general, ways.[1] Small-group analysis has built upon these early descriptive studies. The goal is the development of analytic tools capable of describing small groups in detail. Large-scale experimentation with temporary groups in social laboratories has spearheaded this effort.

[1] A large number of such descriptive studies are summarized in Muzafer Sherif and Carolyn Sherif, *Groups in Harmony and Tension* (New York: Harper, 1953).

SOME INTRODUCTORY CONSIDERATIONS

The approach here is no panacea, no scholarly wonder drug. Thus the completeness of small-group research should not be oversold. It has its significant gaps. Indeed, any attempt to utilize small-group analysis in describing organization behavior represents to some degree (1) trading on the future, and (2) treading on the uncertain. A cursory treatment of some of the difficulties should suffice to make the reader wary.

The futuristic orientation, first, is necessary. Only a sophisticated small-group analysis will permit the differentiation of types of small groups. This ability hinges on two developments: the isolation of the important properties (concepts) of groups; and the perfection of conventions (operations) for measuring differences in such properties. These are the stuff of empirical theory. Empirical theory, in turn, is the payoff of successful research, for such theory has predictive and descriptive uses.

In addition, some concessions must be made to analytical uncertainty. This is the case, in part, because existing theory is fragmentary and perhaps inaccurate. The general use of several operations to study a single concept also contributes to this tentativeness. This is common in early empirical research in any area, but it is nonetheless significant.

These dual problems have not been solved with any finality. Indeed, they are insoluble in a final sense. This must encourage a substantial open-mindedness in coping with the analysis below. The concepts discussed, then, should not be considered as a be-all and end-all of empirical research. They have proved useful in prediction, but it is impossible to be definite about the explanatory "power" of existing concepts and operations. Important ones may not yet have been isolated; some imprecise ones may have temporarily captivated students; and the various concepts utilized below no doubt have different degrees of usefulness in prediction and description.

These factors, however, should encourage caution, not timidity. Such reservations are inherent in the game of empirical analysis. If one does not like the rules, he should not play. But there is no danger as long as we do not delude ourselves about the certitude of any position.

Enough of this general argument. The position may be illustrated by one feature of small-group analysis: the lack of a comprehensive definition of a "small group." This illustration may seem off to an incredible start, the position apparently being that students of the "small group" do not know what they are studying. But the position is not unbelievable. Students of the "small group"—like physicists with their "atoms"—would hardly need to bother with the "small group" if they knew what it was with substantial precision, for then there would be nothing to study. This brief explanation may seem even more incredible, although that is just how things are. But bear with the illustration.

Of course, students of the "small group" have a good general notion of what they are studying. Existing "group" concepts do vary. However, a common working definition, altogether sufficient for present purposes, does underlie much small-group research. Provisionally, then, *a small group is composed of the interrelations of a limited number of people*—with no firm upper limit on the number of members—*who have developed shared ways of perceiving their environment and of behaving within it.* A criminal gang or an adolescent clique, for example, fits this definition. Moreover, there is general agreement that a "small group" is not defined in such formal terms as mere membership in a work unit, a flying squadron, or a classroom.

Such a definition, while useful, leaves open many questions. That it does should not be surprising, for a similar problem bedevils even advanced research. Thus the modern physicist cannot answer the question: What is an atom? Indeed, if he could answer the question, there would be no point in studying physics, because everything worth knowing would be known. Of course, the physicist knows a great deal about atoms, but he never would have accumulated this knowledge had he been overly embarrassed by his failure to answer the definitional question above. The small-group analyst is in a similar position.

The questions left open by the provisional definitions of the small group above can be summed up in the query: How does one recognize a small group? The definition gives substantial help. But, patently, a valid and reliable operation would be required to permit consistent recognition and classification of small groups. Such an operational definition has not yet been developed.

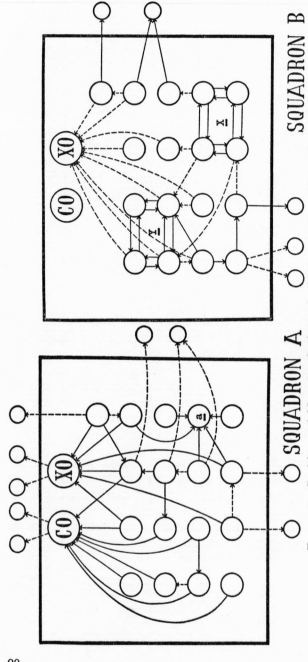

FIGURE 9. *Positive and Negative Sociometric Choices in Two Flying Squadrons*

A solid line designates a positive sociometric choice. A broken line designates a rejection, or a negative sociometric choice. CO designates the commanding officer; XO designates the executive officer.

Source: Reproduced from *Fundamentals of Social Psychology* by Eugene L. and Ruth E. Hartley, p. 379, by permission of Alfred A. Knopf, Inc. Copyright 1952 by Alfred A. Knopf, Inc. The data are from J. G. Jenkins, "Nominating Technique as a Method of Evaluating Air Group Morale," *Journal of Aviation Medicine,* XIX (1948), 12–19.

A brief analysis of one of the preliminary operations helpful in isolating small groups—the sociometric technique—will indicate some of the problems which must be solved. Describing this technique will serve the secondary purpose of demonstrating that formal units (in the case below, flying squadrons) do not necessarily display the behavioral uniformity which characterizes a small group.

The sociometric technique is a simple one. There are some complex technical difficulties inherent in it, but these may be avoided here in the main. The technique involves obtaining and charting the responses of individuals to such questions as: Who would you prefer for a flying partner? and Who would you rather not fly with? Figure 9 charts the positive and negative choices within two flying squadrons active during World War II.

The interpretation of the choice patterns revealed by the technique, however, is a sometimes sticky matter. But some conclusions seem obvious enough from Figure 9. For example, calling Squadron B a "small group" is obviously ill advised. The seventeen internal rejections hardly suggest a fervent togetherness. This is not to say, however, that Squadron B is disorganized. Notice the two "closed" choice patterns, labeled X and Y. The reciprocated choices suggest two small groups with high cohesiveness, which are insulated from each other and from the two formal superiors. The pattern of rejections, both to and from the two clusters of choices, also suggests this conclusion. In contrast, Squadron A has a substantial claim toward being considered a behavioral unit. There are but three internal rejections. The ten rejections directed at individuals who are not members of Squadron A, moreover, suggest an exclusiveness characteristic of small groups. The pattern of positive choices also suggests a similar unity. The formal superiors, CO and XO, are not rejected by any squadron member. The clustering of choices around individual a does suggest at least a latent informal leader, but he does not seem to have organized resistance to the formal superiors. Thus no individuals choosing a reject CO or XO.

Although helpful, such operations as the sociometric technique do not solve all of the problems associated with isolating small groups. But the clusters of sociometric choices do isolate likely (and unlikely) prospects for closer investigation. This is not simply a hope, for such choice-clustering subtly but substantial-

..y influences behavior. Thus it is not surprising that officers rating Squadrons A and B were agreed that A was the superior squadron, with higher morale and involvement in work. Squadron B was the administrative equivalent of Peck's Bad Boy. The sociometric technique helps explain why this was the case. Many of the small-group properties introduced below will similarly help to explain the differences between the squadrons.

Much must be learned, in short, before "small groups" may be classified with the certainty with which a botanist catalogues plants. But, as the following two chapters will demonstrate, considerable sophistication is possible, even if gaps in knowledge remain.

The Relevance of

the Small Group in Organization:

Sources of Group Power

There are, however, factors which support the use of small-group analysis. Two of these are emphasized below in turn: the importance of the small group in understanding behavior in organizations; and the substantial progress which has been made in small-group analysis.

The importance of the small group in understanding behavior in organizations, to begin, can be established in a roundabout (but useful) fashion by explaining the reasons for the small group's control of member behavior. On the most general level, the formation and the influence of the small group seem to be self-starting and self-perpetuating. Thus one student noted: "Our human nature is acquired in primary groups (such as the small group), and in the process of acquiring it we also absorb a taste for primary interaction and motivation to form and join primary groups." [2] Studies of "feral children" strikingly support this view. Thus children who for a time ran wild, or were allegedly raised by animals, did not attain human capacities after

[2] Robert E. L. Faris, "Development of the Small-Group Research Movement," in Muzafer Sherif and M. O. Wilson (eds.), *Group Relations At the Crossroads* (New York: Harper, 1953), pp. 166–67.

recapture despite intensive training. The Wild Boy of Aveyron, for example, had reached only a sixth-year level of performance when he died at the (approximate) age of forty.[3] Deprived of human group life during a crucial period of his development, in short, the Wild Boy never reached full human capabilities.

On a less general level, the small group fills many important needs of its members. Consequently, it may influence member behavior because of the valued services which it provides. Often, in addition, the small group has a near-monopoly on the provision of some of these services. This enhances group power over its members.

Some of these services, the bases of the importance of the small group, are usefully outlined. First, the group may serve as an agency through which its members obtain and evaluate information about themselves and about their environment. For example, individuals seek (and act consistently with) group consensus on opinions and on evaluations of member performance. The finding has massive support in the research literature. Illustratively, people can be induced to perform the strangest behaviors in experimental situations because their fellow group members (who often are accomplices of the experimenter) have led them on. Man often jiggles on the string of social pressure.

Such findings do not demonstrate man's gullibility, but rather his profound and general dependence upon groups. As one student noted of membership in adolescent gangs: "Participation in gang activities means everything to the boy. It not only defines for him his position in the society he is greatly concerned with, but it becomes the basis of his conception of himself."[4] Such rewarding experiences tend to become generalized. Consequently, individuals display a marked sensitivity to group pressures even in highly artificial situations.

Second, the group may create some aspects of reality which affect the behavior of members and non-members. This creation of "social reality" is a crucial group function, nonetheless so because the process is a difficult one to influence from "outside." A formal organization, for example, usually can do no more

---

[3] Arnold Gesell, *Wolf Child and Human Child* (New York: Harper, 1939).

[4] F. M. Thrasher, *The Gang* (Chicago: Chicago, 1927), p. 332. Copyright 1927 by the University of Chicago.

than to attempt to create an environment which encourages the group to follow a friendly path. Thus, commonly, groups develop and enforce limits on production. Such "bogeys" become very real for group members, and for outsiders who happen to come into contact with the group. The reality of such norms may be brought clearly home, for example, to individuals who violate them, for the techniques for keeping group members (and others) in line may run the gamut from more or less friendly cajoling not to be "different" to physical violence. An extreme example covers the full spectrum of such techniques:

> Every [criminal] gang tends to develop its own code of conduct, of which its members are more or less aware and which may be more or less rigidly enforced upon them. . . . Opinion in the group manifests its pressure in the variety of mechanisms through which group control is exerted, such as applause, preferment and hero-worshipping as well as ridicule, scorn, and ostracism. . . . In the gang the member who has broken the code may be subjected to a beating or in extreme cases may be marked for death.[5]

Third, the group may fill a deep need for affiliation and affection. Both needs are quite strong in most humans. Indeed, as a famous impostor has explained the success of his deceptions: "Most people would rather be liked than be right." The small group has an enormous advantage in filling such needs, and thus in controlling its members. Indeed, in the "formal approach," the ideal organization has been purged of emotion and affection.

These needs of man help to explain much behavior. For example, the prevalence of clique formation among adolescents is explained by their curiously in-between state. They are not children and yet are not admitted to adult status. Their need for affiliation (and perhaps affection) is thus particularly acute. The general point is supported in an extreme way by the study of a particularly intense conflict situation in which the normal

[5] *Ibid.*, p. 284.

pressures were complemented by a number of significant forces acting on an immigrant family. As Shaw noted:

> As a protection against the delinquency-producing effects of the gang, play group, and community, the family influence was negligible. Extreme poverty, the lack of group unity which resulted from the widely divergent social backgrounds of the parents and the brothers, and the discontinuity of family traditions, precluded the development of . . . intimate, stable relationships, loyalties and mutual interests . . . . Parental control was almost entirely absent. Consequently, in the absence of restraints in the family, the early controlling influences in the lives of the brothers were limited largely to whatever group or groups they might perchance become associated with. . . .[6]

In a similar way, if to varying degrees, the same tensions encourage the adolescent to find his own way in his peer groups.

Fourth, the group may serve as a defense against forces which group members as individuals could not (or will not) resist. Thus group-enforced restriction of output may protect the individual against management, an effort in which the individual would be relatively powerless.

Relevantly, the "formal approach" seems to encourage the development of small groups opposed to management. The emphasis of the approach upon "partial man," in effect, reduces the likelihood that individuals will view their *roles in the formal organization* as satisfying their needs for belonging and affection. As James Worthy, an acute observer of organization behavior, explained "the apathy of workers, their lack of concern for efficiency, their indifference to finding new and better ways of doing their jobs": "Much of the difficulty lies in the fact that industry, following the tenets of scientific management, has systematically deprived workers of real and effective participation in industry. Industry is reaping what it has sown, for without participation there can be neither initiative nor responsibility."[7]

[6] Clifford Shaw (ed.), *Brothers in Crime* (Chicago: Chicago, 1938), p. 356. Copyright 1938 by the University of Chicago.
[7] Worthy, *Big Business and Free Men*, p. 71.

The small group, then, has many and varied levers for influencing behavior in formal organizations. Thus forecasts of the research place of small-group analysis have been optimistic. As one student noted some years ago:

> The discovery that human society has an actual, dynamic, central structure underlying and determining all its peripheral and formal groupings may one day be considered as the cornerstone of all social science. This central structure . . . is either found or discernible in every form of human society, from the most primitive to the most civilized. . . . In addition, it exerts a determining influence upon every sphere in which the factor of human interrelations is an active agent—in economics, biology, social pathology, politics, government and similar spheres of social action.[8]

The forecast above may seem a bit enthusiastic. The analysis of subsequent chapters will allow the reader to make his own modifications. But the forecast is supported by the preliminary outlined below of the How? and Where? of the relevance of the small group in organization.

How is the small group relevant in organization? Basically, the unity of the small group has a personal or psychological basis. And, moreover, the small group regulates individual behavior and controls (to varying degrees) the conditions of the group's existence within some broader environment. Thus students of organization cannot overlook the small group, for the formal organization is technical, or a-personal, and attempts to control individual behavior for the rational fulfillment of organization purposes. The small group—a behavioral organization—and the

formal organization thus contrast sharply.

This contrast between behavior and the formal organization often has been interpreted simplistically. Much of the literature, indeed, has taken this contrast to imply only that the behavioral organizations (like the small group) constitute a restraint on the degree to which formal organizations can function effectively.

[8] Jacob L. Moreno, "Foundations of Sociometry, and Introduction," from *Sociometry*, IV (February, 1941), 15, Jacob L. Moreno (ed.), Beacon House, Inc., publishers.

This point of view was particularly common in the earlier days of the study of social organization. But the emphasis is still to be found. The small group, of course, can play such a negative role. It can emasculate the most elegant technical intentions, and the small group—or other forms of behavioral organization—would merit study on this ground only. But the small group's role is not limited to resistance; it can make the formal organization more effective as well as less effective.

The contrast between the behavioral organization and the formal organization, in fact, implies the threefold importance of the small group in the accomplishment of the purposes of the formal organization. The negative role need only be acknowledged. Thus a small group may exercise control over its members in matters such as the restriction of output. The emphasis upon the small group, then, complements the emphasis upon authority as a formal, one-way relation.

The positive role of the small group in achieving organization purposes also demands attention. A high output norm, for example, would serve such a purpose. The behavioral dynamics involved may be sketched briefly. A norm supporting high output is often more potent than the most stringent of attempts to coerce effort through formal techniques, for the norm is of the group members' own making; it is not imposed upon them. The difference is a profound one—the difference between being told to do and being anxious to do.

These norm dynamics have been supported by many observations, not the least important of which deal with Soviet industry, in which the possibility of management control of behavior seems most likely. The largely-unknown story of the attempts to encourage work-saving methods in the Soviet Union deserves careful reading by anyone anxious to downgrade the power of the behavioral organization.

Moreover, positively, the small group could complement the technical organization by providing control in areas into which the technical organization has not been extended, or into which it cannot be extended. Illustratively, the small group, by providing affiliation and affection for its members, can make them more secure. This may be of great importance, not only for the general well-being of the individual, but also for his performance in the organization. In the latter sense, for example, the small

97

group could serve organization purposes by reducing the amount of emotional energy an individual expands in worry, lack of concentration on the job, and so on. In any case, the formal organization cannot often (if at all) provide such satisfactions directly. Indeed, to the extent that the formal organization approaches the goals of a-personality implicit in traditional organization theory, the formal organization limits its ability to supply such satisfactions, directly and indirectly.

The small group, then, can lay claim to a substantial importance in organizations. It may influence the achievement of organization purposes in one direction or the other, but it will tend to influence the achievement of these purposes substantially in either case.

That the small group seems literally everywhere in organizations only supports this claim of its importance. Whatever purposes it serves, the small group is a universal element of the "informal organization" which develops within any formal organization. Thus the small group has been called one of the by-products of any attempt at coordinated human behavior. It may be understood. And it may be modified. But it may never be done away with. The prominence of groups even in that most formal of all organizations, the military, forcefully suggests the point.[9]

Where is the small group relevant in organization? "Everywhere" is an accurate, if unrevealing, answer. Consider processes, functions, and levels. The small group is relevant to such organization *processes* as decision-making, for the norms of a small group often constitute the boundaries within which decisions are made. The small group, further, is also relevant in such organization *functions* as personnel management. If, to simplify somewhat, personnel management consists of getting work done through others, the small group must patently be reckoned with. As for organization *levels*, group development is frequent and takes place at all levels. The tendency is to think of the small group as a phenomenon of low organization levels, for much research has centered on the low-level, formal work unit. But the small group is ubiquitous in organization. To illustrate, negotiation and decision-making on higher levels

[9] Burleigh B. Gardner, "The Factory as a Social System," in William F. Whyte (ed.), *Industry and Society* (New York: McGraw, 1946), pp. 4–20.

typically occur in small working committees. Small-group analysis will apply to them.[10]

These are cursory answers to the How? and Where? of the relevance of the small group in organization. But they provide ample evidence that it is not trifling to ask: Where and how is the small group revelant in organizations? Indeed, the question may be one of the more profound ones which may be asked about productive organizations.

This claim of substantial importance for the small group in organizations is not novel, traditional organization theory's neglect of the small group notwithstanding. Thus Chester I. Barnard, a well-known student and practitioner of administration, argued that the very basis of organization is twofold: the successful development of small groups, and their integration into the purposes of the formal organization.[11] What is novel is that the theory to exploit such insights has but recently become available.

SMALL-GROUP PROPERTIES:

INTRODUCTION

The importance of the small group in organization thus can be defended. In addition, there has been substantial progress in small-group analysis which permits a more complete description and explanation of organization behavior than that provided by the traditional theory of organization.

Three related panels of variables will be utilized below to demonstrate this greater completeness. The term "variable" is used here simply as shorthand for any property which is useful in describing small groups. Similarly, "length" is a variable useful in describing my desk. The three panels of variables here are:

    a. a *structural panel*, which consists of variables which characterize the manner in which a group is organized

---

[10] Nicholas T. Fouriezos, Max L. Hutt, and Harold Guetzkow, "Measurement of Self-Oriented Needs in Discussion Groups," *Journal of Abnormal and Social Psychology*, XLV (October, 1950), 682–90.

[11] Chester I. Barnard, *The Functions of the Executive* (Cambridge, Mass.: Harvard, 1938).

TABLE IV

Selected Small-Group Variables

Structural Panel	Style Panel	Population Panel
functional roles	atmosphere	intelligence
status	role style	authoritarianism
leadership	task	response repertoires
status congruency	norms	compatibility
cohesiveness	style integration	
structural integration	threat	

> (e.g., the ranks of group members on the performance of "leadership" behaviors);
>
> b. a *style panel*, which consists of variables which characterize the customary patterns of behavior in a small group (e.g., "authoritarian"); and
>
> c. a *population panel*, which consists of variables which characterize individuals and are relevant to individual performance in small groups (e.g., intelligence).

The reanalysis of the Patent Office case will employ only a few of the variables which have been developed in these panels. These variables are given in Table IV.

SMALL-GROUP PROPERTIES:

THE STRUCTURAL PANEL

Each of the selected variables—beginning with the structural panel—will be described briefly and its relations with other variables will be outlined. Only nominal definitions, about which there is general agreement, will be considered. There is often a wide variation in operational definitions of the same nominally-defined concept. For research purposes, this variation is crucial, but such problems may be avoided here.

1. Functional Roles

"Functional roles," first, refer to sets of behaviors which may be performed in a group. Logical distinctions may be drawn between a large number of supposed roles. Applications of a

TABLE V

Illustrations of the Categories of Behavior
Which Define the Functional Roles

Functional Role	Includes Behavior Classified as
Individual Prominence and Achievement	"forceful" "quick to take the lead"
Aiding Group Attainment	"enforces operating procedures" "oriented toward solution"
Sociability	"socially acceptable to group members" "sensitive to what goes on in the group"

sophisticated statistical technique (factor analysis) to the observed behavior of individuals in groups, however, indicate that only three or perhaps four roles are functionally important *and* independent. The three most frequently isolated functional roles may be described as: Individual Prominence and Achievement; Aiding Group Attainment; and Sociability. These designations are defined in terms of categories which have been developed to observe and to classify behavior. Table V illustrates the types of behavior which have been associated with the three functional roles.[12]

Such classifications are not laboratory curiosities. They have proved useful in the analysis of behavior in work situations. Thus, in conferences and on railroad work units, formal heads who failed to perform a substantial number of behaviors in one or more of the three functional roles had their positions undercut by informal leaders. These informal leaders patently developed in response to a need for the performance of the required behaviors. Relevantly, also, such work units were characterized by low productivity and low satisfaction of participants.[13]

[12] A number of relevant studies are reviewed in Launor F. Carter, "Recording and Evaluating the Performance of Individuals as Members of Small Groups," in A. Paul Hare, Edgar F. Borgatta, and Robert F. Bales (eds.), *Small Groups: Studies in Social Interaction* (New York: Knopf, 1955), especially p. 494.

[13] See, for example, Andrew W. Halpin, "The Leadership Behavior and Combat Performance of Airplane Commanders," *Journal of Abnormal and Social Psychology*, XLIX (January, 1954), 19–22.

2. *Status*

"Status," to continue, refers to the rank accorded an individual for his performance of behaviors within a given functional role ("specific status"). Such a distinction is descriptively useful. Thus groups have been classified on the basis of the agreement of the members in assigning their peers to ranks on the "task facilitation" functional role. Groups with a high degree of agreement versus low-agreement groups on this functional role also tended to have different ranking patterns on the other functional roles. As one student described these differences in three-person groups:

> In summary, role differentiation in the High groups seems to be bi-partite, with an active "task specialist" [that is, a person ranked high on both "group task facilitation" and "individual prominence and achievement"] and a Best-Liked man. In the Low groups [the role differentiation] tends to be tri-partite (as well as more extreme), with an active participator who is neither well-liked nor highly rated on task ability, a more passive task specialist who is not well-liked, and a popular individual who is neither active nor highly rated on task ability.[14]

Status also has an important influence on the quality of small-group behavior. Thus high "status congruency"—that is, high similarity of the ranks of an individual on the three functional roles—is associated with smooth group functioning. For example, groups with high status congruency are more effective in the solution of "internal" group problems, such as providing member satisfaction, and of "external" group problems, such as effective performance of a task assigned by a formal superior.

The finding is expected, for low status congruency patently suggests group conflict about its structure. And such conflict dissipates energies which could have been devoted to task performance.[15]

[14] Philip E. Slater, "Role Differentiation in Small Groups," in Hare, Borgatta, and Bales, *Small Groups*, p. 503.

[15] Christof Heinicke and Robert F. Bales, "Developmental Trends in the Structure of Small Groups," *Sociometry*, XVI (February, 1953), 7–38.

3. Leadership

"Leadership" is of patent importance in the small group, since it may be defined briefly as the capacity to influence the behavior of others in some desired direction. The leadership concept, however, has been a very slippery one. The traditional emphasis has been upon the leader *as a person* with specific traits which are applicable in all situations. This may be called the *fungibility theory of leadership*, for the theory assumes that a leader is a leader in all situations. This emphasis proved abortive. Although such an emphasis underlies traditional organization theory, no universal traits were found. The relevant literature is vast, and thus the failure was not due to lack of effort.

The failure to validate the fungibility theory of leadership, however, led to a more productive concept of leadership as a *generalized function*, changing from situation to situation, to which all group members may contribute. Small-group analysis forced this new conceptualization. Research with functional roles has established that the behavior of leaders (selected by group members or observers) can be described parsimoniously in terms of such functional roles. Group leadership rank, then, is a "general-status" resultant of rank on the three specific-status ranks.

Other research benefits followed from this conceptual break-through. Thus the new concept has permitted the description of leadership in specific cases. And such specific description, in turn, explained the failure of the fungibility theory of leadership. Thus, groups differently weight the three functional roles in assigning leadership rank.[16] Some groups weigh "sociability" most; other groups may weigh "task facilitation" more heavily. The reasons for such differences between groups are not fully understood, but they exist.

Leadership study has profited from this finding. The new concept of leadership thus accounts for the similarities between leaders *and* for the dissimilarities, for the new concept emphasizes situational differences in the environment in which the leadership is exercised. Leadership based upon similar functional

[16] G. A. Theodorson, "Leadership and Popularity Roles in Small Groups," *American Sociological Review*, XXII (February, 1957), 58–67.

103

roles, then, reflects similar situational demands on the leader and his personality. Leadership based upon different functional roles, similarly, reflects different situational demands on the leader and his personality. The fungibility approach to leadership did not permit this degree of specificity. This is, of course, precisely why the early theory was inadequate.

Moreover, the situational concept of leadership contrasts sharply with traditional organization theory in two particulars. The new concept stresses two elements: the degree of similarity between any individual's three ranks on the performance of the three functional roles, and the degree to which the performance of leadership behaviors is distributed among group members. Traditional organization theory recognizes neither element. It assumes, first, that rank in the formal organization alone is sufficient to differentiate "leaders" from the "led." The axiom of one-line authority, for example, reflects this assumption. Traditional organization theory also assumes, second, that *the* leader must perform all (or most) leadership behaviors. The axiom of the unity of command, for example, reflects this assumption.

The test of the two elements stressed by the situational concept of leadership, then, would constitute a check on the validity of traditional organization theory. Such a test has not been performed. Fortunately, however, some preliminary evidence relevant to such a test has been accumulated. (Throughout, it should be noted, only the *informal rankings* are considered. The question of the integration of formal and informal rankings is considered in the last section of this chapter, on "structural integration.") This available evidence may be summarized in terms of two predictions derived from the situational concept of leadership:

    I. the degree to which a group ranks its members similarly on all three of the functional roles of leadership will affect group processes in significant ways; and

    II. the degree to which the performance of leadership behaviors is distributed among group members will affect group processes in significant ways.

The relevant evidence may be abstracted briefly. First, differences in the rankings of group members on the three functional roles have important effects on group processes. To illustrate, define "effective group performance" in terms of high output on task and of high satisfaction of group members. Also define leaders who are ranked highest on all three of the functional roles of leadership as "Great Men." Groups with Great Men have been distinguished from groups without them in these ways:

1. Great-Man groups have higher output on experimental tasks;
2. Great-Man Groups show a lower rate of overt tension, which is reasonably associated with higher member satisfaction; and
3. Great-Man groups have a "friendlier" atmosphere.[17]

Such findings are credible, for groups with a Great Man obviously settled their internal problems quickly and with a high degree of consensus. Such groups, then, most often would be in a favorable position to concentrate on the task than groups who had not agreed so quickly or completely about their status ranks. Thus traditional organization theory comes off second best to the new concept of leadership in the test of Prediction I above.

Second, differences in the distribution of the performance of leadership behaviors also have important consequences for group functioning. Traditional organization theory does not recognize such consequences, but many studies reveal that (up to some as-yet-undetermined point) wide distribution of the performance of leadership behaviors is often associated with more effective group performance. Attempts to monopolize leadership behaviors by one or a few members, in contrast, often depress group performance.[18] Much evidence in this and the following chapter—especially in the section on "atmosphere"—underscores the point. Prediction II above, in short, is supported.

Moreover, relatedly, the sharing of leadership behaviors will occur most often in groups whose members have similar ranks on each of the three functional roles of leadership. This may seem strange. However, the highest-ranked persons in such

[17] Edgar F. Borgatta, Arthur S. Couch, and Robert F. Bales, "Some Findings Relevant to the Great Man Theory of Leadership," *American Sociological Review*, XIX (1954), 755–59.

[18] For evidence of this effect in therapy sessions, see Leonard I. Schneider, "A Proposed Conceptual Integration of Group Dynamics and Group Therapy," *Journal of Social Psychology*, XLII (November, 1955), 174–75.

groups are in a strong position. Consequently, they may allow other group members to perform leadership behaviors in many situations. At the same time, these highest-ranked individuals reserve their right to perform such behaviors when they wish. Moreover, other group members acknowledge the legitimacy of this position. This has the effect of tying group members more firmly in to the group's functioning through personal commitment rather than merely by the force of one person who monopolizes the performance of leadership behaviors. In a group which has a less clear agreement about its rankings on the three functions, in contrast, less leadership sharing is likely. The two or three persons ranked highest on only one or two of the functional roles will tend to reject leadership sharing, since sharing is a threat to their already uncertain positions.

Thus, to complete the argument, the wide distribution of the performance of leadership behaviors will tend to be associated with high agreement on informal rankings. In addition, such agreement tends to be related to effective group performance (as was demonstrated above in reviewing the evidence supporting the first prediction derived from the situational concept of leadership). This, again, suggests the importance of the failure of traditional organization theory to provide for the distinctions implied in the situational concept of leadership.

4. Cohesiveness

The degree of intragroup agreement on status and leadership, in turn, varies with "cohesiveness." Cohesiveness is a measure of the group "social gravitational field." That is, cohesiveness refers to the degree of member attraction to group and, thus, to the degree of power which the group has over the behavior of its members. Three major sources of attraction to group have been studied in the small-group literature. They are: attraction to members; prestige of membership; and the characteristics of the task in which the group is engaged. A group's cohesiveness rises as the attraction to group based upon such elements increases.

Cohesiveness is not recognized in traditional organization theory. Indeed, this theory emphasizes the individual and the formal organization. It thus makes no provision for informal groups, let alone for such properties as cohesiveness. This neglect has a high price, for the direct relation of cohesiveness and the degree of group control of member behavior has been demonstrated often. The usual neglect of cohesiveness (for example, in organizing or disbanding a work unit) consequently shuns social forces of considerable magnitude.

The importance of cohesiveness deserves illustration. To begin, membership in a social group is associated with two effects: the development and enforcement of group standards of behavior, and the maintenance of the mental health of members by permitting easier adjustment to the environment. Given the nominal definition of cohesiveness, groups of high cohesiveness (HiCo) should be more successful on both counts than low-cohesiveness groups (LoCo). A number of existing studies which test this prediction can be reviewed in outline to suggest the nature of cohesiveness and its group effects.

Consider the development and the enforcement of group standards of behavior. The literature clearly demonstrates the greater effectiveness of HiCo versus LoCo groups. Figures 10A and 10B demonstrate this greater behavioral uniformity in HiCo groups. Figure 10A illustrates the finding that, *within* work units, members of HiCo groups tended to have more similar output records (whether high or low) than members of LoCo groups. Productivity was measured as "per cent of standard." Figure 10A thus compares *individuals*. Similarly, Figure 10B reflects the greater tendency for HiCo work units, considered *as groups*, to be higher (or lower) producers than LoCo groups. That is, there were greater differences between the total outputs of the several HiCo groups than between LoCo groups. Again, this reflects the greater control of member behavior in HiCo groups.

Consider, also, the maintenance of the mental health of members and of their adjustment to the environment. Studies again reflect the greater control potential of HiCo versus LoCo groups. Thus in a plant manufacturing heavy equipment, one study reports that the "cohesive work group provides affective support for the individual in his encounters with anxiety-producing aspects of his work environment." To illustrate, members of work units were asked: "Does your work ever make you feel 'jumpy' or nervous?" Several choices were provided. A low numerical score represents relatively high tension.

Figure 11 graphically presents the work-unit score averages on

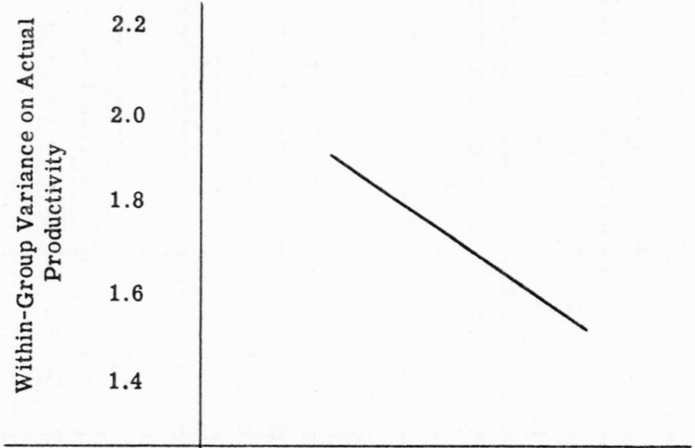

FIGURE 10A. *Group Cohesiveness and Within-Group Variance in Productivity*

Group Cohesiveness	1 - 4 (Low)	5 - 7 (High)
No. of Groups	140	88

FIGURE 10B. *Group Cohesiveness and Between-Group Variance in Productivity*

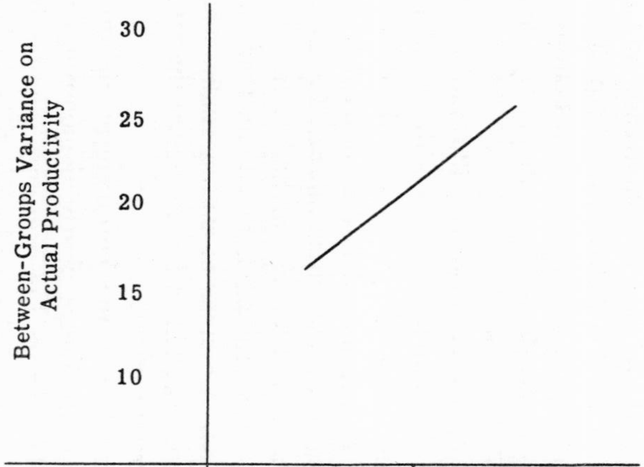

Group Cohesiveness	1 - 4 (Low)	5 - 7 (High)
Number of Groups	140	88

Source: Stanley E. Seashore, *Group Cohesiveness in the Industrial Work Group* (Ann Arbor: Survey Research Center, University of Michigan. 1954), pp. 67 and 71 for Figures A and B respectively.

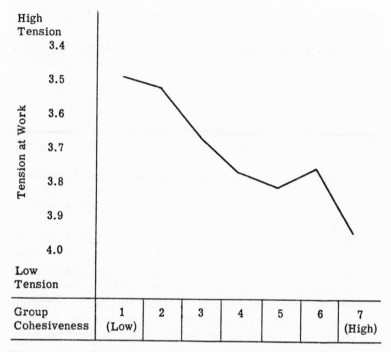

FIGURE 11. *Relation Between Group Cohesiveness and Tension at Work*

Source: Stanley E. Seashore, *Group Cohesiveness in the Industrial Work Group* (Ann Arbor: Survey Research Center, University of Michigan, 1954), p. 49.

tension plotted against a measure of cohesiveness. The association is a pronounced one.

Any group which meets such an important need of its members in such a convincing fashion, of course, would exercise substantial control over behavior. For an individual to reject his group by non-support, in short, would mean that he deprived himself of a defense against the anxiety-producing aspects of his environment. The stakes would have to be high indeed, then, to force such non-support. Interestingly, traditional organization theory seems to raise the stakes. The theory, if followed in organization, would tend to increase cohesiveness. Consider the narrow span of control, or job specialization and routinization. They imply high threat and, consequently, produce high anxiety. In doing so, traditional

109

organization theory would encourage the development of groups with high cohesiveness, for only such groups could reduce anxiety effectively. Traditional organization theory, in short, limits its own effectiveness. Life, in contrast to utopian models, often is curiously paradoxical.

In sum, then, cohesiveness is a strategic group property. Some of the specific processes through which member behavior is controlled further explain the importance of cohesiveness. Four of these processes deserve specific mention, similar relations having been observed in many studies:

1. *amount and intensity of communications:* participation is more equal and intense in HiCo groups than LoCo groups, in keeping with the greater value of participation implicit in the notion of high cohesiveness;

2. *rejection of deviants:* HiCo groups reject those who deviate from group standards more than do LoCo groups; interestingly, communications to deviants tend to be initially more frequent and finally less frequent in HiCo groups: this suggests that HiCo group members first make strenuous efforts to convert the deviant to group opinion, but that when conversion does not result the deviant is convincingly rejected;

3. *willingness to accept influence:* HiCo members are more susceptible to group influence; and

4. *reaction to threat:* HiCo groups are more effective in mobilizing resistance to threat than LoCo groups.[19]

The group with high cohesiveness, then, can influence the behavior of its members through some powerful processes. These processes have two effects: they firmly tie the member to the group, and they shut out the outsider or deviant.

One additional point deserves emphasis. It somewhat ameliorates the neglect of cohesiveness in traditional organization theory. That is, the level of cohesiveness in formal organization may be controlled. Of course, if traditional organization theory were reflected completely in practice, cohesiveness certainly would be low. Short of this apparently unusual state of affairs, however, other techniques also can encourage low cohesive-

[19] Robert T. Golembiewski, "Management Science and Group Behavior: Work-Unit Cohesiveness," *Journal of the Academy of Management,* IV (August, 1961), 87–99.

ness. Thus a "kitty" in a manufacturing situation—the "banking" of some part of an employee's piecework payments for production on "good days" to be applied to his earnings at some future date when his output is lower than he would like it to be—sometimes has been a potent source of suspicion between workers. This tends to keep cohesiveness low, for employees tend to keep the size of their kitties secret, so that their fellow workers will not pressure them to accept jobs for which rates are relatively unprofitable.[20] Group relations are difficult to maintain under such conditions.

5. Structural Integration

Cohesiveness, like the other variables introduced thus far, is relevant to the internal structure of the group. The final class of structural variables is externally oriented. Thus "structural integration" variables tap the degree of congruence of structural properties (e.g., leadership rank) and the corresponding structural properties prescribed by a formal organization (e.g., supervisor). The theory underlying the O & M application, of course, requires no such distinction. Indeed, traditional organization theory assumes that only formal structural relations are relevant.

The distinction between patterns of formal-informal structural linkage is not simply hairsplitting. Consider the crucial matter of communication in an organization. It makes an appreciable difference, for example, who interprets management communications. A formal supervisor with high informal rank often will encourage a friendly reception of communications by work-unit members. An informal leader who arose because the formal supervisor had been rejected often would provide less sympathetic transmission. Indeed, he probably often would tend to be a "central person" who molded together antimanagement sympathies. Reasonably, then, he would try to protect the source of his power. His interpretation of communications, as a result, might not be unbiased.

These patterns have a deep significance in organizations. Illustratively, different patterns of formal-informal linkage have

---

[20] Chris Argyris, *Understanding Organizational Behavior* (Homewood, Ill.: Dorsey, 1959), pp. 85–87.

TABLE VI

*Relation of Men's Perception of a Group Spokesman
to Section Productivity*

Section Gangs on a Railroad
Question: "Is there some one man in the section who speaks up for
the men when they want something?"

	Yes	No	Not* Ascertained	Total	N
Men in high-producing sections	9%	47%	44%	100%	156
Men in low-producing sections	17%	37%	46%	100%	142

* Consists primarily of employees of whom this question was not asked.
Source: Robert L. Kahn and Daniel Katz, "Leadership Practices in Relation
to Productivity and Morale," in Dorwin Cartwright and Alvin Zander
(eds.), *Group Dynamics: Research and Theory* (Evanston, Ill.: Row, Peterson, 1960), p. 558.

important effects on group processes. Thus section gangs on a
railroad tended to give distinctive responses to the question:
"Is there some one man in the section who speaks up for the
men when they want something?" A positive reply, of course,
strongly suggests an informal leader who at least complements,
and may subvert, the formal supervisor. A negative reply implies, although not so forcefully, a high degree of structural
integration. Table VI summarizes the answers obtained and
their relation to work-unit productivity.

In sum, only about 1 in 6 respondents from a high-producing
section reported an informal leader. Almost 1 of every 3
respondents from a low-producing section did so. The differences, of course, are not overwhelming. Thus it is too simple
to conclude that high structural integration of the formal and
small-group organizations is always associated with high productivity, for approximately 1 in every 6 respondents suggests that
low structural integration and high productivity occur together.
In addition, reasonably, in some cases a formal supervisor will
obtain high informal rank in the small group only by becoming
a defender of his work unit and of its low productivity.

But the differences in Table VI do establish this point: when
structural integration is low, it is uncommon that an informal

leader does induce a high level of output; and when structural integration is high, output tends to be high. Consequently, the failure of traditional organization theory to provide for different patterns of structural integration is often a very practical omission. As in many other cases, traditional organization theory lacks specificity.

6

THE SMALL GROUP
AND ORGANIZATION THEORY:
SOME RELEVANT VARIABLES, II

UNDERSTANDING THE STRUCTURE OF A GROUP WILL AID A REANALYSIS of the reorganization of the Patent Office. These structural properties permit an explanation beyond the powers of traditional organization theory, but they do not carry the reanalysis far enough. This chapter concentrates on a panel of variables which will extend the analysis, the style panel. Variables in this panel characterize the tone of group life. They describe modes, or customary patterns, of behavior in groups. Style variables will contribute substantially to a more complete analysis of the reorganization of the Patent Office than is provided by traditional organization theory.

SMALL-GROUP PROPERTIES:

THE STYLE PANEL

The style panel of variables complements the structural panel. Illustratively, knowing A's rank on leadership in a certain group is not enough. The *style* in which A performs the functions of leadership also must be known to permit accurate predictions. The sections below, indeed, are an extended introduction to the subtleties of how the specification of style properties increases the predictive power of group theory.

TABLE VII

Two Leadership Role Styles

Directive	Permissive
1. All determination of policy by supervisor	1. All policies a matter of group discussion and decision, encouraged and assisted by the supervisor
2. Techniques and activity steps dictated by the supervisor, one at a time, so that future steps are largely uncertain	2. Activity perspective gained during discussion period. General steps to group goal sketched, and when technical advice is needed the leader suggests two or more alternative procedures from which a choice could be made
3. Supervisor usually dictates the task and work companion of each group member	3. Members are free to work with whomever they choose and division of tasks is left up to the group

Source: Based on Ralph White and Ronald Lippitt, "Leader Behavior and Member Reaction in Three 'Social Climates,'" in Dorwin Cartwright and Alvin Zander (eds.), *Group Dynamics: Research and Theory* (Evanston, Ill.: Row, Peterson, 1960), p. 528.

1. Role Styles and Group Atmospheres

Markedly different styles of group behavior—or "atmospheres"—result from differences in the role style of supervisors or informal leaders. The structural variable "leadership rank" cannot stand alone. It must be complemented by differences in styles such as shown in Table VII. In sum, the permissive leader attempts to create the conditions for group success. The directive leader, in contrast, stands ready to prevent or punish failure.

Group atmosphere, in turn, has a significant influence on member behavior. The effect is illustrated most markedly when individuals are shifted between collectivities which have different group atmospheres. Figures 12A and 12B vividly portray such atmosphere-induced changes in the behavior of two children.[1]

[1] Kurt Lewin, Ronald Lippitt, and R. K. White, "Patterns of Aggressive Behavior in Experimentally Created 'Social Climates,'" *Journal of Social Psychology*, X (1939), 271–99, describe one study of "atmosphere."

115

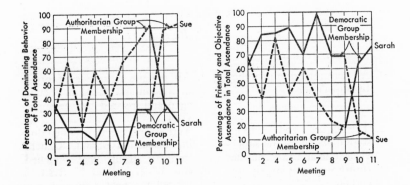

FIGURE 12. *Changes in the Performance of Two Specific Behaviors by Individuals Under Conditions of Two Different Group Atmospheres*
Total Ascendant Behavior = Dominating Behavior + Friendly Ascendance + Objective Ascendance
Dominating Ascendance, example: "Shut up!"
Friendly Ascendance, example: "Let's do coloring."
Objective Ascendance, example: "Give me some of that paint" (might be dominating ascendance, depending upon the tone of voice).

Source: Reproduced from *Fundamentals of Social Psychology* by Eugene L. and Ruth E. Hartley, p. 398, by permission of Alfred A. Knopf, Inc. Copyright 1952 by Alfred A. Knopf, Inc. The data come from Kurt Lewin, Ronald Lippitt, and Sybille K. Escalona, "Studies in Topological and Vector Psychology I," *University of Iowa Studies in Child Welfare* (Iowa City, 1940), XVI, 169.

Moreover—under certain imprecisely-known but general conditions—the permissive atmosphere creates less resistance to the formal supervisor and his goals. Thus, in the famous Lewin experiments, a group often resisted a directive supervisor. And —even if he were successful in monopolizing all leadership functions—the group often rebelled when the supervisor was absent. Task performance was forgotten, and the group tended to disintegrate as a functioning unit. Groups with permissive supervisors did not experience these difficulties.[2]

The finding has a patent importance for organization theory. Of course, the role styles sketched above are extreme types. Behavior in organizations, however, often approaches one or the other style. Supervisory behavior which approaches the directive style runs a substantial risk, for the style is difficult to

[2] Ralph White and Ronald Lippitt, "Leader Behavior and Member Reaction in Three 'Social Climates,'" in Dorwin Cartwright and Alvin Zander (eds.), *Group Dynamics: Research and Theory* (Evanston, Ill.: Row, Peterson, 1960).

116

apply constantly, even when the employee has little skill and his job requires little mobility. The attempt to approach a directive style, then, often will result in considerable loss of effectiveness.

This relation, however, must not be brutalized. The reaction need not be obvious, as in lower output. It might be manifested in more obscure, but no less important, ways. Illustratively, absences might be high; accidents might be more common; or damage and theft might be a great problem. Not all of these consequences affect output immediately, but they all have their costs, whether in terms of dollars or less calculable damage to humans.

Many studies support this prediction. Thus the study of an insurance company revealed that "close supervision" was associated strongly with low productivity. "Close supervision" is defined in common-sense terms such as frequent check-ups, detailed and frequent instructions, and general limits on the freedom of individuals in doing their work. Close supervision, in short, approaches the directive role style. "General supervision," it must be emphasized, does not mean the absence of control by supervisors. The form of control is different, not absent. General supervision stresses the development of objectives monitored by supervisors, with a wide tolerance for differences in employee behavior as long as the objectives are met.

Tables VIIIA and VIIIB illustrate this relation of styles of supervision and output at three organization levels. The relation is a marked one, but it is not monolithic. Thus the direction of results is consistent, although there are exceptions. The results, incidentally, apply to clerical sections in an insurance company. Similar findings have been reported for scientists in research laboratories as well as for a number of other skill levels.

Of course, traditional organization theory implies that a directive role style and close supervision are essential to high productivity. The implication is grossly inaccurate, if such findings as those in Table VIII are any criteria. For, in most cases, the O & M theory predicted incorrectly: of the 48 cases in Table VIII, only 13 showed the predicted relations of close supervision with high productivity or of general supervision with low productivity. Asterisks indicate these 13 cases in the table. This is a 28 per cent record for correct predictions, which does not encourage confidence in the theory from which the predictions are derived.

117

TABLE VIII A

Relation of Closeness of Supervision of Section Head to Productivity

	Close Supervision	General Supervision	Not Ascertained	N
Heads of high-producing sections	6*	5	1	12
Heads of low-producing sections	11	1*	0	12

TABLE VIII B

Relation of Closeness of Supervision of Section Head by His Supervisor to Section Productivity

	Close Supervision	General Supervision	Not Ascertained	N
On high-producing section heads	2*	9	1	12
On low-producing section heads	8	4*	0	12

Source: Robert L. Kahn and Daniel Katz, "Leadership Practices in Relation to Productivity and Morale," in Dorwin Cartwright and Alvin Zander (eds.), *Group Dynamics: Research and Theory* (Evanston, Ill.: Row, Peterson, 1960), pp. 559 and 561.

But a new theory of organization cannot simply call for a change to a permissive leadership style. This is too simple, although it is often advocated. Indeed, many studies contradict such findings as those reviewed above. Illustratively, college students in a directive-condition class received higher marks than students in a permissive-condition class. So varied are the results, indeed, that two students were forced to conclude that "the results obtained . . . are perplexing and leave us doubtful of the effectiveness of the 'group centered' or nondirective . . . methods."[3]

The findings are perplexing, however, only if one neglects all

[3] Henry W. Rieckens and George Homans, "Psychological Aspects of Social Structure," in Gardner Lindzey (ed.), *Handbook of Social Psychology* (Reading, Mass.: Addison-Wesley, 1954), II, 808.

factors other than atmosphere. But such other factors cannot be neglected, and the contradictions in results are more apparent than real. Population variables—some of which are considered in Chapter 7—illustrate the point. Individuals, it is no news, have different personality characteristics. A permissive atmosphere is more congenial to individuals with certain personality characteristics; a directive atmosphere more congenial to individuals with other characteristics. Hence (among other reasons) the contradiction in the research on group atmosphere, for most studies failed to specify the personality characteristics of their subjects.

Thus the diversity of the results of "atmosphere" research should not cause any particular puzzlement. Being puzzled in this connection, indeed, is much like being concerned that batches containing different and unknown proportions of apples and rocks do not always yield the same volume of cider. Granted, this may be overstating the point, for atmosphere research does not cover ground that different. But the general point holds.

The assumed relation of a permissive atmosphere and consequences (like high productivity) favorable to an "external" authority has a further liability. The assumption neglects certain style variables, of which three are particularly important. First, task characteristics have been studied little. But they can be usefully distinguished in terms of two elements: a "degree of structure," which refers to the degree of intimate cooperation necessary in task performance; and a "degree of solution patterning," which refers to such factors as the obviousness of the task solution.[4] Where the degree of structure is high and solution patterning low (that is, a conference on personnel policy, as contrasted with pulling copies of patents), socioemotional disturbances will affect task performance most. There the permissive condition will show to best advantage. Consequently, at least task differences must be specified in predictions of the effects of various supervisory styles.

---

[4] William C. Schutz, "Some Theoretical Considerations for Group Behavior," in Research and Development Board, *Symposium on Techniques for the Measurement of Group Performance* (Panel on Human Relations and Morale, Committee on Human Resources, Department of Defense, October 13–15, 1952), pp. 27–35.

2. Norms

"Norms" are also important intervening variables. The point is straightforward. Norms are the statements of the behavior acceptable in a group. These "gates" admit, or shut out, certain behaviors. Thus a formal supervisor who encouraged a permissive atmosphere in a work unit which had a norm of low productivity would probably reinforce that norm, at least in the short run. The usual temptation, of course, is to associate the permissive condition with more favorable consequences, such as increased productivity.

Other characteristics of norms further underscore their importance. First, the formation of norms is very common in small groups. Thus they are formed even in groups which are composed of previous strangers, who meet only for a short time, and who are unlikely to meet again. And these norms have been demonstrated to influence behavior for a time after their formation. The famous "autokinetic" experiment of Sherif illustrates the point.[5] In the experiment, individuals are shown a small light-source in an otherwise dark room. They are asked to make judgments about the distance the light-source moves during a number of exposures of brief duration. When groups of individuals are asked to make such judgments, they strongly tend to develop a shared estimate of the distance the light moves. These shared estimates persist when, at a later date, the individuals are asked to make such estimates *alone*.

Second, these norms are in important reality—a "social reality"—for group members. Such norms do not depend upon "objective" factors in all cases. Indeed, norms often develop in precisely those areas in which "objective" demonstrations are difficult or impossible. For example, the light-source in the Sherif experiment does not move at all, although it seems to move. Yet the norm influences behavior. Thus demonstrations that a particular norm is "wrong" objectively do not necessarily destroy its power over group members. For example, a work norm which defined a "good day's work" under a work process would tend to continue to influence worker behavior, even when the work process was changed so that it permitted more output with the same expenditure of effort. The factors, then, which are involved

[5] Muzafer Sherif, "A Study of Some Social Factors in Perception," *Archives of Psychology*, Vol. XXVIII, No. 187 (1935).

in the judgment of a "fair day's work" have psychological as well as physiological dimensions. This may seem an obvious point, but it is often neglected.

Third, relatedly, group norms often are the standards used to judge behavior even when these norms violate the rules of a formal organization or of "society." Perhaps more significantly, such norms often will be respected even when the individual prefers to behave differently. The production data below illustrate the power of norms in a clear way.[6]

	Days	Production Per Day
A	1-3	46
	4-6	52
	7-9	53
	10-12	56
B	13-16	55
	17-20	48
C	21-24	83
	25-28	92
	29-32	92
	33-36	91
D	37-40	92

The data present the production record of a member (W) of a small work unit performing a pressing operation. The work norm (informal) was 50 units. When members of the work unit found that member W had begun to exceed that limit (see A to B), other work unit members coerced W into curbing her efforts (B). At (C), the work unit was broken up and only W remained on the job. The increased production (C to D) is some measure of the influence of the norm on W.

Fourth, the member of the small group need not be aware that the norms of the group are influencing his behavior. Indeed, norms are more effective in controlling member behavior when they are unobtrusive, as when the individual simply cannot conceive of behaving any other way.

In sum, norms are the starch which keeps the small group functioning as a system, in contrast to a number of individuals. Consequently, norm violations are a threat to a group's existence.

[6] Lester Coch and John R. P. French, Jr., "Overcoming Resistance to Change," *Human Relations,* I (December, 1948), 519-20.

Such violations tend to be severely sanctioned as a result, with sanctions ranging from social ostracism to physical punishment, or in extreme cases, death. A cohesive group, however, need not employ sanctions continuously, for members tend to develop consciences about group norms. That is, they feel guilty about violating norms, or are frightened of the sanctions which may greet a violation. Discipline, in short, becomes internalized.

The norm concept thus is patently a crucial one in small-group theory. The concept's relations with other variables underscores this importance. For example, the degree to which norms influence behavior varies with cohesiveness. This is expected on logical grounds, for the greater the attraction of a group for its members, the more likely the performance of group-approved behaviors. Consistently, also, guilt feelings about the violation of norms are greater under conditions of high cohesiveness.[7]

3. Style Integration

The simple relation of permissive supervisory style and group performance which is favorable to the formal organization, also neglects "style integration." "Style integration" refers to the degree of consistency between the goals, norms, and behavior adopted by the informal group and those required by the formal organization. To illustrate, consider the formal supervisor who employs a permissive style in a group with a low-productivity norm. This supervisor might gain high informal status. To do so he probably would have to become a party to the norm enforcement, however. Thus structural integration of the formal and informal leadership ranks would be high, but style integration would be low.

The tendency for norms to determine supervisory behavior is well illustrated by a study of children's play groups in a day nursery, which deals with the effect of group norms on children who were introduced into groups after norm development had taken place.[8] The original group members might be described as "normally followers." In contrast, the children who were introduced after the norm development were "normally leaders."

[7] Glen Rasmussen and Alvin Zander, "Group Membership and Self-Evaluation," *Human Relations*, VII (May, 1954), 239–51.

[8] Ferenc Merei, "Group Leadership and Institutionalization," *Human Relations*, II (January, 1949), 23–24, 25. Italics supplied.

122

That is, they were children who were older and were judged as "domineering, imitated, aggressive rather than submissive, and . . . had initiative" in the day nursery from which the "normally followers" were drawn. The period of norm development was described in this way:

An assembly was considered a group when it developed a relatedness, with . . . rules, habit, traditions, entirely of its own. . . . Only such habits were considered traditions which were not found in the day nursery, but had developed during the experimental period. This gave us an objective criterion of the point at which an assembly constituted a group. (Pp. 23-24.)

The results of this experiment suggest that group norms often direct the leader or supervisor. As the experimenter summarized the results of those cases in which the "normally leaders" were able to gain control of groups:

. . . the same definite tendencies could be observed in all experimental units: the group absorbs the leader, *forcing its traditions on him.* The leader *takes over* the habits and traditions of children who are younger than himself and who in the day nursery had been his underlings following his guidance. Now he engages in those activities which the group had developed before he entered it. His own undertakings either remain unsuccessful or gain acceptance *only in a modified* form suiting the traditions of that group. (P. 25.)

the leader adjusts to bend toward est. group norms. This is necessary for leader to be part of the grp.

Thus the distinction between structural and style integration has many applications in organizations. Such a distinction is not provided for by traditional organization theory. It assumes that a formal-informal distinction does not exist, that structural and style integration are complete.

4. Threat

The final style variable is the degree of threat in the group environment. The common notions of "threat" are sufficient to indicate the conceptual ground which will be covered. Differences in threat underlie many of the variables in the style panel. Thus the different effects associated with role styles and group atmospheres, to illustrate, hinge upon the degree of threat to group members. That is, the directive role style has a higher threat potential for most subjects than the permissive role style.

Threat is no stranger to traditional organization theory. Indeed, it presumes the utility of a high degree of threat. Three of the propositions underlying this theory, especially, reflect this presumption. The limited span of control, first, clearly reflects an intention to create high threat on the job through close supervision. Similarly, the conception of authority as a formal, one-way relation also implies a high degree of threat, for the presumption is that the individual is—or, more properly, should be—impotent against formal authorities. Routinization and specialization, in addition, also imply a high degree of threat, as it is patently easier to monitor behavior closely when the unit of work is of limited and simple dimensions. Similarly, the person who performs routine tasks is easily replaceable. He thus has little countervailing power over formal superiors.

The theory underlying the O & M (Organization and Methods) application, then, assumed that *all* individuals *could* operate most effectively under high-threat conditions. But the theory also implied much more: that *all* individuals *would* operate effectively *only* under such conditions. The underlying assumption, of course, is that all (or enough) workers require threatening conditions to force their effort. As one official articulated what is apparently a common impression:

> I'll tell you my honest opinion. Five per cent of the people work, ten per cent of the people think they work. And the other eighty-five per cent would rather die than work.[9]

Practice seems to follow the lead of the traditional organization theory, if in a modified way, for employees often have countervailing power to (more or less) blunt formal authority, contrary to the traditional theory. For example, a supervisor explained his failure to use budget data to encourage *greater production* in this revealing way: "No, no, I couldn't even use a

[9] Chris Argyris, *What Budgets Mean to People* (New York: Controllership Foundation, 1952), p. 11.

budget in front of my people. *I just wouldn't dare. . . . We wouldn't get any production.*"[10]

Much recent research supports this supervisor's view, for high performance is often associated with low, rather than high, threat on the job. In sum, the O & M theory is not specific enough. That is, traditional organization theory conceives of but one response to threat, acceptance. At times, this response will occur and the theory will permit accurate prediction. But there are other responses to threat which do not lead to acceptance. Moreover, there are some low-threat techniques which can induce high productivity.

Traditional organization theory, then, does not cover all relevant cases. Some of these cases will be discussed here. First, the several responses to threat (and their consequences) will be analyzed. Second, a low-threat, group-oriented technique will be compared to traditional management methods for achieving high efficiency. In sum, the following discussion will demonstrate the simplicism of traditional organization theory, and it will also demonstrate that, in some cases, the theory will attain that which it seeks to avoid.

4a. Threat: Acceptance and Rejection. Patently, a threat-inducing command may lead to a high level of performance. The conditions under which such acceptance will occur, however, are not at all clear. In contrast, traditional organization theory assumes that acceptance will occur always (or most often).

The inadequacy of traditional organization theory can easily be demonstrated. The specific conditions in which it will be inadequate, however, pose a problem whose answer can only be outlined now. Consider the hypothesis that the greater the threat by management in support of a particular policy, the greater the conformity of employees to that policy. This hypothesis, of course, is consistent with the O & M theory.

Such a hypothesis has in fact been tested in a study of how threatening messages affect conformity to certain rules of dental hygiene.[11] To explain, a Strong Appeal emphasized such conse-

---

[10] *Ibid.* Italics supplied.

[11] Irving L. Janis and Seymour Feshback, "Effects of Fear-Arousing Communications," *Journal of Abnormal and Social Psychology,* XLVIII (January, 1953), 81.

TABLE IX

*Effect of the Illustrated Talk on Conformity
to Dental Hygiene Recommendations*

Type of Change	Strong Appeal	Moderate Appeal	Minimal Appeal
Increased conformity	28%	44%	50%
Decreased conformity	20%	22%	14%
No change	52%	34%	36%
Net change in conformity	+8%	+22%	+36%

Source: Based on data in Irving L. Janis and Seymour Feshback, "Effects of Fear-Arousing Communications," *Journal of Abnormal and Social Psychology*, XLVIII (January, 1953), 84.

quences of failure to follow the rules as pain from toothaches, and cancer, paralysis, blindness, or other secondary diseases. The Minimal Appeal mentioned no consequences worse than mouth infections and cavities. A Moderate Appeal emphasized intermediate consequences. The experimental subjects got the point. For example, about one-third of the subjects given the Minimal Appeal felt "somewhat worried" or "very worried" about the condition of their teeth. Nearly three-quarters of those exposed to the Strong Appeal experienced such worry.

One week before the appeals were made, the subjects were rated on their conformity to five basic rules of dental hygiene. The five rules were emphasized in each of the three appeals. One week after the appeals were made, the subjects were again rated on their conformity to the five rules. The object of interest, of course, was the effect of the three appeals on the individuals' conformity to the rules of dental hygiene.

The results are arresting, for they are in stark opposition to commonly-held expectations, as Table IX witnesses. In sum, the high-threat appeal barely broke even in influencing conformity to the five rules of dental hygiene. Only 28 per cent of those exposed to the Strong Appeal increased their conformity, while 20 per cent decreased their conformity. In contrast, 50 per cent of those exposed to the Minimal Appeal increased their conformity, while only 14 per cent showed a decrease.

The question of threat, then, is a complex one. Indeed, there are three possible explanations of the results obtained: hearers tend to avoid the fear-arousing issue, either by misunderstanding or not paying attention; hearers tend to react aggressively against the speaker, and punish him by rejecting his statements; or hearers may build up defenses against thinking about the fear stimulus again.

Similar rejection of fear-arousing communications occurs in organizations. Relatively full employment, unions, and the like, patently, would encourage such rejection. In addition, the reactions reflected in the experiment would be more intense if they were reinforced by group sanctions in an organization. A group will be most cohesive—and thus most able to control the behavior of its members—under conditions of a threat which is not overwhelming. Consequently, management actually may compound its problems of control by the use of fear-arousing techniques, unless it is willing to be ruthless. This difficulty would be greatest when a strongly-held group norm, such as a work-restricting norm, was at issue.

The implications of the experiment, however, should not be pushed too far. Under certain conditions, fear-arousing communications may have a more impressive record. Thus the threat may be overwhelming and resistance futile in the short run. Even in this case, however, it is unlikely that the threat can be sustained indefinitely. Hostile reactions can be expected when things "ease up."

The dental-hygiene experiment, moreover, is not in all respects comparable to an organization situation. Thus the subjects in the experiment could rather easily reject the communication if its fear-arousing potential were too high. In organizations, one may be able to "walk away" from similar communications only by quitting one's job. This may be a significant hardship. Moreover, threat might be more or less continually applied in an organization. The speed of an assembly line, for example, might be used for this purpose.

4b. Threat: Frustration and Its Characteristics. But if threatening stimuli in organizations may be less escapable than in the dental-health experiment, this does not necessarily make threat more effective. Consider a second general reaction to threat. An individual's progress toward goals he desires often will be thwarted by threat. This is another way of saying that *frustration* is a likely reaction to threat.

127

One cannot trifle with the literature on frustration. It is massive, and must be interpreted delicately in the bargain.[12] Moreover, the prolixity and complex nuances of the literature make for very heavy going and also make the attempt to integrate several approaches a more or less chancy matter. As if this were not reason enough for caution, efforts are presently being made to integrate the concept of "frustration" in a general theory. The distinguished psychologist O. H. Mowrer, for example, has made such a recent effort in what is usually called "learning theory."[13] Consider Amsel's integrative approach. He noted:

> . . . an adequate theory of instrumental behavior must involve three types of goal event: (a) *Rewarding events*—usually the presence of stimuli which evoke a consummatory reaction appropriate to some condition of deprivation; (b) *Punishing events*—noxious stimulation at the termination of a behavior sequence; and (c) *Frustrative events*—the absence of or delay of a rewarding event in a situation where it has been present previously.[14]

These may prove sufficient categories to encompass "goal events," but it would be presumptuous to assume that anyone knows with any precision the ways in which such integrative efforts will affect the concept. Thus particular care, and substantial understatement, are necessary in the interpretation of the "frustration" literature.

With all due respect to the problems of dealing with the concept in a very precise way, a somewhat heavy-handed approach will suffice for present purposes. This is not arbitrary, for it is possible to extract a central core of meaning from the literature.

[12] Laurance F. Shaffer and Edward J. Shoben, Jr., *The Psychology of Adjustment* (Boston: Houghton, 1956), pp. 98–124, review many relevant studies of humans and animals. Abram Amsel, "The Role of Frustrative Nonreward in Noncontinuous Reward Situations," *Psychological Bulletin*, LV (March, 1958), 102-19, reviews a very substantial body of such studies, his emphasis being upon experimentation with animals. The treatment here attempts to steer clear of the "debates" in the literature concerning whether frustration is a "state" or an "event," whether it is "emotional" or "nonemotional," and so on.

[13] O. Hobart Mowrer, *Learning Theory and Behavior* (New York: Wiley, 1960), especially pp. 403–11.

[14] Amsel, "The Role of Frustrative Nonreward," p. 102.

This central core—because of the frequency with which it has been validated from study to study—seems unlikely to be dropped from any future development of the concept. This relative certainty provides a firm basis for the present effort. Less may be said than the literature can support, but we may be the more certain of it because of the strict ground rule which has been set.

It is convenient to begin with an outline of the concept "frustration," providing we do not become too enamored of the particular terminology in which this working concept is couched. Thus there is general agreement that "frustration" involves the non-fulfillment of some premise upon which an individual has acted. Consider a chimpanzee which has become accustomed to getting water by pressing the handle of a spigot. If the water source is turned off, the chimpanzee will experience the non-fulfillment of one of his behavioral premises when it presses the handle of a spigot.

A second major emphasis completes our rough map of the conceptual terrain presently covered by the "frustration" concept. The concept is increasingly tied to *fear*, as well as to disappointment of behavioral premises. Indeed, these may simply be two ways of viewing a single reaction. This relation of fear and frustration is typically expressed in such terms as: "Thus all frustration would definitely connote the presence of fear, which is not, however, sufficiently overwhelming to cause a complete disappearance of the original goal-oriented tendency."[15]

Within this general description of the concept, several other areas of agreement seem clear. Thus increasingly fewer efforts are made to tie frustrating sequences to a particular reaction. The classical approach—following the pathfinding *Frustration and Aggression* of Dollard, Doob, Miller, Mowrer, and Sears— held that frustration and aggression were related in a simple stimulus-response chain.[16] The current view is more complex. Illustratively, Brown and Farber noted that

[In] this treatment of frustration as a determinant of behavior . . . no attempt has been made to specify precise-

[15] N. Bull and E. Strongin, "The Complex of Frustration: A New Interpretation," *Journal of Nervous and Mental Diseases*, CXXIII (1956), 532.

[16] John Dollard, Leonard Doob, Neal Miller, O. Hobart Mowrer, and Robert R. Sears, *Frustration and Aggression* (New Haven: Yale, 1939).

ly which responses will appear in thwarting situations. The present theory does lead to the [expectation] that responses associated with frustration in one situation will tend to appear in other thwarting situations. But there is nothing in the theory . . . to imply that aggression, for instance, will occur more frequently than withdrawal . . . or [regression].[17]

Some of these terms in this description will be more carefully defined presently. For now, our friend—let us call him Chimp A—may be used to illustrate the commonly-held notions outlined above. The present position is that the specific responses of many chimps to the same frustrating experience cannot be predicted accurately.[18] But if we know Chimp A well enough, his behavior when the water is turned off may be predicted with some certainty. Chimp A, for example, may bite his trainer at the first available opportunity nine out of every ten times the water is turned off. In addition, although with less certainty, the reaction may be predicted to occur when the chimp faces other frustrating conditions. (Our example may seem a bit hard on the trainer, but at least he should know what to expect.)

Also, relevantly, frustration is often accompanied by what the specialists call "intensification of on-going behavior." Thus Chimp A may evidence his frustration by repeated efforts to fulfill his premise concerning the water spigot, as by repeated and vigorous pressing of the spigot handle. This is a very common finding in the literature, whether animals or humans are considered.[19] On some occasions, however, the subject may lose interest in his original goal (e.g., getting a drink) and devote his attentions to the (real or fancied) obstacle to his original goal.[20]

[17] Judson S. Brown and I. E. Farber, "Emotions Conceptualized As Intervening Variables—With Suggestions Toward a Theory of Frustration," *Psychological Bulletin,* XLVIII (November, 1951), 490.

[18] As Mowrer noted of the white rat which is specially bred for laboratory experimentation: ". . . even a highly docilized strain of rats still have some spunk and spirit left. . . ." *Learning Theory and Behavior,* p. 405.

[19] A series of relevant experiments with animals documents the point. See A. Amsel and Jacqueline Roussel, "Motivational Properties of Frustration: I. Effect on a Running Response of the Addition of Frustration to the Motivational Complex," *Journal of Experimental Psychology,* XLIII (May, 1952), 363–68.

[20] Bull and Strongin, "The Complex of Frustration," p. 531.

130

It is in such cases that the trainer gets bitten rather than the spigot handle pressed. In either case, an intensification of behavior occurs, apparently reflecting a heightened motivation to achieve the original goal.

These few comments provide a degree of orientation to the literature on frustration. This accomplished, the next order of business is to begin the more direct application of the "frustration" concept to life in organizations. The transition will be gradual. Thus some of the difficulties of using "frustration" to predict behavior will be outlined, and particular attention will be devoted to the difficulties which arise because of the several possible reactions to a frustrating condition. This will build toward a set of predictions of the several effects frustration may have on output in organizations.

The move from the "frustration" literature to behavior in on-going organizations must be made cautiously. This need for caution is derived from three major sources of difficulty in the prediction of behavior under frustrating conditions. First, to complicate matters at the outset, frustration may occur along with either acceptance or rejection of a fear-arousing communication.

Second, people are not smooth marbles similarly affected by similar forces. Individuals differ in their tolerances to frustration. Moreover, different situations are frustrating to different individuals. To explain, most of the subjects in Lewin's experiments, who were reared in the "American culture," strongly preferred the permissive role style and atmosphere. Most of the children disliked the directive role style and atmosphere. They were frustrated by it. Some children, on the other hand, preferred the directive role style and its associated group atmosphere. Thus one child—perhaps significantly the son of an Army officer—said, "[The directive supervisor] was best. . . . [He] was strictest and I liked that a lot . . . he decided what we were to do"[21] Such children enjoyed the situation which had frustrated many other children. Their reaction is not a typical one in the small-group literature, but the reaction does emphasize the importance of the personality differences which are discussed in the next chapter.

Third, prediction also is difficult because frustrated behavior

[21] R. Lippitt and R. K. White. "An Experimental Study of Leadership and Group Life," in Theodore M. Newcomb and Eugene L. Hartley (eds.), *Readings in Social Psychology* (New York: Holt, 1947), p. 319.

may have four major characteristics, more than one of which may be present at the same time. Each of these has been produced experimentally in social laboratories, so their probable effects can be discussed with some confidence. These four characteristics are aggression, regression, fixation, and resignation. Each of them will be considered below in turn.[22]

The term "aggression" is used here to refer only to those reactions of rage—either of anger or of hate—which occur when an individual is continually thwarted in his attempts to control his environment. Typically, then, "aggression" in this sense refers to a specific desire to inflict pain or cause suffering.

But aggression is not a simple phenomenon. To begin, there are three general *sources* of aggression:

1. a specific individual or group with little power over the individual;
2. a specific individual or group with great power over the individual; and
3. general sources of discontent, e.g., economic conditions.

To compound the difficulty, the *target* of an individual's frustration is not necessarily the source of his aggression. Thus, given Source 2, direct aggression is difficult and/or dangerous; and with Source 3, direct aggression is impossible. Even with Source 1, the frustrated person may have strong feelings against direct aggression. Assorted dogs, cats, wives, and children may fall unsuspecting heir to the work-site frustrations of husbands. Or the individual may take out his aggressions on himself, and perhaps develop an ulcer or a psychosomatic illness.

The consequences of an aggressive reaction to frustration, then, are problematical, for an individual may direct his aggression inwardly, and punish himself by producing more. Or a "scapegoat" may be found who is the target of many aggressive acts but the source of few. Indeed, a self-punitive high producer is a likely candidate for scapegoat. Output restriction would be likely, and employee aggressions induced by the restriction would be visited upon the high producer. But the picture is very iffy. Thus if the scapegoat is an inept worker, he may have the opposite effect of sustaining higher productivity of other members of his unit. They must maintain superior performance

[22] See, particularly, the discussion in J. A. C. Brown, *The Social Psychology of Industry* (Baltimore: Penguin, 1954), pp. 254-75.

or lose their target for aggression. Or the "scapegoat" may be another department, against whom aggression can take such forms as forwarding defective items which may be counted against the record of the scapegoat department.

Thus an individual or a group can express aggression in a number of ways which will affect the formal organization differently. Frustration, however, can seldom be controlled so that only consequences favorable to the formal organization result. Thus one student noted that

> When frustration is of a minor degree or applies to only a few members, the resulting resentment may be fairly constructive and directed more or less rationally against the sources of the grievances. But when it is more severe and affects a larger number of people, it is liable to become generalized, wholly irrational, and directed against quite innocent individuals. The existence of a frustrating atmosphere in a factory may be easily diagnosed by the presence of such symptoms as excessive criticism of management, malicious gossip, the voicing of superficial grievances, damaging of equipment, . . . absenteeism and neurosis.[23]

Curiously, management apparently often attempts to meet these symptoms with their cause. That is, stricter discipline may be enforced or tighter work schedules set. The author described the circular process in this way: "This leads to further frustration, more resentment, more destructiveness, and merely aggravates the situation. If carried far enough, the workers may be cowed into submission, and the final result will be a smouldering hatred which is likely to poison management-worker relations for a long time. . . ."[24]

The second characteristic of frustration is *regression*. Regression refers to the tendency of frustrated people to abandon constructive attempts at problem-solving and to engage in more "childish" behaviors. Some measure of the effect of regression is provided by an experiment which placed children in a mildly frustrating situation. The children played initially with some very desirable toys. Their behavior, including the constructive-

[23] *Ibid.*, pp. 250–51.
[24] *Ibid.*, p. 251.

ness of their play, was closely observed and scored. After a time, the children were separated from the desirable toys and were given less desirable ones with which to play. The experimenters concluded that the degree of differentiation and organization of the children's play was equivalent, on the average, to that expected of children some 17.3 months younger in mental age. That is, the average child regressed nearly one-and-a-half years under a very mild frustrating stimulus.[25]

Regression in organizations is a very tricky phenomenon. It might have favorable consequences on some relatively simple tasks. In many cases, however, regression would be job-inhibiting, for it is associated with such consequences as lower emotional control, greater susceptibility to rumor, or wanton destruction of materials and equipment. The effects are wondrous to contemplate, should the members of a group of high cohesiveness react regressively because of their frustrated attempts to achieve a common goal. Unlike the individual who regresses, the group member has a ready source of support and protection. Regressive reactions supported by a group thus could be extreme.

The third characteristic of frustration is *fixation*, or the compulsive continuation of behaviors which have ceased to have adaptive value. To explain, a threat may have two different effects upon the individual threatened. In the first place, the threat may discourage the repetition of the act. The consequences of the threat, then, are avoided by avoiding the act. This is, of course, the intention of the threat. But the threat, paradoxically, may have the effect of leading to the fixation of that act. Thus, in some cases, the punishment of a child for some action may be futile, for the punishment merely compels him to perform it. This curious consequence seems to depend on a kind of psychological pleasure-pain calculation. Even though the act is punished, in short, the performance of the act, on balance, has desirable consequences. The frustration of not performing the action is disliked more than the punishment for performing the action.

If fixation occurs as a consequence of threat, predictions derived from the theory underlying the O & M application would be inaccurate. Instead of facilitating change, threat

[25] Roger G. Barker, Tamara Dembo, and Kurt Lewin, "Frustration and Regression: An Experiment With Young Children," *University of Iowa Studies in Child Welfare*, Vol. XVIII, No. 1 (1941).

would reinforce the *status quo* and compel resistance to change. If group members express their frustration by fixation, it goes almost without saying, unfreezing group attitudes will prove quite a chore.

Ample reasons suggest that fixation often occurs as a reaction to frustration, although stringent enough measures might force abandonment of the reaction. Consider an effort by management to change a group norm which restricts output. Reorganization would be a common technique for attempting to increase production. Indeed, just this technique was employed in the Patent Office. Reorganization need not be doomed to failure, but its chances of success will depend as much upon *how* the reorganization is introduced as upon what the reorganization proposes to do. Thus, given management's initiating role, frustration and fixation often will accompany attempts to reorganize, for any group must control its environment in order to reduce the anxiety of its members. This fact, of course, encourages individuals to join groups and to maintain their membership, because most individuals prefer low levels of tension. Any change (for example, in output) not sanctioned by the group, then, implies frustration of the common desire to lessen anxiety. The difficulty may be greatly compounded by reorganization, since the "moving around" attendant on reorganization only adds to the upset of traditional patterns of behavior. Hence tension increases. Such efforts by management, then, may simply raise the odds favoring the fixation of behavior which previously served to reduce tension.

The possibility of fixation, of course, does not rule out reorganization or any other technique of change. Fixation, however, does suggest some of the limits on the success with which these techniques may be applied. Change is certainly possible. Change may sometimes be accomplished by bulling the matter through, no holds barred. There may be no alternative, in fact. But the approach may have aftereffects which are more serious than the original problem. Some of the feathers ruffled in the process of bulling a change through may stay that way for a long time. Accomplishing change more tidily involves altering a group norm without threatening the power of the group. This is as delicate as it sounds, and the matter will be considered later in some detail.

The fourth characteristic of frustration is *apathy*, or *resignation*. The state of resignation is one in which the individual "gives up." That is, he ceases his attempts at problem-solving and abandons himself to his environment. Resignation seems to be the result of extended frustration. A young Austrian carpenter during the Great Depression illustrates the process toward resignation and the state itself. When he lost his job, the carpenter—a married man—at first reacted aggressively. He was deeply resentful and desperately tried to find work. After many unsuccessful attempts, he ceased his struggling. As he explained it, "I decided not to go anywhere any more. And for months, lying in the sunshine, I wait quietly for the day when my wife will tell me that she has spent the last money and that the grocer does not want to give us credit. But it lasts very long, and I ask myself *how fate will finally decide.*" [26]

Predicting the responses to threat of apathetic individuals cannot be definite. They might respond with docility to management directives which are threatening, and thus might be high producers on certain types of jobs. This is not likely, however. In the first place, the resigned person may be quite sanguine about threats—he may be content to see "how fate will decide." Moreover, an apathetic individual seems unlikely to provide even trivial adjustments required by the work situation. On many jobs, this lack of adaptability would be a source of considerable loss of productivity.

In sum, the consequences of a fear-arousing communication which induces frustration cannot be predicted easily. O & M theory grossly oversimplifies when it implies that the greater the threat, the greater the adherence to management directives. Figure 13 summarizes the more complex analysis above. The conclusion implied in this figure is an important one: traditional organization theory is likely to be in error as often as it is correct.

These four reactions to frustration are a useful set of concepts for analyzing behavior in organizations. Thus this analysis is not a mere exercise. The point can be established most directly by outlining the potential for frustration implicit in the act of organizing. O & M theory accentuates this potential. Consider the following types of situations which have been found to have a high potential for frustration:

[26] Paul F. Lazarsfeld and Bohan Zawadzki, "The Psychological Consequences of Unemployment," *Journal of Social Psychology*, VI (1935), 237.

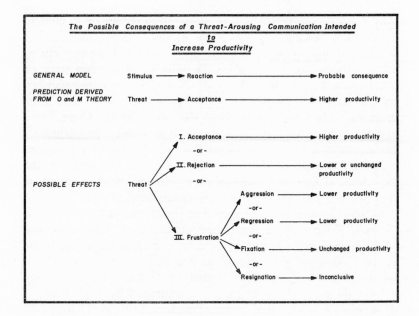

FIGURE 13.

1. arbitrary change of a desired condition;
2. preventing the completion of a task;
3. inducing a sense of failure and of low ability;
4. interference with expression and assertion; and
5. unsatisfactory leadership.[27]

Traditional organization theory, then, cannot claim a low potential for frustration; for specialization has the effect of inducing Situation 2, and the limited span of control seems based upon the necessity of inducing Situations 3 and 4. Moreover, the directive style of supervision prescribed by traditional organization theory often will encourage employees to conclude that Situation 5 exists. Finally, traditional organization theory presumes that Situation 1 has favorable consequences, as is evidenced by the suddenly-announced reorganization of the Patent Office.

But traditional organization theory should not be taken too much to task. It is a step forward to recognize frustration and the waste of physical and emotional resources to which it often leads.

[27] Hilde Himmelweit, "A Review of Recent Experimental Work," in T. H. Pear, *Psychological Factors of Peace and War* (New York: Philosophical Library, 1950), pp. 164–70.

Any organization theory which attempts to reduce or to control frustration, however, faces a difficult task.

The developing research on frustration should aid this effort, but overoptimism is not a luxury which the existing state of our knowledge permits. Thus two notes of caution are necessary to conclude this introduction to frustration. First, only four reactions to frustrating conditions were considered. These, however, are not necessarily sufficient to fit all cases. "Substitution," for example, may be a common reaction.[28] The four reactions discussed above are the most firmly established ones in the experimental literature. Hence they will aid comprehension, if they do not provide complete understanding.

Second, considerable evidence suggests that frustration and "learning," broadly defined, are closely tied. Much of the research deals with low-level behavior, or what has come to be called "instrumental behavior," as opposed to "higher-level" behavior. For example, the abolition of "habits" (e.g., tripping a lever on a signal) in animals is encouraged by frustration, if frustration is not crucial in inducing such behavioral changes.[29] Future research will have much to say on this topic.

Provisionally, there seem to be sharp limits on the easy transfer of the "frustration-unlearning" hypothesis. This hypothesis requires the prediction that the "unlearning" of a group norm can be accomplished only (or mainly) by frustration massive enough to override the satisfactions which the norm had provided. Small-group analysis suggests some alternatives to this type of treatment. A brief survey of the concept "participation" will illustrate these limits.

4c. A Contrast to Threat: "Participation" and Its Consequences. There is a high potential for frustration in the act of organizing, which the traditional theory of organization does little to lessen.

[28] For example, experimental animals have displayed a type of behavior which suggests "substitution" rather than "fixation." As Eglash explained: "Whereas fixation suggests rigidity or perseveration, the fixated animal remains as flexible as the normal. [It often acts, indeed, with] a surprising ingenuity." The adaptation may take the form of a wide variety of efforts by the animal which frustrate the experimenter. Albert Eglash, "Fixation and Inhibition," *Journal of Abnormal and Social Psychology*, XLIX (April, 1954), 242. Anyone who has observed organization behavior will have many candidates for "substitution" responses to frustration.

[29] Mowrer, *Learning Theory and Behavior*, pp. 403–11.

This high potential, of course, sets a substantial order for any organization theory. Some interesting experiments, however, suggest at least a partial remedy for the often-unintended consequences of threat. These experiments employ the control potential of the small group. One example will serve to illustrate the important applications of small-group theory.

The example involves a work unit of eighteen hand pressers whose job was to be changed slightly.[30] In accordance with usual factory routine, the production department restudied the job and set a new piece rate. Immediately before the change was instituted, a brief meeting of the employees was held. The pressure of competition was cited as the reason for the change, and the time-study man carefully explained the new piece rate. The employees were then set to work. The results suggest the high frustration potential of the usual factory routine, reinforced by management and time-study threat:

> The [employees] improved little beyond their early efficiency ratings. Resistance developed almost immediately after the change occurred. Marked expressions of aggression against management occurred, such as conflict with the methods engineer, expression of hostility against the supervisor, deliberate restriction of production, and lack of cooperation with the supervisor. There were 17% quits in the first [40] days. Grievances were filed about the piece rate, but when the rate was checked, it was found to be a little "loose." (P. 329.)

Experiment I, then, did not encourage uneventful change. The broken line in Figure 14 graphically portrays the sharp drop in productivity after the transfer. The drop was sustained for approximately five weeks, although the figure only portrays the experience of the first eighteen days. Except for the marked absence of resignation, the characteristics of frustration are patent.

The relearning period having failed, the work unit was broken up and its members were scattered to new jobs around the plant. Two and a half months later, Experiment II began. Its purpose

[30] Cartwright and Zander, *Group Dynamics*, pp. 329 and 331. The study is by Lester Coch and John R. P. French, Jr.

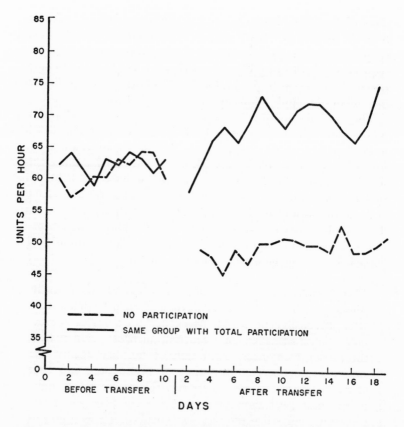

FIGURE 14. *The Comparison of the Productivity Effects of the "No Participation" and the "Total Participation" Procedure on the Same Work Unit*

Source: Dorwin Cartwright and Alvin Zander (eds.), *Group Dynamics: Research and Theory* (Evanston, Ill.: Row, Peterson, 1960), p. 331.

was to harness the control potential of the small group to organization purposes. Experiment I, in contrast, made no attempt to develop the structural or style integration of the work unit. This is consistent, of course, with the assumption in traditional organization theory that the individual has but a single relevant source of authority. It just did not work well.

The technique employed in Experiment II was the "total participation" of the work unit in the redesign of the new job. Since only thirteen of the original eighteen members remained, a high degree of informality and give-and-take was possible. The participation took place in the frame of management's "general plan" and involved the solicitation of recommendations of work-unit members in matters such as designing the work and time study. "Total participation," then, may be briefly described as permissive in style, with low threat, the aim being the high structural and style integration of a small group with the formal organization. The group's high cohesiveness would enable it to develop and enforce norms with some power behind them.

The unbroken line in Figure 14 shows that the experience of Experiment I was not repeated. The productivity drop due to relearning was slight, and work-unit members went on to achieve substantial productivity increases. Unlike Experiment I, also, there was no marked aggression in the work unit nor were there any "quits" in the nineteen days following the changeover.

Traditional organization theory cannot explain either the failure of Experiment I or the success of Experiment II. Small-group analysis fills the gap by providing knowledge of style and structural properties and of the ways these properties affect performance.

Small-group analysis, then, suggests a way to live with that apparent dilemma posed some pages before: changing group norms without threatening the group and thereby encouraging its resistance. Traditional organization theory falls before this dilemma, for it does not recognize norms, or for that matter, groups. Worse still, the O & M theory can (and in the Patent Office, did) aggravate matters. Thus the properties of the traditional theory challenge the influence of the group. The point will be demonstrated in detail in Chapter 8.

Small-group analysis, then, supports a new maxim for organization study and practice: What you do not know can hurt you very badly.

4d. "Participation": Its Explanation in Terms of Conflict. The differences between the two output curves in Figure 14 are impressive. But the reader may hesitate to accept the results, which may seem to have occurred for no good reason. Why, indeed, should such a technique as "participation" have the

141

observed effects? This may be the question on the reader's mind. The question is a good one to put to any research. It is a useful rule of thumb to distrust any research claims unless they can be explained in terms of other things one knows, unless they "make sense" in terms of one's total experience.

Consider the concept "conflict." It should clarify the "participation" results in terms of other things which have been learned about behavior. Some elegant experimental work stresses the usefulness of considering three types of conflict situations, building upon the seminal contributions of the late Kurt Lewin toward the study of conflict and its resolution.[31] In the usual shorthand, these conflict situations may be named and described in this way:

1. *Approach-Approach*, in which the conflict results because the individual must decide between two similarly attractive courses of action;

2. *Approach-Avoidance*, in which the conflict results because the individual, in order to perform some attractive action, must remain psychologically "close" to a situation or action that is unattractive to him; and

3. *Avoidance-Avoidance*, in which the conflict results because the individual is faced by two similarly unattractive courses of action.

These conflict situations tend to encourage specific reactions. *Approach-Approach* situations, first, do not seem to cause much difficulty. That is, there seem to be few humans who react like the burro who was halfway between two equally succulent-looking piles of hay, but starved because he could not make up his mind which way to go. *Avoidance-Avoidance* situations, second, tend to encourage the individual to "leave the field," that is, to avoid the two threatening possibilities by performing a third action. Difficulties do arise when it is not possible for the individual to "leave the field," e.g., sticking with a job, no matter what, during a severe depression. If leaving the field is not possible, the individual becomes tense and may vacillate. Organizations, to be sure, provide a mine of examples of such behavior.

[31] Kurt Lewin, *A Dynamic Theory of Personality* (New York: McGraw, 1935); and his "Behavior and Development as a Function of the Total Situation," in Leonard Carmichael (ed.), *Manual of Child Psychology* (New York: Wiley, 1954), pp. 918–70.

142

Approach-Avoidance situations, third, pose a particular problem, for there is no possibility for the relatively easy resolution of the conflict. That is, the individual is drawn psychologically toward the attractive alternative which, however, also draws him toward the unattractive. The individual, of course, may decide to give up the attractive alternative so as not to experience the unpleasant consequences of achieving it, but this also causes conflict.

These general considerations may be given some flesh and blood. An experiment by Hovland and Sears illustrates the different degrees of conflict associated with the three types of situations.[32] In the experiment, subjects (Ss) were trained to respond to two stimuli in these ways. They were to draw lines on a piece of paper in response to their observations of the positions of a red and green light. If they observed a green light, they were to represent the position of the light (as right or left) on paper by drawing a line *toward* the corresponding corner of the paper. If they observed a red light, Ss were to draw a line *away* from the position in which they had observed the light.

After this conditioning, Ss were exposed to an experimental design such that the three types of conflict above were induced by various combinations of two red and two green lights. For example, the Approach-Approach situation was induced by showing green lights at both the right and left positions. Figure 15 graphically depicts the experimental treatment for the three conflict conditions. The figure also summarizes the typical reactions of the Ss. The (+) and (−) signs, of course, denote the directions toward which and away from which, respectively, Ss were trained to draw lines. From another point of view, the (+) represents the direction in which an "acceptable" line may be drawn, the (−) the direction in which only "unacceptable" lines may be drawn.

How is the experiment to be interpreted? Consider the elements which it provides one to work with. The experiment, obviously, simulates the three types of conflict situations. Moreover, it provides two measures of the degree of conflict felt by

[32] Carl I. Hovland and Robert R. Sears, "Experiments on Motor Conflict. I. Types of Conflict and Their Modes of Resolution," *Journal of Experimental Psychology*, XXIII (1938), 477–93. Some simplification of procedure is made above.

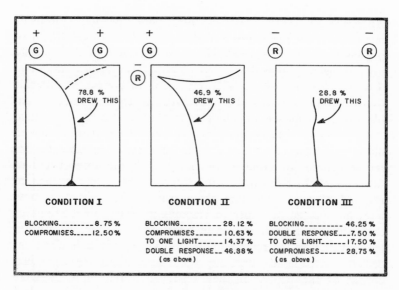

FIGURE 15. *Three Types of Conflict Situations and Their Effects on Motor Responses*

Source: Adapted from Carl I. Hovland and Robert R. Sears, "Experiments on Motor Conflict. I. Types of Conflict and Their Modes of Resolution," *Journal of Experimental Psychology*, XXIII (1938), especially 479–80, 491.

the Ss, although it is difficult to determine which measure reflects greater conflict. "Blocking" is one such measure. That is, in cases, the Ss could not bring themselves to provide the motor response of drawing some line. The Ss felt the strain of "blocking." Thus the inhibition of motor response was commonly accompanied by tension-relieving behavior such as swearing or giggling. "Compromising" is a second measure of conflict. A "compromise" resulted, as in Condition III in Figure 15, when Ss "split the difference" between competing demands. That is, Ss could not "go away from" the red light on the right without going toward the red light on the left. The conflict was compromised by doing neither but by doing something.

Bearing these features in mind, Figure 15 may be made to yield interesting information. As expected, the Approach-Approach condition caused no great difficulty. Only 9 per cent of the Ss "blocked," while 79 per cent drew lines to one or both of the corners of the paper. Only 12 per cent of the Ss compromised. Conditions II and III reflected more conflict.

144

Thus most individuals "compromised" in the Approach-Avoid-ance situation. They felt the conflict of drawing the line toward the green light *and* toward the red light, when their training was that the line should be drawn away from the red light. Twenty-eight per cent of the Ss "blocked" in Condition II. "Blocking" was most common, however, in the Avoidance-Avoidance condition: 46 per cent of the Ss "blocked," and an additional 29 per cent chose the "compromise" illustrated in Figure 15.

Without doubt, then, Conditions II and II caused substantial conflict. The substantial "blocking" in Condition III may be interpreted as a leaving of the field. Similarly, the prevalence of "compromising" in Condition II suggests that Ss were not able to avoid the conflict easily.

These situations may not seem to do justice to the complexity of life as we live it. This is indeed the case to a degree (for experiments are meant to abstract from, or simplify, reality). The point, however, should not be conceded too cheaply, for real-life situations approximating those of the Hovland-Sears experiment are not lacking, although we face many conflict situations which are more uncertain than those of the experiment. In addition, the pervasive social training each one of us undergoes provides very substantial opportunities for conflict of a sharp nature, if the conflict based upon the rather superficial training of the Ss is any criterion.

The Hovland-Sears type of analysis, however, can handle a greater complexity. The experiment, to explain, included a situation which seems to have many real-life analogues. This was a compound, or double, Approach-Avoidance situation. Hovland and Sears gave this illustration of the type: "a man has two desirable appointments at the same hour, the neglect of either of which will produce punishment or disappointment." We humans know the dilemma well, for the essence of life is the allocation of scarce resources.

The compound Approach-Avoidance situation was simulated by displaying both red and green lights at both the right and left locations. In this situation 72.5 per cent of the Ss "blocked" and an additional 5.0 per cent "compromised," suggesting very substantial conflict. There was no way out for most Ss but leaving the field.

Conflict, then, has its price, whatever the type of situation

145

which induces it. The Hovland-Sears experiment suggests some of these costs. More pointedly, considerable experimental evidence shows that three main effects of intense conflict may be expected. As Shaffer and Shoben summarized that evidence:

> First, a severe conflict arouses a strong *emotional response*, with many evidences of visceral and muscular tension. Second, the response to a conflict shows a *wide generalization*, spreading to stimuli that were only remotely or incidentally associated with the original situation. Early discriminations that formerly were made without effort can no longer be achieved. Third, the effects of conflict have a *notable persistence*. The behavioral effects of an experimentally induced conflict may last for months or even years, and are not diminished by rest or by lack of further reinforcement.[33]

The resulting state, Shaffer and Shoben note, is well described as anxiety, "an apprehension, an unpleasant blend of dread and hope referred to the future." [34]

The practical implications of such findings seem straightforward. To emphasize only the extremes, life in organizations would be better for all concerned if massive efforts were made to limit compound Approach-Avoidance situations, at the same time that massive efforts were made to increase Approach-Approach situations. Conflict, from the look we have had of it, is something organizations easily can have too much of. Consider only the effects of high anxiety on communications in organizations. Even the most innocent communication, in this state, may seem threatening to the recipient. The sender, in turn, may be puzzled by the obstinacy of his subordinates in what seem to be "clear-cut cases." He may decide to "take the kid gloves off." The employees, in time, will be able to congratulate themselves that they saw it coming all along, and they can busy themselves with a freer conscience in building those informal defensive arrangements which can frustrate the most intricate attempts at top-level control through formal means.

This has been the long way around of making a simple point.

[33] Shaffer and Shoben, *The Psychology of Adjustment*, pp. 119, 121.
[34] *Ibid.*, p. 121.

146

Perhaps the essence of "participation"—and of such of its variants as "group decision-making"—is the attempt to emphasize Approach-Approach situations and the low conflict they imply. Consider the attempt to increase output although a group norm favors low output. Group membership normally will have a positive attraction for its members which is not easily shaken. If the increase in output is to have a positive attraction, group members must have come to accept the increase as their norm. A management order for higher output may be accepted in cases in which the working relations are friendly enough, or management's control is tight enough. But such situations do not seem to be common, to say the least. In most cases, then, "participation" alone will avoid tainting the increase in output with a negative attraction, easy enough to do even under the best circumstances.

Traditional organization theory—in contrast to "participation" —seems to encourage compound Approach-Avoidance situations. In the Hovland-Sears experiment, of course, this situation induced the most conflict.

The Patent Office experience suggests that the O & M theory induced a compound Approach-Avoidance situation. To explain, two alternatives faced the copy pullers. First, the copy puller could strive to maintain the informal group and the satisfaction he derived from it, while running the risk of the considerable sanctions which management could muster. Second, he could strive to increase production and respond to the formal organization, for, let us not neglect the point, his organization affiliation was the source of many satisfactions, such as wages, security, and the feeling of loyalty and belonging. But this course posed its difficulties. It threatened the power of the group from which the copy puller also derived satisfactions and it exposed him to the contempt of, and the social isolation from, those fellow group members with whom he had established strong bonds.

Altogether, this was not a happy position for the copy puller. The resulting conflict could be expected to be of significant proportions, and the impact of this conflict upon the operations of the Copy-Pulling Section, even over a long period of time, could be great.

To tie two lines of thought together, finally, there seem to be complex relations between conflict **and frustration. Each may** lead to the other under various conditions which cannot be sketched here.[35] We may content ourselves by observing that conflict and frustration often may be found together. Indeed, in an important sense, conflict and frustration are two vantage points for interpreting the same behavior.

[35] Brown and Farber, "Emotions Conceptualized as Intervening Variables," p. 481, for example, conclude that "frustration is the consequence of either (1) the simultaneous activation of two competing excitatory tendencies or (2) the presence of a single excitatory tendency and an inhibitory tendency." This sounds much like a conflict formulation, of course.

7

THE SMALL GROUP
AND ORGANIZATION THEORY:
SOME RELEVANT VARIABLES, III

SMALL GROUPS CONTAIN PEOPLE; BUT SMALL GROUPS ARE NOT simply several people. The small group develops properties which may be described independently of member characteristics.

This may seem obvious, but elaboration will prove useful. The reader may usefully think of molecules and atoms in the physical sciences as a parallel. The properties of molecules may be studied on their own level, without reference to the constituent atoms. For example, the properties of water may be studied quite apart from the fact that each molecule of water is composed of two atoms of hydrogen and one of oxygen. That is, the freezing point of water may be determined, its specific gravity may be ascertained, and so on, all without relevance to its constituent elements. Notice also that the molecules of water have characteristics which are distinct from the characteristics of the component atoms. The crucial factor is the way in which the constituent atoms are organized: organization is the factor which differentiates one molecule of water from two atoms of hydrogen and one of oxygen.

Much the same may be said of the small group. The small group is something different from the people who are its members. It—like the molecule—is the set of structural and style relations *between* its constituent units.

Small-Group Properties:

The Population Panel

The analogy above concerning "levels of organization" in the physical and social worlds may be carried further. The small group can be studied on its own level, in terms of cohesiveness, norms, and the like. But, as in the physical sciences, the characteristics of a group's atoms often must be studied. Persons, of course, are themselves a level of organization distinct from the group. Very disorganized people—schizophrenics, for example —require help. Similarly, atoms and molecules are distinct levels of organization.

The point may be supported by analogy. The *kind* of hydrogen in water may substantially influence its characteristics. Thus "heavy water," composed of a relatively rare breed of hydrogen atom, has uses in atomic research which "regular water" cannot serve. One cannot explain the differences between the two types of water on the molecular level of organization, one must distinguish the hydrogen atoms of which various batches of water are constituted. The same type of distinction holds, in many cases, for small groups.

The analogy may be extended further. If you are merely to drink the water, you need not be concerned with its constituent atoms. Gross description suffices to keep you away from hydrochloric acid when you stand in need of a mild refresher. But bigger payoffs than the satisfaction of thirst require atomic as well as molecular description.

This tale of the atom applies to small groups also. Bigger payoffs in the application of results require knowledge of the relation of group properties and member characteristics. Knowledge of group properties does not suffice, for example, to construct groups beforehand so that they will have certain desired properties. And such construction is of great importance.

The population panel of variables eventually will permit clear distinctions between the characteristics of members of small groups. Differentiating the characteristics of group members and determining their impact upon group behavior, however, is not a simple job. Indeed, the task is gargantuan, for the study of personality is no less than the study of the patterns of thought, feeling, and action which differentiate people. "Personality" is an abstraction which attempts to relate the observed behavior of an individual with his needs and his environment. The difficulties of classifying the properties of the group *on its own level*, of course, have already been sketched. The problems of the study of personality *and* group properties add to this already-substantial research burden.

No small wonder, then, that research has isolated few of the relations of the personality characteristics of group members and the properties of the small group. But the existing work is all the more valuable because of its scarcity. Some of the highlights, therefore, will be reviewed below.

1. Individual Needs and Group Control

In broadest terms, a small group exists because it fills certain personality needs of its members. The degree to which a group fills such needs of individuals, in a real sense, determines the limits within which an individual will permit his behavior to be group-controlled. Some of the services provided by the group have been outlined in the previous chapter.

Whatever the reasons, many individuals develop a generalized need to allow groups to control their behavior. This effect has been observed even in very temporary groups under circumstances in which the individual was forced to make substantial concessions to good sense. A typical illustration of group influence involves one naive subject and several stooges in experimental groups. The stooges (by prearrangement) make atrocious estimates of the length of a line. Table X reflects the magnitude of group influence under such artificial conditions.[1] This influence is marked even when no instructions are given to subjects, and it sharply increases when the subjects are given instructions to behave as members of a group. These findings suggest how easily group patterns may be induced. Given the weightlessness of the reasons why the naive subjects should misperceive so often—that is, why they should allow the group to influence them—the degree of control is astounding. Interest-

[1] Morton Deutsch and Harold B. Gerard, "A Study of Normative and Informational Social Influences Upon Individual Judgments," *Journal of Abnormal and Social Psychology*, LI (November, 1955), 629, 631, and 632.

TABLE X

Group Influence on the Perceptions of Naive Subjects in Instructed and Uninstructed Collectivities			
	Possible Number of Errors of Judgment		
	Memory Series	Visual Series	Total
Experimental Treatment	12.00	12.00	24.00
	Actual Average Number of Errors of Judgment		
	Memory Series	Visual Series	Total
Group Instructions	6.87	5.6	12.47
No Instructions	3.15	2.77	5.92

Source: Derived from Morton Deutsch and Harold B. Gerard, "A Study of Normative and Informational Social Influences Upon Individual Judgments," *Journal of Abnormal and Social Psychology*, LI (November, 1955), 632.

ingly, the naive subject seldom realizes that he is being taken in by the stooges, and even when he does, he most often goes along with their judgments.

2. Group Atmosphere and Intelligence

The small group, then, often influences behavior. But this is little help in predicting behavior precisely. Specific population characteristics must be related to specific properties of groups.

An experiment employing a variation of the parlor game Twenty Questions illustrates the specifics which much be investigated. The game, of course, involves the guessing of unknown items by asking questions of a moderator. No initial information is given beyond the fact that the object is animal, vegetable, or mineral.

The experiment utilized groups composed according to atmosphere (authoritarian and permissive) and according to member intelligence (bright and dull). Table XI below gives two measures of the efficiency of the four types of groups studied. In sum, the differences consistently favor the greater efficiency of the "brights" under a permissive condition and of the greater efficiency of the "dulls" under an authoritarian condition. To illustrate, the Permissive-Dull group was able to solve only half as many problems as the Authoritarian-Dull group.

The results suggest the intimate interaction of personality

TABLE XI

Two Measures of the Problem-Solving Efficiency of Groups
Under Conditions of Differing Intelligence and Atmosphere

Condition	Efficiency Criterion	
	Questions Per Problem	% Problems Solved
Permissive-Bright	15.5	100.0
Authoritarian-Bright	18.5	87.5
Permissive-Dull	31.0	37.5
Authoritarian-Dull	24.5	75.0

Source: Allen D. Calvin, Frederick K. Hoffman, and Edgar L. Harden, "The Effect of Intelligence and Social Atmosphere on Group Problem-Solving Behavior," Journal of Social Psychology, XLV (February, 1957), 64.

characteristics and group properties. The O & M theory, however, does not provide for such distinctions. That theory prescribes a high-threat, authoritarian condition, which is likely to encourage productivity losses, especially on difficult tasks and on those tasks which require effort substantially below the mental capacity of the operators. The O & M emphasis upon specialization, of course, often will have the latter effect. The widespread educational opportunities in this country, of course, make this point particularly important.

3. Group Atmosphere and Authoritarianism

A particularly important line of recent work has been the study of the so-called authoritarian personality. "Authoritarianism" is a personality dimension which is not easily defined, but its importance is suggested by evidence from many sources.

Authoritarianism is peculiarly relevant to organization theory, for the "authoritarian personality" describes closely the characteristics which are implied in traditional organization theory. This kinship can be most readily suggested by a longish description of some of the characteristics which students have assigned to the concept "authoritarianism." Thus Flowerman, for example, emphasized these characteristics:

From the findings . . . has emerged this composite psychological portrait of the Authoritarian Man:

He is a supreme conformist. [He] conforms to the nth degree to . . . authority. But conformity is no voluntary act for him; it is compulsive and irrational. It is an attempt to find security by merging with the herd, by submitting to some higher power or authority. Not only does he feel compelled to submit; he wants others to submit too. He cannot run the risk of being different and cannot tolerate difference in anyone else. . . .

Authoritarians see the world and its inhabitants as menacing and unfriendly. Being so threatened, so anxiety ridden, they must seek security somehow, somewhere. The best security for the authoritarian is to surrender to a powerful authority. . . .

He doesn't have to wield the power himself so long as he can be near power, sharing it vicariously. . . .

He is rigid and shows little imagination. He is a mechanical man, a kind of robot who reacts to only a limited number of ideas and can't be budged out of the channels in which he has been conditioned to operate. This doesn't mean that [he] is a person of low intelligence and imagination. . . .[2]

The utility of the "authoritarianism" concept may be demonstrated in two ways. First, consider differences in authoritarianism and differences in the degree of acceptance of formal leaders. Formal leaders acceptable to authoritarians, in brief, would be individuals with high power relative to, and capable of imposing strong repressive sanctions on, their subordinates; with formal positions and prerogatives which sharply differentiate them from their subordinates; and with the capacity to induce significant love, admiration, or fear in their subordinates. The military provides the most marked example of the attempt to meet these conditions. Thus it is possible to predict that

1. all other things being equal, formal military leaders who have the conventional traits of the "good officer" will be

[2] Samuel H. Flowerman, "Portrait of the Authoritarian Man," *The New York Times Magazine* (April 23, 1950), pp. 9, 28. Italics supplied.

TABLE XII

Authoritarianism, Acceptance of Formal Leader with Conventional "Good Officer" Traits, and Re-Enlistment Intent

| | | Authoritarianism | |
	High	*Medium*	*Low*
Leader Acceptance			
Above median	59%	52%	36%
Below median	41%	48%	64%
Totals	100%	100%	100%
Re-Enlistment Intent			
Yes, or Undecided	38%	34%	24%
No	62%	66%	76%
Totals	100%	100%	100%

Source: Nahum Z. Medalia, "Authoritarianism, Leader Acceptance, and Group Cohesion," *Journal of Abnormal and Social Psychology*, LI (September, 1955), 209, 210, and 211.

accepted most by people who have strong authoritarian tendencies; and

2. all other things being equal, individuals with strong authoritarian tendencies would be more likely to re-enlist than individuals with weak authoritarian tendencies.

Table XII presents the results of the tests of these two hypotheses. These results support the hypotheses. That is, individuals with strong authoritarian tendencies decidedly leaned toward the acceptance of "good officers" and toward the contemplation of re-enlistment. Individuals with weaker authoritarian tendencies leaned the other way. The results in Table XII cannot be dismissed so summarily, however. Their interpretation is quite a sticky matter. An educated guess would be that the differences between degrees of authoritarianism would be even greater, in the absence of certain problems with the design of this experiment, but this is crystal-ballish. A more restricted interpretation is that the results are more suggestive than definitive. Thus not all high authoritarians reacted the same way. Moreover, a number of technical factors, whose discussion is beyond the limits of this work, limit the confidence which can be placed in the results.

Second, the style properties of groups also may be predicted from the authoritarianism of their members. Groups of high performers of authoritarian behaviors (HiA) are compared to groups of low performers (LoA). Existing studies are quite elaborate. The results, however, may be illustrated briefly: HiA and LoA groups strongly tend to develop behaviors which are consistent with the directive and permissive atmospheres, respectively. More explicitly, the detailed analysis of the role styles of those chosen as leaders by group members of HiA versus LoA groups sharply reveals the differences expected from the general theory of authoritarianism. Thus individuals who emerged as leaders in LoA experimental groups displayed greater sensitivity to other group members, performed more behaviors rated as "leadership," and were more effective in helping their groups toward the completion of the experimental task than leaders who emerged in HiA experimental groups. Similar findings, although they did not always reach accepted levels of statistical significance, also support this picture of the interacting influence of personality characteristics and leadership behavior. Compared to emergent leaders in HiA experimental groups, for example, LoA leaders were more friendly, less aggressive, less autocratic, and showed less of a tendency to isolate themselves from the group.[3] The pattern, of course, is consistent with the population characteristic "authoritarianism."

A similar interaction of personality characteristics and group characteristics also should exist in on-going organizations, with important consequences for organization theory. Illustratively, consider a work unit with a group style which reflected the personality characteristics of group members. Such style properties would be very difficult to change permanently, for change would run afoul of resistance induced by deeply-rooted personality characteristics. Traditional organization theory, of course, does not provide for such personality differences. Predictions derived from that theory, then, will not always apply, as was the case, for example, in the Patent Office.

[3] William Haythorn, Donald Haefner, Peter Langham, Arthur Couch, and Launor Carter, "The Effects of Varying Combinations of Authoritarian and Equalitarian Leaders and Followers," *Journal of Abnormal and Social Psychology*, LIII (September, 1956), 210–19.

4. Response Repertoires

The sections above may give the impression that it is impossible to change group style. The impression is without foundation, for the sections have dealt in the main with extreme scorers on various personality characteristics. Thus the "bright" subjects of Section B had American Council of Education test scores (used as measures of "intelligence") which averaged 133.9. The "dulls" in contrast had scores which averaged 86.2.

There are few extreme scorers on most personality dimensions, however. Most people tend to fall somewhere in between. The extreme scorers are studied, of course, because differences are most likely to show up when the extremes are compared.

The great "in between," however, need not be neglected. Thus studies of group atmosphere have demonstrated that many individuals have wide "response repertoires." That is, many individuals are able to provide the behaviors induced by various group atmospheres. This situational flexibility may be very marked. As one student explained:

The concept of "response hierarchy" appears to be useful here. Faced with similar group positions and, hence, similar situational requirements, individuals of different personality types will initially respond in somewhat different fashion to the extent that the required response is located differently in the individuals' response hierarchies. In other words, the required response will probably occur sooner the higher the response in the hierarchy. However, assuming that this required response is in the individual's repertoire and that there are no response inhibiting factors, it is likely that the required response will eventually occur. Over time, then, the individuals of different personality types will come to behave in similar fashion.[4]

An experiment was designed to test the usefulness of the "response repertoire" concept. An artificial communication network was designed so that certain positions ("central positions")

[4] Leonard Berkowitz, "Personality and Group Position," *Sociometry*, XIX (December, 1956), 210.

would handle many communications, while other positions ("peripheral positions") would handle few. The net was a Y-type, with one central position (CP) and three peripheral positions (PP). Schematically, PP could receive communications

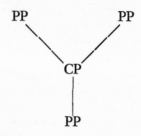

only from CP; CP, however, could receive communications from all other positions. In half of the cases, individuals whose usual behavior was "dominant" or "ascendant" were placed in the central positions. In the other cases, individuals low on dominant or ascendant behavior were placed in the central positions.

Differences between the "consistent" and "inconsistent" assignments were evident briefly. But all individuals soon adapted to the requirements of their communication positions, whatever their usual behavior. Thus in the first trial the Highs (high scorers on ascendance) in the central positions tended to complete their problems before other group members. Lows in the same position failed to utilize their central positions in the communication net to as full advantage in early trials. The behaviors highest in their repertoires were non-ascendant. But by Trial III there were only minor differences between Highs and Lows in the central position.

Thus many subjects—on situational demand—were able to supply behaviors which they did not normally display. The choice of behaviors was not a matter of indifference to the subjects, however, for the response repertoires of most individuals are rank-ordered in terms of definite preferences. Thus, to illustrate, groups of authoritarians tend to develop a directive atmosphere if they are given relative freedom. These individuals probably could be constrained to perform behaviors consistent with a permissive atmosphere, but the performance of low-preference behaviors over a substantial period of time would have such effects as decreased satisfaction.

Research with response repertoires has a major implication for organization theory: the preferred behaviors of the employees must be known. Then it is necessary to create the conditions under which the performance of such behaviors is often required. This may seem like a great deal of bother, for most people can perform a wide variety of behaviors. But the continued performance of low-preference behaviors is likely to involve a high cost, always for the individual and often for the formal organization.

This problem is neglected in O & M theory, for that theory attempts to make do with two empirical assumptions replacing the sophisticated theory required. First, the theory assumes that most individuals empirically can and will perform authoritarian-type behaviors without any organizational or personal loss. This assumption is inaccurate.

Second, the O & M theory assumes that the performance of such behaviors will permit substantial control of member behavior for organization purposes. Much of the evidence in this chapter, however, suggests strict limits on the validity of this assumption. In addition, the normative question of whether or not individuals ought to be induced to perform authoritarian-type behaviors also requires consideration.

5. Work-Unit Compatibility

The usefulness of constructing work units so as to minimize the conflict resulting from differences in population characteristics is implied in the "response repertoire" research. Existing work underscores this point. Schutz, for example, developed a measure of an individual's orientation toward interpersonal relations which tapped these three (assumed) behavioral predispositions of individuals:[5]

1. a *dependence-counterdependence* (or power) *orientation,* which attempts to assess the individual's predisposition for "following rules, following the leader, becoming a leader or power figure, and in general, conforming to, manipulating, and/or controlling the power structure";
2. a *personalness-counterpersonalness orientation,* which attempts to assess the individual's predisposition to work "within a framework of close personal relations . . . get-

[5] W. C. Schutz, "What Makes Groups Productive?" *Human Relations,* VIII (November, 1955), 429–66.

ting people to like him, being a 'good guy,' . . . liking others, . . . treating people differentially—not on the basis of status—but on the basis of personal liking"; and

3. an *assertiveness orientation*, which attempts to assess the individual's tendency to make his views felt in a group.

These orientations derived from the individual's earliest relations with others and were fundamentally retained through adulthood. Schutz explained his interest in these orientations in this way:

> . . . the dominant reason for a group's productivity depends on the extent to which its members can get along together—their "compatibility." The more energy a group expends on interpersonal problems arising from lack of compatibility the less energy they devote to the task at hand. Further, the conversion of interpersonal hostility into obstructive task behavior, as in unreasonable criticism, is a subtle and amazingly large source of nonproductivity. (P. 429.)

Schutz constructed compatible and incompatible experimental collectivities, for example, by assigning all high scorers on personalness to compatible groups and by assigning both high and low scorers on personalness to incompatible groups.

The results of such assignment supported expectations. Thus high-compatibility groups were more productive, in general, on experimental tasks, were more satisfied with their group membership and performance, had higher status congruency, and so on, than low-compatibility groups. The results require one note of caution, however. Compatibility and the more successful solution of "internal" group problems (e.g., friendliness of members) are reasonably associated, but a compatible group need not be a high producer. Indeed, a compatible group could be higher or lower on the solution of such "external" problems as productivity than a less compatible group, for compatibility is associated with the ability to develop and enforce norms. Such norms need not sanction high output, but might sanction low output as well.

These findings are consistent with much of the evidence in the sections on the structural and style properties of the small group. This consistency further supports the findings reviewed directly above. Thus incompatible groups should tend toward lower cohesiveness. The direct experiment to validate this prediction has not yet been made, but the circumstantial evidence is very strong. For example, incompatible groups have only middling success in controlling the behavior of their members (e.g., in output) or in meeting the needs of their members (e.g., in keeping member satisfaction high). Greater success in such matters, of course, is associated with high cohesiveness.

The findings above, then, challenge traditional organization theory, which assumes that there is no "assignment problem," save that of finding individuals physically capable of performing a job. This presumption reduces the usefulness of the theory.

8

THE SMALL GROUP AND ORGANIZATION THEORY: A REVISIT TO THE PATENT OFFICE

THE O & M THEORY AND ITS ASSOCIATED METHOD HAVE TWO defects, both of which may be spotlighted by using the small-group variables. Thus, it will be shown, the theory underlying the O & M application neglected important behavioral factors. Consequently, predictions derived from the theory often were inaccurate. Moreover, a second emphasis will demonstrate, the O & M theory also permitted accurate predictions. This accuracy is not altogether praiseworthy, for the predictions often were based on the wrong or inadequate reasons.

These two defects of the O & M theory, then, demonstrate that it has substantial inadequacies. For an adequate empirical theory must be a unique *and* convincing explanation. The O & M theory, to a substantial degree, is neither.

SOME PRELIMINARY NOTES

Three restrictions, however, qualify this focus of attention on small-group analysis. First, the implied position is *not* that O &

M techniques and theory are worthless. The emphasis upon the small group complements, rather than merely subverts, the O & M approach. The aim is the outline of some of the conditions under which the O & M theory does not apply.

Second, the emphasis upon the small group is not the only behaviorally-relevant approach to organization phenomena. For example, abnormal psychology is necessary to understand the organization behavior of SS Colonel Rudolph Hoess, the commander of the Nazi World War II terror camp at Auschwitz. Hoess, who administered the murder of many Jews, was in such a mental state that after his capture he could not perform simple tasks like multiplication, except in a revealing way. After puzzling over such a problem for a long time, Hoess would say, "Yes, of course, I had to figure out problems like that all the time—how many days it would take to burn so many corpses, etc." [1] The shrinkage of Hoess's personality is also reflected in his comments concerning moral qualms about the murders he administered:

> Don't you see, we SS men were not supposed to think about these things; it never even occurred to us. . . . We were all so trained to obey orders without even thinking, that the thought of disobeying an order would simply never have occurred to anybody. . . . [2]

Third, action sequences must be reconstructed. Every effort to verify this account of the reorganization was made, but few of the necessary records are available, and the recollections of participants, understandably, could be stirred incompletely and only with difficulty. Consequently, this effort is hypothetical as well as empirical. To illustrate, the pervasiveness of small-group ties in the BC Copy-Pulling Section cannot be demonstrated. It must be inferred. Three things, however, are clear. The case report strongly suggests the pervasiveness of BC group membership in the Section, as do the recollections of some who were involved in the reorganization. But formal membership in

[1] G. M. Gilbert, *The Psychology of Dictatorship* (New York: Ronald, 1950), p. 248.
[2] *Ibid.*, p. 255.

the Section does not define the behavioral system which is a small group, and an individual normally has a number of simultaneous (and often conflicting) group affiliations.

These latter two points, patently, raise some difficulty. For precise boundaries cannot be drawn for the social unit whose existence in the Copy-Pulling Section is presumed. Nor can its importance, relative to the other group affiliations of the copy pullers, be demonstrated directly.

These considerations do not invalidate this analysis, for the account, judging by the best available evidence, is not wildly wide of the mark. Indeed, many elements of this analysis explain satisfactorily to participants in the reorganization events which they did not really understand at the time. At best, then, this analysis can provide a useful description and explanation of a sliver of behavior in organizations. Even at the worst, however, it will be useful, for the analysis will portray the interaction of small-group properties which are important in many organization situations. From a teaching standpoint, indeed, whether the "best" or the "worst" condition prevails is not particularly relevant. The lesson for the student is the same, whether or not a reorganization of the Patent Office ever took place. Such a reorganization did take place, and major characteristics of it seem to have been captured in the following analysis. All this is pure gain, setting a problem of theory in the workaday world.

THE GENERAL PROBLEM:

THE SMALL-GROUP VIEW

On the most general level, the small-group analyst would approach the reorganization of the Copy-Pulling Section from quite a different vantage point than the O & M (Organization and Methods) teams. To describe this vantage point briefly, the small-group analyst would describe the backlog in terms of low structural and style integration.[3] Structurally, integration was low at two vital points in the Patent Office. Thus the Copy

[3] "Production Planning in the Patent Office," pp. 6–7.

Sales Branch "enjoyed considerable autonomy except when a crisis arose" because of the work load of its formal superior. The size of the backlog which forced high-level intervention suggests that this structural autonomy was substantial indeed.

Moreover, the Patent Copy-Pulling Section—one of the constituent units of the Sales Branch—also was characterized by low structural integration. The head of the Section, to suggest the point, faced many difficulties. For example, the exigencies of war aided the copy pullers in resisting their superior, for personnel were very scarce. In addition, the assignment of copy pullers to one of the BC parallel lines of operation also limited supervisory control. Indeed, copy pullers seem to have blunted attempts at control by arguing that they were dependent upon the particular line in which they worked and thus could not control their behavior as the Copy-Pulling Section supervisor desired. A similar argument seems to have been used on other supervisors who attempted control: the desired changes, it was argued, were not possible because of the orders of the head of the Copy-Pulling Section. The BC parallel work system, in short, complicated the Section Head's control problems. Finally, copy pullers held their jobs for relatively long periods. Thus stable social relations on the job developed. Before the war, in contrast, the Copy-Pulling Section was a temporary way station. The unattractive task was used to test the motivation of new employees of the Patent Office. Those who remained on the job were promoted with some regularity. The postwar use of promotion as a safety valve against work-restricting practices was reduced.

Style integration in the Copy-Pulling Section, to continue, also was low, for "a depressing effect on the morale of the group" resulted from a number of factors. They were lack of advancement possibilities, undesirable working conditions and physical surroundings, and the employment of transfers who kept their wartime classifications and salaries although they were higher than those of non-transfers who long had done the same or similar work. Consequently, the copy pullers had a strong tradition that pulling 300 copies was "a day's work." This group norm opposed formal organization goals when the rapid increase in postwar demand occurred.

Problem Analysis:

The Small-Group View

The small-group analyst can apply a more sophisticated theory to this problem than that employed by the O & M teams. The variables described in the two preceding chapters constitute the vitals of this theory. :

This extended analysis will consider behavioral factors which were induced by the formal work-process changes, and behavioral factors which were independent of the formal work-process changes. The O & M theory is not adequate to describe or predict these behavioral changes. However, the techniques and organization patterns utilized by the O & M specialists sometimes do suggest some solid, if implicit, behavioral theory.

1. Norms and Work Process

Work-process changes and behavioral factors had an interacting influence in the reorganization of the Patent Office. This accounts for the early failure of the reorganization, for it was stymied initially by the BC norm of pulling only 300 copies per day. This norm was a social product, quite independent of the AC changes which were designed to induce greater productivity. Being a social product, also, the norm was not destroyed by the simple act of formal reorganization. The BC norm was broken in the later AC stages, of course. (Remember BC means "before the reorganization"; and AC means "after the reorganization.")

An interesting argument may be developed from the very observation of the BC norm. The 300-copy norm to explain, was not necessarily a function of the physical characteristics of the BC work process. Consequently, changing the BC norm through "group decision-making" techniques might have increased production markedly. No work-process changes need have been made. The technique also could have been used in developing new work patterns, in contrast to the "command them" approach of the O & M teams.

Group decision-making, then, is an alternate technique for inducing change. The technique employs small discussion groups presided over by a trainer. It encourages the development

166

and enforcement of group norms, although the "direction" of the norm depends heavily on the trainer's skill. Generally, however, the results of the technique have been favorable, resulting in increased productivity and so on. The general reasons for such an effect may be briefly sketched. Group decision-making is a low-threat technique. Consequently, it avoids the resistance common when individuals are simply ordered to change their behavior. The technique also affords the group members substantial participation in decisions which affect them. The decision, then, becomes a product of one's own membership group rather than an edict from some distant formal organization. Traditional organization theory, in contrast, employs high threat and low (or zero) participation. As a result, it falls heir to difficulties which group decision-making avoids.

Group decision-making is more than an alternative, however. It is often a high-powered alternative. Its effectiveness, in comparison with techniques derived from the O & M theory, has been demonstrated impressively. For example, significant increases in productivity have been achieved with the technique on jobs set by time-and-motion analysis on which workers were already producing near the purported job ceiling. Figure 16 dramatically supports this point. The ceiling on output for the job in question had been set by time-and-motion analysis. Seventy-five units per day were considered the approximate physical ceiling for the job as it was laid out; 60 units were considered "standard."

Traditional organization theory would despair at the prospect of increasing output on this job, at least without reorganizing the work process. This despair would be unwarranted in one case; in another, it would seem applicable at first glance.

Despair about raising output did not apply to a group of workers who were allowed to set their own work goals. These workers, incidentally, already were producing near the purported job ceiling. No changes in work process were made, but the average output rose by one-sixth, to 87 units per day (see the upper curve in Figure 16).

Traditional organization theory seemed right on the nose in a second case, yet was wide of the mark. Management, simultaneously with the use of group decision-making, attempted to increase the production of all other experienced workers by

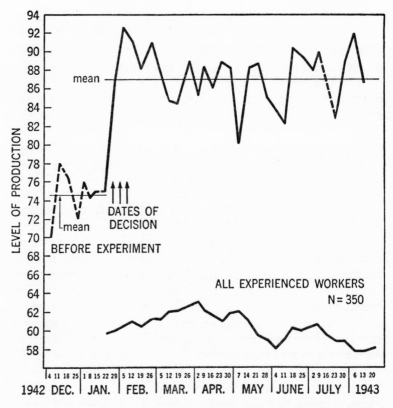

FIGURE 16. *The Effects on Productivity of Group Decision-Making versus Management Exhortative Techniques*

Source: Kurt Lewin, "Group Decision and Social Change," in Theodore M. Newcomb and Eugene L. Hartley (eds.), *Readings in Social Psychology* (New York: Holt, 1947), p. 343.

employing traditional exhortative techniques. The lower curve in Figure 16 reflects the results of such efforts, which do not compare favorably with those of group decision-making. Traditional organization theory, then, seemed correct in its despair that output could not be increased without reorganization. But the conclusion is superficial. The failure to increase output merely indicated the limits of the traditional theory.

Traditional organization theory can no more explain satisfactorily the resistance to increased output in the second case than it can explain its absence in the first. But mystical explanations

168

TABLE XIII

Typical Responses to General Success and Failure

General Success	General Failure
raise goals	lower achievement standards
gain interest in work	lose interest in work
gain confidence	lose confidence
increase persistence to future goals	give up quickly
increase ability to cooperate	fear any new task or methods
increase ability to adapt readily	expect failure
increase emotional control	escape by daydreaming
	increase difficulty of working with others

Source: Chris Argyris, *What Budgets Mean to People* (New York: Controllership Foundation, 1952), p. 21.

are not necessary. The concept of threat provides a start toward an explanation. As was demonstrated in Chapter 6, threat tends to have negative consequences. Consider, to illustrate, the summary in Table XIII of many studies of the ways in which individuals respond to consistent success (which, in general, is nonthreatening) and consistent failure (which, in general, is threatening and frustrating).

The explanation of findings such as those reflected in Figure 16, then, is straightforward. Time-and-motion analysis is a high-threat technique, and especally so when (as in the Patent Office) the employees are informed of changes only in bits and pieces. Traditional management exhortative techniques can be characterized similarly. Group decision-making, in contrast, is a minimal-threat technique. It thus tends to reduce the defensive efforts of employees and to encourage the development of group norms at a higher level than before. Less threatened because it is their own decision, in short, group members can safely give more of themselves. Thus group decision-making avoids the danger in changing output norms by preserving the group to make and enforce the change.

These generalizations hinge upon an important condition, however. Group members must make the final decision, and they must feel they do. Pseudo-participation—the attempt to con employees into ratifying a decision which has already been made—is not likely to be effective.

169

This qualification does not detract from the usefulness of participation. Patently, change of the formal work process was insufficient, and perhaps unnecessary, to induce the AC productivity increase in the Copy-Pulling Section. In addition, even the later AC level of output (600 copies) may have been raised by the group decision-making technique. To explain, the reorganized work process probably permitted higher productivity than the BC process. For example, the AC layout permitted a higher density of work assignments, but this potential does not seem to have been fully exploited. The resistance of copy pullers in the transition, first, suggests that the AC "experimentation" did not approach the physical capacity of the job set-up. Moreover, the five filing units had roughly equal work loads, but the units had different floor areas. The probability, then, is that the unit with the most area would be the bogey-setter. Thus, at least, the filing units with the more advantageous layouts probably did not exploit the full possibilities of the AC work process.

This is not to say that such participation devices as group decision-making are some kind of a never-fail, all-purpose tool. Such devices cannot, for example, do management's job. They cannot of themselves create the environment within which genuine participation is possible. Nor can they set the general framework for such decision-making in terms of organization objectives and solid planning. These management cannot avoid. Moreover, as in all things human, one has to give in order to get. Real participation cannot be bought cheaply, but requires constant cultivation and proof that it really means something. This, in cases, may deprive management of the power over men which management thought it had. What happens when participation leads to a decision which management generally does not favor, in short, often will determine the future usefulness of any participative devices.

If not a cure-all, however, this analysis of participation does suggest the gaps in the O & M theory. Empirically, behavioral factors of some importance were neglected. Of course, an intimate interaction often exists between the physical work environment and social products which develop in it. For example, common skill and job requirements have been found to induce strikingly similar social patterns, even in an organization with many field offices.[4] Thus the position here is not that norms exist independently of such factors as organization structure. The point here, rather, is that when social products such as norms develop, their influence is likely to persist even when (for example) the organization of work is drastically altered. This happened in the Copy-Pulling Section.

Except under peculiar conditions—for example, with a highly-skilled work unit performing a strategic process—it is true that the BC norm probably could not have prevented change permanently. But this does not excuse the neglect of norms, in theory or practice, for knowledge of norms could have eased the transition in this case, and is important in any case.

Normatively, also, their neglect obscured a value choice. The choice, of course, was between group decision-making and the high-threat techniques utilized in the later AC stage.

2. Cohesiveness and Work Process

The small-group analyst need not be content with such a cheap victory over the O & M theory. A more elaborate analysis of the breakdown of the BC norm is possible and will also add a new theme, for traditional organization theory did suggest techniques capable of destroying the BC norm. The techniques worked temporarily, but they were based on inaccurate or inadequate premises.

The BC Copy-Pulling Section, to begin, had characteristics which suggest high cohesiveness. Moreover, threat (up to a certain point) will increase group cohesiveness and the tenacity with which a group will defend its norms. The early AC persistence of the BC norm, then, suggests this characterization: originally high cohesiveness increased by the threat of the reorganization and the trickle-down manner in which it was inaugurated.

The aim here is to sketch those factors which carried threat

[4] The interaction of the "external" system and its social products has been neglected most often. For an example of a recent recognition of the neglect, see William F. Whyte, *Man and Organization* (Homewood, Ill.: Irwin, 1959). Much evidence supporting Whyte's position may be found in Leonard R. Sayles, *Behavior of Industrial Work Groups* (New York: Wiley, 1958).

171

beyond the "certain point" in the later AC stage, which reduced cohesiveness, and induced the breakdown of the BC norm of pulling only 300 copies per day. The suggested analytical tack, then, is to extract from the case report those factors which would reduce member attraction to group, that is, cohesiveness. Decreased cohesiveness reduces norm potency, or the degree to which the group influences member behavior.

The three bases of cohesiveness isolated in the literature—prestige of membership, task attraction, and attraction to members—conveniently serve as finer analytical guide lines for this effort.

2a. Prestige of Membership. The prestige of informal-group membership in the BC Copy-Pulling Section, to consider the first base of cohesiveness, contributed to high cohesiveness. Thus the BC structural and style autonomy of the Section no doubt were considered prestigeful by most Section members. That is, both the setting and enforcing of the BC norm were handled informally in the Section. This control of the environment beyond the capacity of isolated individuals is vital. It has a double-barreled effect: it aids group control over the behavior of its members, and it makes the group attractive to its members.

The AC changes, in contrast, sharply reduced the prestige of informal-group membership. This may seem an obvious point, and in total effect it is. But the magnitude of the reduction can be understood only by carefully analyzing a number of factors which contributed to the total effect. First, the "experimental" assignment of definite work loads "to be done before a given deadline" signalled the end of the BC structural and style autonomy. Moreover, this "experimentation" had a high threat potential, which added to the threat generated by the work-process change itself. Second, many of the copy pullers were particularly vulnerable to the "experimentation," for they were, in the main, elderly, long-service employees. The possibility of release had a particularly pronounced impact, considering the general and sharp civil cervice cutbacks promised for the post-war period. Third, a work-force reduction of approximately 20 per cent in the Copy-Pulling Section during the first half of 1946 gave substance to any such fears.[5] Fourth, inferential evi-

[5] "Production Planning in the Patent Office," p. 12.

172

dence also suggests that the primary BC norm enforcers were among those separated (see the discussion of status changes below).

These factors were well suited for inducing quota-busting and upward-oriented competition in the "experimentation" of the later AC stage. The limited skill involved in copy pulling, moreover, did not provide a very substantial defense against these increases in threat.

The formal work-process change may be credited with inducing these forces, but the O & M theory does not always explain their effects adequately. For example, the theory does not provide for cohesiveness. Thus it could hardly explain the ways in which the "experimentation" reduced cohesiveness and norm potency.

Other changes, which were at least in part independent of the formal work-process change, also increased attraction to the formal organization and decreased the attraction of the particularistic BC allegiances. The introduction of an over-all personnel program for the Patent Office, for example, was conceded to be a "helpful coincidental development" in the increased productivity of the Office staff. It may have been more important, since it increased the attraction of the formal organization and reduced the reason for informal-group membership.

2b. Task Characteristics. The characteristics of the copy-pulling task, to consider the second cohesiveness base, also reflect a BC to AC diminution in member attraction to group. Under the BC system, the copy puller could control his job to a substantial degree. He also had some opportunity for job enlargement and rotation. Illustratively, BC copy pullers did their own sorting. They could arrange a satisfactory itinerary through the files, perhaps with a partner. Moreover, the work pace was informally regulated.

The AC changes provided a sharp contrast: sorting and copy pulling were set up as separate work processes; individual copy pullers were assigned to individual segments of the files; and two levels of supervision with a narrow span of control were provided. These AC changes sharply reduced copy-puller discretion and no doubt reduced task attractiveness. They certainly increased on-the-job threat.

173

More generally, available evidence supports the implied conclusions that routinization and job diminution increase the threat in the work environment, and that in turn threat reduces task attraction. In a negative sense, the generally high dissatisfaction of workers on assembly lines illustrates the extreme reaction by many employees to routinization.[6] Indeed, the most efficient lines often are those which decrease threat, as by job rotation. This excerpt typifies available findings:

> While the boss was away, some factory workers in Endicott, New York, switched jobs, just to break up the boredom. Result: it turned out to be just what the doctor ordered. By the time the switch was discovered, the men were all doing so much better that the boss decided to rotate jobs in his department—an International Business Machines plant—as a matter of policy. That was a year ago. Since then manufacturing costs in the department have dropped about 19 per cent.[7]

In addition, similarly, the very successful use of morons on routinized tasks (which had been performed more spottily by "normal" employees) strikingly suggests the common revulsion to routinization. The Works Manager of an electronics firm reported, after a year of experience with several morons, that

> In every case, these girls proved to be exceptionally well-behaved, particularly obedient, and strictly honest and trustworthy. *They carried out work required of them to such a degree of efficiency that we were surprised they were classed as subnormals* for their age. Their attendance was good, and their behavior was, if anything, certainly better than any other employee of the same age.[8]

In a positive vein, the successes of firms (such as IBM) with job enlargement during periods of rapid growth—when usual recommendations insist upon job routinization—also suggest the

[6] Argyris, *Personality and Organization*, p. 276.
[7] *Newsweek*, March 22, 1954, p. 79.
[8] From *The Making of a Moron*, by Niall Brennan, p. 16. Copyright 1953 Sheed and Ward, Inc., New York. Italics supplied.

lack of specificity of the theory underlying O & M applications.[9]

In sum, then, the AC changes had the effect of reducing the attractiveness of the task. This, in turn, reduced cohesiveness and the strength of the 300-copy norm. Interestingly, the O & M teams explained that these task-relevant changes had quite another purpose. They were cited as consistent with the machinelike need for "rhythm," and so on, ascribed to copy pullers who could be high producers. This formal theory seems accurate, for output did increase. Most probably, however, this is a case of being correct for the wrong or inadequate reasons. A behavioral explanation of the increased output seems less simplistic. The AC changes raised output (only temporarily, however), not because they increased "rhythm," but because they had the unintended effect of contributing to the breakdown of the BC norm by lowering cohesiveness. This norm was the roadblock to increased output.

This contrast of behavioral and formal theories raises two points. First, the contrast illustrates one of the major difficulties in scientific work. Many theories may seem to explain the same phenomenon. Thus scientists accord great importance to findings which disprove a theory, for such findings demonstrate what is not the case. Findings which support a theory, in contrast, do not reveal what is the case. They permit only the cautious conclusion that the theory is not inconsistent with available evidence.

Second, one can understand how the O & M theory attracted adherents. Successful O & M applications (and there were many) were interpreted incautiously. Negative findings, moreover, were not given proper attention. For example, the concept "hoard and spend" often more accurately describes worker expenditure of effort than "rhythm."[10] It permits the worker to control his job, as well as to respond to changes in his physical state. The notion of "rhythm," of course, reflects the mechanical view which traditional organization theory has of the employee. The utopian method of the O & M theory, of course, encouraged the neglect

[9] F. L. W. Richardson, Jr., and Charles R. Walker, *Human Relations in an Expanding Company* (New Haven: Labor and Management Center, Yale University, 1948).

[10] Argyris, *Understanding Organizational Behavior*, pp. 85–87.

of such negative findings by settling for logical consistency rather than empirical validity.

Some characteristics of the AC work process, specifically the areal assignment, probably also had the effect of improving the work environment. To explain, assignment of copy pullers to specific segments of the files with responsibilities for maintenance improved working conditions. BC, all copy pullers worked in all storage areas. Apparently no one had specific responsibility for maintenance. Thus the rationalization that it was "the other fellow's" fault was always available. Such improvements also may have removed physical blocks to increased productivity.

These improvements in working conditions probably reduced the importance of small-group membership as a defense against a management which neglected the interest of its employees. The 300-copy norm, in short, was one way of "getting even" for poor working conditions and the slighting of the employee they would be taken to imply.

Although the reorganized work process contributed greatly to the monitoring of this clean-up, there are two required observations. First, such improvements might have been accomplished without any work-process change. The development of a "good housekeeping" norm might have sufficed. The (presumed) high cohesiveness of the BC group in the Section, of course, at least implied the control potential to police such a norm.

This control potential might have been employed, similarly, in the informal handling of work assignments. The experience of the sales force in a clothing store is relevant. The sales people were on commission and tended to neglect stock and inventory work, for which no one had specific responsibility. This is similar to the BC Patent Office situation. The problem in the clothing store was settled informally.[11] One employee permanently elected to perform stock and inventory work, and the others agreed to divide the total commissions on an equal-share basis. The arrangement was successful in terms of employee satisfaction and service to patrons. Some reasons for this success

[11] Nicholas Babchuk and William J. Goode, "Work Incentives in a Self-Determined Group," *American Sociological Review*, XVI (October, 1951), 679–87.

seem patent. Primarily, the employees made their own decision. They could thus police it without fighting it. Moreover, the original commission plan had a high threat potential. Thus sales people would compete for one another's customers, and the like. The sharing of commissions avoided many of these difficulties and was welcomed (that is, employees were forced to perform low-preference behaviors by the commission system). The arrangement was unknown to management, which assumed quite different notions of how employees are motivated.[12]

To cite another limit on crediting the Patent Office clean-up to the work-process change, the development of a "good housekeeping" norm might have been necessary even with the change in the work process.

The area system, finally, also may have had the *task-relevant* effect of reducing (or destroying) group influence in such matters as work restriction. The old system gave pullers a common interest (i.e., conditions in the entire storage area). The BC system also permitted a high degree of social contact on the job. Both elements often lead to group development.[13] In contrast, the area system set imposing barriers to the social interaction upon which group development and norm enforcement are based. It isolated copy pullers in segments of the files, and it set the stage for interunit, or intersegment, competition as well. The interests of the newly-appointed supervisors, plus the pressure of the AC "experimentation" and time schedule, also would tend to increase these competitive and divisive pressures. This hypothesized social competition *cum* divisiveness, of course, is consistent with the setting of the new bogey at about twice the level of the BC norm.

But the area system might not only dilute BC group influence. Derivative pressures might also induce a new behavioral style, or atmosphere, in the AC filing units. Thus the AC changes imply leader-centered groups and a directive atmosphere. The before condition, in contrast, seems to have been member-centered and permissive.

[12] See the list of dominant assumptions in terms of which Argyris, *Personality and Organization,* pp. 123–62, describes management's understanding of the factors which motivate their employees.

[13] These group-formative elements are stressed by Muzafer and Carolyn Sherif, *Groups in Harmony and Tension,* pp. 192–208.

That increased productivity resulted under these conditions may seem strange, for much of the literature implies that a directive atmosphere would decrease productivity as a reaction to formal restraints, and much research supports this position. The explanation is tenable. Credibly, a permissive atmosphere implies the greater possibility of tying group influence over members to organization purposes. This avoids the defensive reactions often induced by a directive atmosphere. In addition, it precludes the necessity of constant and direct supervision, which is difficult even under conditions of low task skill and fixed work positions.

But the small-group literature also contains many contrary findings.[14] The reason is that existing studies most often manipulate only the atmosphere variable. The effects of three "intervening variables" credibly explain the mixed results in the literature. First, individuals with "response repertoires" skewed toward authoritarian behaviors would enjoy a directive atmosphere and be high producers. Indeed, some individuals might be high producers only under directive conditions.[15]

Moreover, second, even individuals who seldom display authoritarian behaviors might be high producers in a directive atmosphere, *given certain conditions.* In one case, for example, a small plant with an atmosphere of great suspicion, competitiveness, difficult working conditions, and limited worker participation in decision-making—in short, with characteristics directly opposed to those suggested by the "human relations" literature—had high output. The "certain conditions": threat was sustained at a very high level, and "naturally" so, for many of the employees were transients or had physical characteristics, such as deformities, which limited their employability in larger concerns in the industry.[16] A similar set of threatening conditions —employee age, fear of release, the pressure of the time schedule and of the new supervisors—seems to have existed in the Copy-Pulling Section.

[14] See the summary in Rieckens and Homans, "Psychological Aspects of Social Structure."

[15] Consult the instructive case of Administrator H in Harold D. Lasswell, *The Political Writings of Harold D. Lasswell* (Glencoe, Ill.: Free Press, 1951), pp. 127–35.

[16] William J. Goode and Irving Fowler, "Incentive Factors in a Low Morale Plant," *American Sociological Review,* XIV (October, 1949), 618–24.

Evidence suggests that the long-run maintenance of such "certain conditions" is problematical, especially in a relatively free society. Sustaining threat at high levels, for example, may prove an unrewarding chore. The task seems to have been difficult enough in the Copy-Pulling Section, indeed, to have encouraged its abandonment. In addition, threat seems to have boomeranged, for output dropped sharply. Subsequent analysis will consider these reactions to the AC threat. Consistently, also, earlier consideration generally supported the prediction that high threat will tend to encourage negative reactions. It is possible, however, to explain how threat can have at least temporary effects which differ from usual predictions. Although it is not possible to be very precise, the threat induced in experimental situations is (at most) "mild." Crudely, the threat is substantial enough to induce negative reactions in the subjects, but it can be opposed. Threat, in the natural state, can be pushed beyond the "mild" stage; the consequences will differ from those observed in social laboratories.

Third, the copy-pulling task was less likely to suffer productivity loss due to the directive atmosphere than tasks which are more difficult and require greater interpersonal cooperation. The "human relations" literature often assumes that all tasks have a high degree of structure and low solution patterning.

Deutsch's study of "cooperation" and "competition" in laboratory collectivities illustrates the usual assumption. The study also spotlights the not-so-usual awareness of the interaction of atmosphere and task characteristics.[17] Deutsch predicted that competitive groups would be less efficient than cooperative groups. The prediction was supported, however, only for certain relatively difficult problems involving significant interpersonal cooperation (such as the discussion of a human-relations problem). For a puzzle problem, in contrast, no significant differences existed between the two conditions. Deutsch concluded that the puzzle task required so little cooperation and had such obvious solutions that problem "blocking" was difficult even in the competitive condition.

These factors related to the AC task suggest that the theory underlying the O & M application missed some important bets. Sometimes, in sum, the O & M theory led to inaccurate predic-

---

[17] Morton Deutsch, "The Effects of Cooperation and Competition Upon Group Processes," in Cartwright and Zander, *Group Dynamics*, pp. 414–48.

tions (as in the expectation that the AC work process would increase productivity). At other times, the O & M theory permitted accurate prediction, but for the wrong reasons. This was the case, for example, with the AC area form of organization, which had the real (if unarticulated) effect of contributing to the breakdown of the BC norm.

Small-group analysis contributes to making traditional organization theory more precise. But small-group analysis does not meet all of the problems raised above. For example, given the relation of work process and personality, the value problem is still open. That is, what kind of behavior ought to be induced in organizations? The question is complex. But it cannot be avoided in O & M applications by such question-begging answers as: Behavior which results in high productivity ought to be induced. Research has shown that there are at least two sets of such behaviors. Attention thus must be paid to the normative side effects of alternate ways of empirically achieving the same goal.

2c. Attraction to Members. The attraction to members in the Copy-Pulling Section, to consider the third cohesiveness component, also probably dropped AC versus BC. This would contribute to decreased cohesiveness and to the weakening of the BC norm. Three major elements were involved in this reduced attention to members of the Copy-Pulling Section: changes in force levels, changes in the behavior of individuals, and changes in the status of individuals.

i. Changes in force levels. Changes in force levels, first, probably reduced cohesiveness significantly. Thus it is an informed guess (made for reasons outlined below) that those with the greatest BC attraction for others were released. Moreover, the AC reductions operated in the short run to decrease attraction of the remaining members, whoever they were, for they were all potential competitors for retention.

ii. Changes in behavior. Changes in the behavior of Section members, second, probably also decreased the attraction-to-members component of cohesiveness. The argument is straightforward. Group atmosphere has a significant influence upon the behaviors which will be chosen by most individuals from their response repertoires. Moreover, the pressure of group atmosphere on an individual to display or experience low-pref-

180

erence behaviors over time is threatening. Frustrated behavior is a likely consequence.

Frustrated behavior may hinder, or help, task performance, so firm general predictions are reserved for the foolhardy. The Lewin experiments, for example, reflected both effects. Children subjected to group atmospheres they disliked engaged in much aggressive behavior. When the adult supervisor was present, task performance did not suffer. When the supervisor was absent, however, task performance deteriorated rapidly. Many signs of regressive behavior were observed. Materials and output were destroyed, fights broke out, and the like.[18]

The Copy-Pulling Section similarly reflected both positive and negative effects of frustration caused by requiring undesired behaviors of the copy pullers. Thus the BC atmosphere was permissive and the AC atmosphere was directive. It is reasonable, then, that the employees retained in the Section often performed low-preference behaviors. The implied increase in threat did not immediately aid task performance. The sharp AC resistance by the copy pullers, indeed, suggests it had the opposite effect.

This early resistance to the reorganization seems to reflect one, perhaps two, characteristics of frustration: fixation, and perhaps aggression. Their effects were negative: productivity did not rise.

The increases in threat in the later AC stages overwhelmed this initial reaction, however. Productivity rose in the intermediate run. The key change was the dilution of group control and the breakdown of the BC norm, although frustration levels probably increased. Experimental evidence supports this general position. For example, when "cooperative" versus "competitive" instructions are given to individuals who are to perform tasks in experimental situations, the major contrast is the lack of the performance of behaviors which develop and support group control over members in the "competitive" situation.[19] The reorganization, as it were, changed such "instructions" by threat in the short run.

But the source of frustration remained. Resignation to the

18 White and Lippitt, "Leader Behavior and Member Reaction in Three 'Social Climates.' "

19 Deutsch, "The Effects of Cooperation and Competition Upon Group Processes."

frustration did not occur, and over the longer run, the reaction to frustration hindered effort. Suggestively, another reorganization of the Copy-Pulling Section was necessary in 1948. Some evidence indicates that this reaction took the form of minor (but constant) complaints and nagging failures to make minor work adjustments. Both elements can make a drudgery of work. Both reflect strong overtones of regression. Again, frustration caused by the long-run performance of undesired behaviors would have negative effects on productivity. The discussion in Chapter 6 of the "conflict" concept also seems relevant to explaining the necessity of the 1948 re-reorganization. The re-reorganization, and the difficulties which precipitated it, suggest the impact of the three general costs of intense conflict: strong emotional response, wide generalization, and notable persistence.

iii. Changes in status. Status changes, third, also probably resulted in reduced attraction to members. These changes seem to have induced higher productivity in the intermediate run. But this occurred in spite of, rather than because of, the recognition of status. The importance of the neglect of status can be demonstrated by considering the instability of status ranks induced by the reductions in force and by the promotion of certain copy-pullers to supervisory positions, and the probable release of the top BC performers of leadership behaviors.

First, status instability contributed to decreased cohesiveness, for status reshuffling is a prime creator of conflict.[20] All indications point to a particularly tender situation in the Copy-Pulling Section. Consider these two points. High status congruency suggests high cohesiveness and strict enforcement of norms. The conflict over status, then, could be expected to lower cohesiveness and to contribute to the breakdown of the 300-copy norm. Moreover, high BC performers of leadership behaviors (see below) probably were released. The personality characteristics necessary to achieve high status on all three major functional roles of leadership—individual achievement, group task facilitation, and sociability—are rare. Hence replacement of high leadership performers without a deterioration of effectiveness would be unlikely.

Moreover, even if all Section employees had been retained, status instability was still important, because the promotion of

[20] Christof Heinicke and Robert F. Bales, "Developmental Trends in the Structure of Small Groups."

some copy pullers to supervisors raised the problem of the integration of formal and informal leadership structures. The problem is a general one.[21] There is reason to believe it was acute in the Section. Thus BC informal leaders were substantially free from formal supervision, that is, they performed the leadership functions. But few (if any) of the BC informal leaders were likely to be promoted, for promotion was based on productivity. And, because of considerations to be reviewed soon, BC leaders were not likely to have high output records.

Probably, then, the reorganization deprived the BC informal leaders of the performance of functions which supported their pre-eminence. Severe personality disturbances often follow such deprivation.[22] In any case, it encouraged resistance to change by those most able to mobilize resistance. The reorganization, in short, made problems for itself.

In sum, then, the attraction-to-members component of cohesiveness would fall whether or not reductions in force were made. Status instability was implicit in the way the AC changes were made.

A second and related consequence of status changes which reduced the attraction-to-members component of cohesiveness also requires analysis: the probable loss of the top BC leadership performers. The relation of status and conformity to group norms supports this prediction. Studies of the relation of status and norm conformity have yielded mixed results.[23] Thus studies have demonstrated that status and conformity to norms are directly related. Other studies have demonstrated an inverse relation. The findings, however, are not necessarily incompatible. Dittes and Kelley, for example, explain the apparent contradiction in terms of such intervening variables as: (1) whether the situation in which the conformity is observed is "public" or relatively "private"; (2) whether or not the individual observed

[21] For a treatment of this problem in the unlikely context of a maximum-security prison, see Gresham Sykes, *The Society of Captives* (Princeton: Princeton, 1958), especially pp. 53–58.

[22] Thus Doc of the famous Norton Street Gang, for example, suffered severe headaches and dizzy spells when circumstances prohibited his performance of leadership functions. See William F. Whyte, *Street Corner Society: The Social Structure of an Italian Slum* (Chicago: Chicago, 1952).

[23] See, respectively, for research supporting and denying this relation of status and conformity to norms: Fritz J. Roethlisberger and William Dickson, *Management and the Worker* (Cambridge, Mass.: Harvard, 1939); and E. C. Hughes, "The Knitting of Racial Groups in Industry," *American Sociological Review*, XI (1946), 512–19.

highly values his group membership and status; and (3) whether or not the individual feels secure in his status.[24] To explain, given a private situation, low valuation of status, and high security of status, a high-status individual might be a low conformer. This is contrary to usual predictions, which are based upon status and conformity only.

In the Copy-Pulling Section, however, the norm observance situation was public, it was likely that individuals highly valued their membership and status, and their security was probably low. Thus high BC status would probably be associated with rigid norm observance and with resistance to increased production. BC informal leaders, consequently, would tend to be the more "visible" low producers. This, in turn, raises the probability of their release.

The release of the BC informal leaders would encourage the breakdown of the BC norm and increase production. The costs, however, are substantial. They include certain social dislocation, probable resistance to the formal organization when conditions permit, and the likely loss of individuals who had demonstrated their capacity for leadership.

SOME CONCLUDING THOUGHTS

This explanation via small-group analysis differs in fundamental ways from the O & M explanation of the productivity experience of the Patent Office. The latter is couched in terms of traditional organization theory. The explanation here is more complex, but it also seems to reflect reality more adequately than traditional organization theory. There is, then, ample reason to respecify traditional organization theory to include this greater complexity. Indeed, empirical theory—whether goal-based or not—has no other reasonable alternative.

Such respecification would constitute a theoretical advance, but it would be a highly practical addition to traditional organization theory as well. Evidence of this practicality dots this chapter. The following chapter spells out the point more explicitly and more systematically.

[24] James E. Dittes and Harold H. Kelley, "Effects of Different Conditions of Acceptance upon Conformity to Group Norms," *Journal of Abnormal and Social Psychology*, LIII (July, 1956), 100–107.

9

THE NEGLECT OF
THE SMALL GROUP:
SOME MISSED OPPORTUNITIES
IN THE PATENT OFFICE

THE NEGLECT OF THE SMALL GROUP IN THE THEORY FROM WHICH
the reorganization of the Patent Office was derived had a very
practical aspect. Indeed, all theories have very practical aspects.
There are, however, important differences between theories.
"Good" theories pay off; "bad" theories cost.

In the broadest sense, the cost of the O & M theory is reflected
in the apparently unrecognized destruction of the group affiliations of the copy pullers in order to increase production. The
point is not simply that the reorganization failed in its early
stages. More important, the destruction of these group affiliations would have the probable consequence of increasing job-relevant interpersonal problems which would hinder performance
in the longer run. Illustratively, a group with high cohesiveness
serves to reduce the anxiety of its members. Given a low-output
norm, the destruction of the group enforcing the norm would
probably increase production in the short run. But such a course
would be likely to have unfavorable consequences in the longer
run. These would be most prominent on tasks which require
constant cooperation, but few jobs so isolate workers — both
socially and functionally — that high levels of threat would not
affect task performance negatively over the long run.

This chapter takes a more specific approach to the unnecessary costs of the reorganization. The analysis will be a three-pronged one, stressing the neglect of the behavioral consequences of the 1946 reorganization. First, status changes will be emphasized. This discussion taps the influence of what might be called the behavioral organization on the formal organization.

Second, the neglect of the behavioral consequences of the form of organization prescribed for the Patent Office also will be analyzed. The neglect implied unnecessarily high costs in the reorganization. This second element might be characterized as the effect of the formal organization on the behavioral organization.

A third emphasis more sharply suggests that the magnitude of the costs of the missed opportunities to induce and reinforce change were great indeed. The Copy-Pulling Section was again reorganized in 1948, and the reorganization followed vastly different lines than the one of 1945–46.

NEGLECT OF BEHAVIORAL CONSEQUENCES:

STATUS AND PROMOTION

The neglect of status—like the neglect of other behavioral elements—reflects the imprecision of the theory underlying the O & M application. But it also implies the loss of substantial opportunities to ease and to reinforce change. Thus this neglect is intensely practical, as well as theoretical.

This claim of double-barreled importance requires solid substantiation. The evidence here will be centered upon promotions. The major questions which will be asked, in effect, are:

1. How were the promotions handled?
2. What were the consequences of this handling? and
3. How might the promotions have been handled more deftly?

The handling of the AC promotions provides a major illustration of the missed opportunities to encourage change through an awareness of status. This evaluation stands despite the favorable consequences of *any* promotions in the Copy-Pulling Section. To explain, the lack of postwar promotion opportunities had been a sore point in the Section. Reasonably, in fact, the lack of such opportunities may have helped turn the informal leaders and their groups toward an output-restricting norm. There was no real alternative, in short, for the ambitions of those individuals in the Section who were capable of exercising leadership. The promotions, then, had "something going for them."

The opportunity of the promotions went begging, for the high-productivity criterion for the promotion of supervisors excluded the BC informal leaders. This left no course open for the informal leaders except resistance. The extended opposition to increased production in the early AC stage reinforces this surmise. This resistance might have been reduced if at least some BC informal leaders had been utilized to aid change. Formal status and the induction of higher productivity are the *quid pro quo*.

Such a line of argument must be tempered by two reservations. First, BC informal leaders might not have successfully encouraged higher output. Thus an informal leader may be more a captive of group norms than their creator. Norm-breaking efforts by an informal leader thus might result only in making the leader unacceptable to the group. Even in this case, however, higher production might result, for the leader's defection might leave the group without anyone as capable of rallying members in support of their norms. However, cases exist of groups which retained their identity even under conditions of rapid change of personnel.

Second, the BC informal leaders might not want the formal supervisory positions. This is not an unusual case, since accepting the position of foreman implies attitudes more consistent with those of management than with those of work-unit members. Many feel the price of "leaving the guys," physically as well as psychologically, is too high a price to pay.[1]

1. The Promotions: Self-Choice versus Above-Choice

In any case, the method of selection of supervisors in the Section, while consistent with the O & M theory, implied substantial adverse effects on productivity. To explain, students have argued that peer representation, or even self-choice, be utilized in such matters as promotion.

---

[1] Such cases are common. Whyte, *Street Corner Society*, for example, cites the case of an individual so committed to his group ties that he did not take an opportunity to further his education.

TABLE XIV

*Differences in Attitudes and Rank in A Formal Organization:
Attitudes Toward the Behavior of Non-Commissioned Officers*

The Issue	(per cent who agree with each statement)		
	Privates	Noncoms	Officers
"A noncom should not let the men forget that he is a noncom even when off-duty"	39	54	81
"A noncom has to be very strict with his men or else they will take advantage of him"	63	81	90
"The harder a noncom works his men the more respect they will have for him"	10	18	42
"On a fatigue detail, a noncom should see that the men under him get the work done, but should not help them do it"	36	37	68

Source: Samuel A. Stouffer, *et al.*, *The American Soldier* (Princeton: Princeton, 1949), p. 408.

On a negative tack, to stake out the rationale for the position, management and employee criteria for promotion tend to differ. For example, Table XIV presents some data illustrating such differences. Three levels of organization in the United States Army are represented. The regularity of the differences requires no underscoring. Differences in opinions between the ranks do vary from issue to issue, but the regularity and sharpness of these differences support the point of this paragraph with something to spare.

Such differences in attitudes by organization levels have this important implication: choices by management will tend to neglect the needs and desires of the supervisees. This induces resistance to the formal head, and encourages the emergence of informal leaders. Finally, output would be likely to suffer, especially on tasks which have a high degree of structure and a low degree of solution patterning.

The argument, then, may be blocked out fully. High style integration (reflected, e.g., in high productivity) often will accompany high structural integration (which occurs when the formal supervisor has high informal leadership rank). Traditional organization theory, however, does nothing to bring about this integration; indeed, it often inhibits it. Elements of small-group theory provide some hope. Consider the relation of group compatibility and performance, which suggests the usefulness of such simple techniques as self-choice, or peer representation, in the choice of formal supervisors. Self-choice implies high structural integration: the person informally chosen is made the formal supervisor. This does not guarantee high style integration, but it does increase its probability. Low structural integration, in this regard, is far more of a long shot.

A study of small conferences illustrates this relation of structural and style integration. In some conferences, the chairmen (or formal heads) did not perform leadership behaviors. "Lessened group cohesion and lessened satisfaction" characterized such conferences. A measure of productivity also was inversely related to the degree to which other conference members had to take up the leadership slack. Such findings are suggestive, for "leadership sharing" behaviors imply low formal-informal structural integration. And this implies high conflict, which disrupts group functioning.

One reservation concerning this argument, however, must be stressed. The formal supervisor with high informal rank may have had to support group norms opposed to the formal organization. Thus it is not enough to be "accepted by the men." The terms of acceptance are crucial: group norms must be specified. To illustrate, Adams studied the congruence of formal and informal status in Air Force crews. He reported direct relations of the degree of congruency and social performance scores (e.g., friendliness). Both both low *and* high congruence were associated with low technical performance. This latter finding requires explanation. The "low" finding suggests the impact of status conflict on the productivity of the group. Adams offered two explanations for the "high" finding. High status congruency, first, implies fewer attempts by the aircraft commander to organize activity. Second, it implies a cohesive informal group which protects crew members from the threat which might be applied from "outside" to spur activity.[2]

The "above" pattern of assignment, moreover, does not con-

[2] Stuart Adams, "Status Congruency as a Variable in Small Group Performance," *Social Forces*, XXXII (October, 1953), 16, 18, 19, and 21.

tribute to group compatibility. Self-choice tends to do so. The point is significant. Schutz's work, to explain, suggests the difficulty and the payoffs of developing the analytical tools which will permit "external" assignment for compatibility. An IBM machine, for example, might be employed to determine the proper "mixes" of group members suited for specific purposes. Schutz's work is a step toward the creation of analytical tools necessary to produce these desired "mixes" of member characteristics. But much remains to be done.

Applications need not wait on this sophisticated work, however. Self-choice, in effect, permits the "internal" creation of compatible work groups. That is, group members themselves determine the group "mix." Formal authorities, of course, lose much of the control they would have in "external" assignment, and self-choice may not result in the proper mix of abilities for a particular task. But the "internal" assignment for compatibility by self-choice often produces results consistent with the goals of the formal organization. To illustrate, self-choice versus the "above" assignment of members of work teams on a construction project proved to be more efficient as measured by an index of labor costs, an index of material costs, worker satisfaction, and turnover rate. Consider labor and material costs only. Self-choice crews turned out almost four houses per hundred more than above-choice crews.[3]

This coin of self-choice, however, has another side. Self-choice may sometimes—although apparently not often—simply reinforce existing opposition to the formal organization. This was the sad experience of a warden who allowed his prisoners self-choice of cellmates. He found to his horror that the most troublesome prisoners had chosen one another. Consequently, his disciplinary problems were multiplied.

2. Liabilities of the New Supervisors: General

The lack of awareness of status changes also implied other lost opportunities to ease or reinforce change through the promotion of the new supervisors. Four of these opportunities are of partic-

[3] Raymond H. Van Zelst, "Validation of a Sociometric Regrouping Procedure," *Journal of Abnormal and Social Psychology*, XLVII (April, 1952), 299–301.

ular importance. Most prominently, the new supervisors were probably not the BC high performers of leadership functions. Thus they had to establish their claim to informal leadership, and their probable low BC status did not make the job easier. Moreover, the new supervisors probably could not be expected to display more than maudlin leadership talent.[4]

Second, assume that the weighting of the functional roles in determining leadership did not change greatly. The new supervisors would be rated low at least on the sociability function of leadership (which probably had a heavy weighting in BC leadership), for the high productivity of the new supervisors suggests low popularity, if not social isolation.[5] Obviously, the quota-buster will not be accorded high status in a group of high cohesiveness enforcing a norm of low productivity, status and norm observance being directly associated. Moreover, the high-cohesiveness group would decisively exclude the quota-buster after having failed to convert him. In addition, available evidence stresses the social insensitivity of the quota-buster. Thus he may withstand the social pressures to which others succumb, but he probably could not provide the sensitivity to behavioral problems required of the new supervisors.

Indeed, the high producers probably were scapegoats in the Section. They were, that is, the targets of substantial aggression before the reorganization. The simple act of promotion would not destroy these group evaluations. Indeed, the reorganization probably increased hostility toward the supervisors, although less of it may have been expressed overtly.

This suggests a nasty dilemma faced by any attempt to change human behavior. The deviant from original group opinion may be most temperamentally suited for performing the behaviors required for change, but he also will have great difficulty in establishing satisfactory working relations with other group members. To make a deviant the formal supervisor of the group— even though he is able to supply the behaviors required by the

[4] Evidence suggests that self-choices are more accurate indicators of success in organizations than choices of superiors. For example, see Robert J. Wherry and Douglas H. Fryer, "Buddy Ratings: Popularity Contest or Leadership Criteria?" *Sociometry*, XII (February-August, 1949), 179–90.

[5] For a sketch of the "rate buster" as a social isolate, see Melville Dalton, "The Industrial 'Rate-Buster': A Characterization," *Applied Anthropology*, VII (Winter, 1948), 5–18.

formal organization—is probably asking for trouble, for it virtually assures low structural and style integration.

Relatedly, the new supervisors probably would be frustrated in their early attempts to exert leadership, whatever their capabilities. Fixation would be a likely consequence. That is, supervisors would be likely to exaggerate precisely those behaviors which had not endeared them to employees in the Section. It is also human to "get even." The supervisors would have not only their pre-reorganization experiences to feed this understandable aggression, they also would have the post-reorganization resistance of the copy pullers to intensify any desires to even the score. But "getting even" would complicate the supervisors' problem of gaining real, as well as formal, power. This would increase supervisory frustration. Moreover, informal leaders would be likely to develop in the several filing units. This would induce conflict, reduce structural integration and, in the long run, probably reduce output. Consequently, frustration would increase, and . . . but the point should be clear: a nasty circular process is at work.

Third, especially significant tensions could be expected when a supervisor had one or more high-ranked BC leadership performers in his filing unit. The task, plus the formal controls developed, might tamp the high conflict potential for a while, but the situation would be very likely to have serious long-run effects.

3. Liabilities of the New Supervisors: Lack of Power

The consequences of the neglect of status had the combinatory effect of reducing supervisory effectiveness. A fourth factor also weakened the position of the supervisors, for the AC work-process changes sharply limited the "power" of the new supervisors. The time schedule, coupled with the unit-segment organization of the files, operated to make the supervisor a clerical middleman. He had little discretion; consequently, he had little leverage to control the copy pullers. Yet the system of controlling orders in two daily batches (rather than direct control by segments or units) put the supervisors directly on the spot with their superiors. All supervisors might be reproached for a problem in a few segments, for the superiors would not tend to follow the difficulty to its source. The situation reeked of difficulty and high threat.

This position of the "man in the middle," of course, is common. Thus even in a maximum-security prison, the guards—the first-line supervisors—experience substantial cross-pressures. Prisoners often inform upon guards, sometimes with real cause, sometimes not. Lack of cooperation or riots illustrate more direct ways of informing on guards whose behavior is thought inappropriate by the prisoners. These countervailing powers of the captives, coupled with the fact that the guard must coax a certain productivity from the prisoners on the tasks they perform during the prison workday, provide a substantial leverage for the prisoners *over* their keepers. At the same time, top management—the warden—is ranking guards in terms of their ability to "control" their prisoners. "Control" is defined in terms of a satisfactory level of output plus the absence of passive or violent resistance by the prisoners. Thus guards looking forward to promotion operate within very real limits. This problem, common in many work situations, is heightened by the more unique danger that a "tough" guard may bring physical violence upon himself or his family.[6]

Because it is common, the problem of the "man in the middle" is of great significance. Two "solutions" suggest the point. The supervisor might seek to gain informally what the formal organization does not provide. The supervisor, then, might become a more effective spokesman for his work unit than for the formal organization. Many forces encourage such a course, for, most often, the supervisor must make some sort of peace with the work unit. If he does not, resistance is very likely to develop. The supervisor then will be marked down by his superiors as unable to control his men, i.e., as an ineffective supervisor. Moreover, most people need to be liked. It is a unique person who is able to function effectively in the face of continuous expressions of hostility toward him. And even if the supervisor has an asbestos personality, the productivity of his unit probably will be reduced by the very hostility which he is able to withstand.

[6] Sykes, *The Society of Captives.*

At the very least, supervisors often will operate in a state of continual threat from above and below. Frustration, then, may be expected. Illustratively, supervisors in one study were found to handle threat, or pressure, in at least three ways:

1. to channel it into interdepartment strife and to constantly blame fellow foremen for the difficulties which exist;

2. to channel it into "line" versus "staff" conflict and to constantly blame the difficulties on the budget people or the production control people;

3. to "internalize" the pressure in one of two ways:

   a. to remain apparently calm and non-emotional and to restrain themselves from "blowing off steam" while at the same time they work excessively: this is "inward aggression";

   b. by "checking up" on all the employees, making a show of giving commands and demanding immediate action: this is "outward aggression."[7]

These three ways of adapting to threat reflect all of the characteristics of frustration, save resignation. Aggression, for example, is reflected in various forms in all three of the adaptive variations. Regression, moreover, seems to be reflected in Adaptation 1, which substitutes emotional release (by assigning blame) for problem-solving. In addition, Adaptation 3b suggests fixation, for the supervisor persists in just those behaviors which will encourage pressure from his work unit.

Each of these ways of handling pressure tends to have negative effects. Even 3a, for example, often would have such consequences. The seemingly paradoxical plight of the foreman who is "too capable," to explain, is a common one in the literature of the shop.[8] By setting unattainable standards for his own work, the foreman causes work-unit members to despair of ever satisfying him. Hence, workers commonly curb their efforts. This protects them from the almost-certain failure which would result from their attempts to attain their foreman's standards.

The picture is no monochrome, however. Sometimes such a

[7] Argyris, *What Budgets Mean to People*, p. 19.

[8] The case of one such supervisor is presented in the case, "The New England Power Company," in Rossall J. Johnson, *Personnel and Industrial Relations* (Homewood, Ill., Irwin, 1960), pp. 521–27.

194

supervisor can inspire heroic effort. The subtle chemistry causing one or the other of these two possible effects cannot be detailed. Trouble seems likely to follow the foreman who is self-punitive, who needs to punish himself in his work rather than derive satisfaction from it. The "guy who works as if he wanted to kill himself" is quickly recognized by most people, who try to protect themselves from him.

The other possible adaptations to pressure even more clearly reflect the negative effects which are likely to accompany them. For example, channeling tension into interdepartmental conflict (Adaptation 1, above) will probably be time consuming and unproductive as well. Consider this resolution of the charge of a $3,000 error on a customer's order:

> For two months, supervisors of the departments most likely to be blamed waged a continuous campaign to prove their innocence. Each supervisor blamed the others. . . . The supervisors actually spent hundreds of man-hours arguing and debating among themselves. Emotions were aroused, people began calling each other names. Finally, two of the supervisors refused to talk to each other. Conflict reigned. . . .
>
> But the supervisors were not the only persons in conflict. The division manager was also in conflict. He had to make the decision. To charge any supervisor with such an error would certainly invite hostility from that supervisor. This hostility might have further effects in the future. . . .
>
> A meeting was held with the interested supervisors. The problem was discussed until just about everybody and everything that could be blamed, were blamed for the error. The division manager finally "gave in." He decided to place the error under "general factory loss." No department would be affected.[9]

Perhaps this story had a happy ending. In any case, the "solution" did not approach the problem, and this abortive effort had a very high price tag.

[9] Argyris, *What Budgets Mean to People*, p. 19.

TABLE XV

Relation of Foreman's Perception of Opportunity for Planning to Section Productivity

Question: "Are you able to plan your work ahead as much as you would like?"

Foremen of Sections with Productivity of:	Can Plan Ahead as Much as Needed	Sometimes Have Trouble in Planning Far Enough Ahead	Usually Cannot or Hardly Ever Plan Ahead
97–101%	37%	42%	21%
91–96%	51%	32%	17%
86–90%	29%	41%	30%
80–85%	29%	46%	25%
50–79%	14%	40%	46%

Source: Robert L. Kahn and Daniel Katz, "Leadership Practices in Relation to Productivity and Morale," in Dorwin Cartwright and Alvin Zander (eds.), *Group Dynamics: Research and Theory* (Evanston, Ill.: Row, Peterson, 1960), p. 561.

The failure to reinforce formal status with power, in addition, had the second consequence of missing an opportunity to induce and reinforce change. To explain, high-power supervisors tend to have high-producing units, which informally accept them. Low-power supervisors, in contrast, tend to have low-producing units. Moreover, the latter work units often develop informal spokesmen who are rivals of the formal supervisors. The reasons for such relations are not obscure. People normally act deferentially toward powerful figures, and differences in power, if they are not arrogantly flaunted, need not breed resentment.[10] The formal supervisor who is merely a glorified file clerk, in contrast, is a convenient and safe target for derision or contempt.

Table XV illustrates the importance of supervisory "power." It reveals the relation of supervisory power (defined in terms of the opportunity to plan ahead on the job) and productivity (measured as "per cent of standard"). All supervisors on the job and level, of course, have similar authority. To interpret Table XV, the foremen of high productivity sections had high power. This is reflected in three ways in the table. These foremen versus foremen of low-producing units more often feel they can plan ahead as far as needed, tend less often to

[10] Recall Berkowitz' experiment with the "response repertoire" concept. Its results are consistent with this position.

feel they sometimes have trouble in planning enough, and much less often report that they can rarely or never plan ahead adequately. The ability to plan, of course, implies significant control of the work environment.

The pattern of results in Table XV probably is less sharp than it might be, for the foremen were asked for *their judgment* of their ability to plan ahead. But, since the foremen probably had different standards, their answers are not strictly comparable. Foremen of high-producing units probably would feel that a great deal more planning was necessary than would foremen of low-producing units. Thus the foreman of a high-producing unit who reports he cannot plan far enough ahead may fool you. He may exercise more power through planning than the foreman of a low-producing unit who reports he can plan as far ahead as he wishes.

But, whatever the case, the data in Table XV do support the importance of the power of the supervisor. Employees, in short, differentiate supervisory power. Organization theory can do no less. But—as in the O & M theory—it has done much less.

4. The New Supervisors: Their Adaptation

The analysis to this point sometimes has a hypothetical nature. Because of the fact, it may seem to have missed the important possibility that the lesson of the promotion of the high-producing copy pullers may have been well learned by personnel in the Section. Consequently, they may have changed their estimate of the requirements of leadership to suit the AC situation. The new supervisors, as a result, would have achieved high structural and style integration with little difficulty.

This is a possibility, to be sure, but the odds seem great that it is a remote possibility. Such a change, it seems certain, did not occur in the short run. The intermediate-run success of the reorganization seems to suggest such a change, but the re-reorganization of the Copy-Pulling Section in 1948—to be analyzed in detail later—demonstrates that the new supervisors did not function effectively. Moreover, frustration apparently did not lead to resignation on the part of the copy pullers.

Interestingly, indeed, the new supervisors in the Copy-Pulling Section apparently attempted to gain the support of the copy pullers. The purpose was obvious: to gain the cooperation required to meet the daily work load without great emotional strain. The evidence, to be certain, is not conclusive, but it appears that the AC "experimentation" had raised output to approximately 800 copies per puller per day. Once the backlog was reduced, however, output seems to have stabilized to approximately 600 copies per day. The new supervisors seem to have supported this reduction.

Such an attempt by the new supervisors is credible. The supervisors-to-be, before the reorganization, did not have to cultivate the support of other copy pullers. Indeed, they probably alienated them, for the supervisors-to-be were violators of the 300-copy norm. As supervisors, however, they would have to cultivate such support. Thus their promotion implied a new situation to which they had to make some accommodations. Such situational changes, as research with the "response repertoire" concept demonstrates, often affect behavior substantially. Once the backlog had been reduced to control levels, some relatively painless accommodations by the supervisors were possible. The Section had approximately 45 copy pullers in the early AC stages. Their capacity at 800 copies per puller, per day, would be 36,000 copies. The average work load was approximately 20,000 copies per day. Only 22 copy pullers would have been required for this load, given an 800-copy bogey. Thirty-three pullers actually were retained, and the work load was approximately 600 copies per day.

The foremen need not have been alone in supporting some reduction in output. Other forces may have been aiding such an accommodation. Although there is no conclusive evidence, the management of the Patent Office could have accepted some looseness in output standards. This would provide a work-force "cushion" which would provide a hedge against increases in demand or against cuts in appropriations by Congress. The copy pullers, of course, would not object to such an accommodation.

Neglect of Behavioral Consequences:

Organization Forms

The neglect of the behavioral consequences of the AC form of organization also implied the loss of a major opportunity to

198

induce and ease change in the Patent Office. The point can be demonstrated through the comparison of the probable effects of two forms of organization: the "flat" form and the "tall" form.

1. Two Contrasting Organization Forms: The "Flat" and the "Tall"

The "tall" form of organization is implicit in the traditional theory of organization. It derives especially from the notion of a limited span of control, which sets the limits for the supervisees of any one man at a modest few (recall the "three and seven" rule). Thus an organization of forty individuals might have as many as four levels. Hence the designation "tall" form of organization.

The "flat" form of organization, in contrast, derives from different properties than those which underlay the Patent Office reorganization. The major properties of the "flat" form can be abstracted in these terms:

1. a conception of authority as a multi-line relation, with both horizontal and vertical components, and with social and psychological as well as formal characteristics;
2. a conception of management which emphasizes the creation of the general conditions under which employee motivation can occur, rather than the attempt to police employees by close supervision;
3. a conception of the individual as more than a physiological being, whose identification with the organization often can be encouraged by a "flat" organization, serving at once the needs of the individual and the purposes of the formal organization; and
4. a conception of the individual who has psychological needs whose fulfillment is encouraged by significant discretion on the job, e.g., as in job enlargement versus the job reduction implicit in O & M theory.

In an organization of forty people following such guide lines, there might be two or three levels. Hence the designation "flat" form of organization.

Without going into details, the major properties of the "flat" form of organization patently reflect a theory, just as do the properties underlying the "tall" form. The difference is, of course, that the properties of the "flat" form attempt to pay

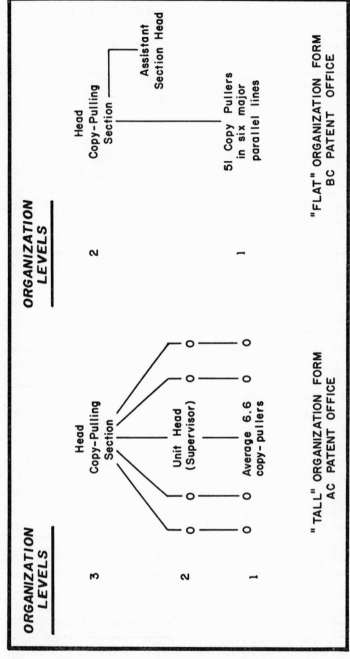

FIGURE 17. *"Tall" and "Flat" Forms of Organization*

more attention to man *as he is found* in the American "work environment," rather than to man *as he is assumed to be.*

These rudimentary distinctions will permit greater understanding of the reorganization of the Patent Office, for the reorganization of the Copy-Pulling Section followed the "tall" form. The "flat" form describes the BC organization of the Section. Figure 17 presents charts of these two forms of organization, along with other information which helps establish some obvious differences between them.

2. Some Behavioral Consequences of the Two Forms of Organization

These two forms of organization have significantly different behavioral consequences. Some of these consequences—e.g., those related to job reduction ("tall" form) versus job enlargement ("flat" form), and to close supervision ("tall" form) versus general supervision ("flat" form)—have already been analyzed. The purpose here is to outline the broader range of behavioral consequences associated with the two forms of organization. The subsequent analysis, however, leans upon one crutch. The assumption is made throughout that the individuals involved have response repertoires which favor permissive behaviors. The assumption seems to be a useful one for general prediction in the American work environment. In addition, the personnel of the Copy-Pulling Section also seem to have favored such behaviors. Thus there is a firm rationale supporting the assumption made, although this rationale has its limits. More refined prediction would require the specification of personality differences such as those introduced in Chapter 7.

Six major points will outline the different behavioral consequences of the two forms of organization. The approach is not all-or-nothing. The emphasis is upon general tendencies.

1. The threat induced by the "tall" organization form tends to be greater than that induced by the "flat" form. This, of course, is consistent with the intention of the narrow span of control. Thus the "tall" form will more often suffer from the negative effects of threat. Any attempt to change from one form of organization to the other—especially when the original form developed informally—will induce these negative effects. The

reorganization of the Copy-Pulling Section, of course, was just such a change.

2. The "tall" form tends to intensify the need for defensive informal groups. These groups help to control the threatening work environment. Resistance to the formal organization is common. Thus, in a real sense, the "tall" form sows the seeds of its own diluted control.

3. The "tall" form tends to encourage lower structural and style integration than the "flat" form. The "tall"' form presents a picture of the organization towering far above the individual, with authority figures sharply differentiated from him. This reduces the likelihood of the individual's identification with the formal organization and with his superiors. It also increases the possibility that—whenever possible—the individual will attempt to combat the formal organization with informal organization. Sparse evidence also suggests that lower morale and satisfaction also characterize membership in "tall" organizations.[11]

4. The "tall" form will tend to encourage, indeed it is designed to ensure, decision-making toward the top of the hierarchy. This close supervision of the "tall" form makes the intervention of any higher level in the decision-making of any lower level quite possible. The "flat" form, in contrast, encourages (if it does not force) general supervision. Any organization level is thus likely to have considerable autonomy, subject to general review (as supervision in terms of the accomplishment of major objectives rather than in terms of the close direction of specific work steps).

The practical behavioral consequence is the passage upward of many problems for solution in the "tall" form, and of few problems in the "flat" form. In effect, then, the "tall" form places a great part of the day-to-day burden of operations on the upper organization levels, even if subordinates are not consciously "passing the buck" up the hierarchy. Little confidence can be placed in the capacity of the new AC supervisors to provide such administration in the Copy-Pulling Section.

Of course, some problems should percolate up to higher organization levels than those at which they originate. But, on the other hand, if upper organization levels are deeply involved in

[11] James C. Worthy, "Factors Influencing Employee Morale," *Harvard Business Review* (January, 1950); and "Organizational Structure and Employee Morale," *American Sociological Review*, XV (April, 1950), 169–79.

operations, the functions of management (such as planning, creating environment which motivates exceptional performance, etc.) are likely to go begging. Thus, it may be argued that the difference between the "tall" and the "flat" forms is a difference of degree only. But this difference in degree may change the style of administration radically.

In capsule form, too many problems will find their way up the hierarchy in the "tall" form. In contrast, organization superiors in a "flat" form must be alert, lest they be cut off from important problems. This vigilance, to illustrate, was not exercised in the BC Patent Office. The Section Head had, in effect, lost control to the informal leaders among the copy pullers. For a time, this relation was tolerable and output was satisfactory. But with the postwar increase in demand for patent copies, attempts at overhead control proved ineffective, so complete had been the lack of top-level vigilance. The copy pullers were not set loose within general limits. They were set loose, period.

5. Relatedly, the "tall" form also tends to discourage the initiative of individuals at intermediate supervisory positions. As James Worthy has noted, initiative implies the ability to make one's own mistakes and to learn from them. This learning process seems to be encouraged in the "flat" form, but not in the "tall" form. The "tall" form may have certain short-run advantages, if top-levels are not overloaded, for it permits a more experienced handling of problems on which lower supervisory levels might make mistakes. But the "tall" form has important disadvantages. Thus it cuts off the intermediate manager from the educational experience involved in seeing a problem through to its decision and implementation. Moreover, the "tall" form would encourage careful "playing by the book" rather than creativity when it is required.

Illustratively, in Sears, Roebuck's medium-sized stores, those with a "tall" form were less efficient from a sales standpoint than stores with a "flat" form. Moreover, the "tall" stores contributed much less than their share of the management personnel considered promotable. The "flat"-form stores, in contrast, contributed more than their share.[12]

6. Relatedly, also, the "tall" form has the effect of reducing

[12] James C. Worthy, as abstracted in Whyte, *Man and Organization*, pp. 11–16.

the power of intermediate supervision. The relation of low supervisory power and low productivity was discussed above. The negative effect of the "tall" form on supervisory power, then, is a significant one.

This effect of the "tall" form on supervisory power has important consequences. Define "power" as the ability to influence the work environment in significant ways. Now consider a first-line supervisor in a "tall" organization. He often would find it convenient to request his superior to make a particular decision. Indeed, the superior might demand to do so. Two major consequences would follow: there would be an inevitable and often appreciable time lag between problem isolation and a decision; and it would become obvious to the supervisor's work unit that he did not have control. These consequences imply a diminution of supervisory power and, hence, effectiveness.

In the "flat" form, in contrast, a different problem obtains: restricting the power of intermediate supervisors to controllable limits *when necessary*. Superiors in a "flat" form of organization cannot supervise the work of their subordinates in detail, even if they desired to do so. The broad span of control prevents this. Illustratively, the BC informal leaders were able to derive considerable power from the then-"flat" organization of the Copy-Pulling Section, but top level failed in its task of setting the informal leaders free *within an area* which would permit their control when necessary.

Do not jump to a simplistic conclusion, however. Executives, restrain yourself from wholesale changes to "flat" organization structures! To explain, organization members will not always have response repertoires which favor permissive behaviors, and the "flat" form requires such behavior. The experience of Sears, Roebuck is instructive. As noted, medium-sized stores in the Sears chain—without any overhead planning—tended to develop either a "tall" or a "flat" form of organization. The "flat" form was found to have certain advantages.

But many factors hindered a changeover. Consider the transfer of a manager who had developed a "flat" form to a store with a "tall" form. The manager soon reported that he did not need the intermediate supervisors. Slowly, he changed the store's organization to the "flat" form. The manager who had developed a "tall" form behaved similarly. He developed a layer of intermediate supervisors when he was assigned to a store which had operated under a "flat" form of organization.

In sum, personality changes—as well as formal organization changes—often are required for a marked changeover to the "flat" form. Some of the required personality changes would be of a significant character. This is implied, for example, in the following general description of managers who favored the "flat" form (referred to as "X type" below) as opposed to those who favored the "tall" form("Y type" below):

> The manager of the X type store . . . appeared to be an individual with an optimistic view of people. He spoke freely of his faith in his subordinates. He seemed to take pride in the successes they achieved on their own initiative. On the other hand, the manager of the Y type store seemed to have a much more pessimistic attitude. He felt it was very difficult to get good hard-working people any more. . . . James C. Worthy comments, "These managers often seemed to expect the worst of their people and generally found their fears justified. They found that people had to be watched, that their work had to be checked closely— otherwise no telling what might happen."[13]

The conclusion to be drawn from such findings, however, is not that personality change is impossible. Significant changes can be wrought in even the supervisory habits of a score of years or more.[14] The conditioning of management personnel, however, often poses the most substantial barrier to the changes implied by the "flat" form. This would at least be the case of management personnel who cut their administrative teeth on the O & M theory!

Neglect of Behavioral Consequences:

The 1948 Re-Reorganization

The preceding analysis demonstrates the imprecision of the theory reflected in the 1945–46 reorganization of the Patent

[13] *Ibid.*, p. 13.
[14] Paul R. Lawrence, *The Changing of Organizational Behavior Patterns* (Cambridge, Mass.: Harvard, 1958).

TABLE XVI

Copies of Patents Sold, Patent Copy Sales Branch
1946–1951

Fiscal Year	Copies of Patents Sold
ending June 30, 1946	4,540,625
1947	3,250,237
1948	3,445,112
1949	app. 4,400,000
1950	app. 4,600,000
1951	4,869,768

Source: Data are from the *Annual Reports* of the Commerce Department for the fiscal years 1946–51.

Office. This theoretical imprecision would burden, if it does not imply the breakdown of, the work of the Copy-Pulling Section.

The most telling proof of the inadequacy of the theory which underlay the 1945–46 reorganization, however, is provided by the *re-reorganization* of the Section in 1948. The 1948 change followed quite different lines than the 1946 reorganization. This suggests, of course, the failure of the O & M theory to provide for the behavioral consequences of organization forms.

Problems of communication to, and control of, the five units seem to have forced the change. A number of factors which may have caused such problems have been reviewed above. Output in the Copy-Pulling Section also dropped sharply in fiscal 1947, the first full fiscal year after the 1946 reorganization. It is not known to what degree this drop reflected slackened demand or output restriction. In any case, sales increased markedly after the 1948 reorganization. Table XVI presents the relevant data.

Two Reorganizations Contrasted: 1946 and 1948

The reorganization of 1948 contrasts very sharply at a number of important points with the 1945–46 reorganization. Figure 18 presents a useful outline of some important features of the 1948 change. On the broadest level, then, the basis of organization was again shifted to order source. Separate copy-pulling units

206

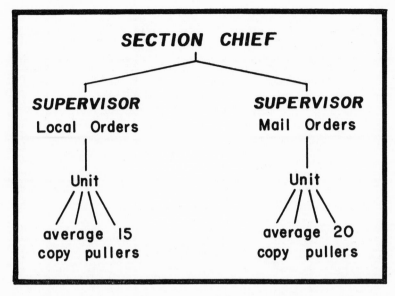

FIGURE 18. *1948 Formal Organization, Copy-Pulling Section*

were organized for orders which had a local source (that is, those received at the windows of the Patent Office) and for orders which came through the mail.

Other important characteristics of the 1948 reorganization may be listed and commented upon briefly.

1. The first-line supervisors' span of control was sharply increased. This, of course, made detailed supervision far more difficult. Increases in productivity could probably be expected from this change alone.

This 1948 organization violated the "three and seven rule." (The force levels in Figure 18, however, are illustrative only.) The "violation" had its point, though. The Local Orders Unit apparently developed a norm of fast service, a norm consistent with the intention of the reorganization. The 1945–46 reorganization did not reduce the waiting period for local orders as opposed to mail orders, and a differential was considered important.

2. Job-enlargement possibilities were increased. Thus copy pullers now perform the "fine sorting" of their orders. More-

207

over, job rotation is commonly used as a reward for effective performance. In addition, deserving copy pullers as a matter of policy may train on a variety of jobs.

3. The discretion of copy pullers in their control of the work pace was increased. For those processing mail orders, only one batch of orders is scheduled each day. In contrast, two batches were scheduled under the 1945–46 reorganization. This 1948 change permits the copy puller more latitude in arranging his workday and in accommodating to his own "rhythm." The degree of threat in the work environment, moreover, also was reduced by the 1948 change. Pullers working on local orders faced a greater time pressure, but their work load—determined by daily demand—is reportedly well within the output expectations of the pullers.

4. The power of the two 1948 supervisors was increased. Thus the supervisors control the assignment of copy pullers to other tasks, as well as the assignment of particular batches of orders to the copy pullers (see Section 6, below). The new supervisors thus controlled job rotation and training, probably important factors to many copy pullers.

In addition, the 1948 reorganization encouraged supervisors to concern themselves with general supervision, planning, and creating a favorable work environment. The broad span of control contributes to this end. Moreover, the tendency was abetted by the Section Chief's general control over the two units. This general oversight was encouraged by the experience with the 1946 organization, by the different problems of the two units based upon the source of orders, and by the satisfactory output levels which have been maintained.

5. New work bogeys were developed for mail orders to allow for the differential walking distances between probable "hits" in the various sections of the files. The bogeys developed under the 1948 reorganization range from *600* to *1,800* copies per day for different sections of the files. This adds substance to the speculation above that the least physically advantageous AC unit had been the bogey setter, for the low range of the new work standards approximates the highest output induced by the AC "experimentation." Of course, the 1,800 bogey is far above the AC standard. There are no work standards for local orders except daily demand.

Moreover, the work standards for mail orders apparently

are not strictly enforced. Certainly their enforcement does not approach the intent of the 1945–46 system. This probably puts the point too moderately, in fact. For example, officials could not remember the last major disciplinary action due to a failure to meet standards. One gets the impression that the work force is not all that disciplined, but rather that a relatively high output encourages a certain "looseness" in enforcing standards. Relatedly, a number of technical features build in substantial possibilities for such "looseness." The practice of job rotation and training, in addition, also contributes to the looseness of the application of standards.

These changes imply a reduction of threat. O & M theory would predict a drop in production as a consequence. Output, however, has been very satisfactory. Indeed, the total number of copies pulled has increased substantially, but the number of copy pullers has increased only slightly.

6. Copy pullers have a very high turnover, compounded of promotions and drop-outs. Both factors seem to contribute to high output, by encouraging attachment to the formal organization and by reducing the possibility of the development of stable, defensive informal groups. High turnover, although it has its costs, acts as a social escape valve. One would expect that, on tasks which are more difficult and require greater interpersonal cooperation, the costs would begin to outweigh the returns.

These characteristics patently contrast with the 1945–46 reorganization. The differences may be of degree, rather than of kind, but they are substantial. Thus the 1948 reorganization moved toward the "flat" form of organization as far as the copy pullers were concerned. It did retain characteristics of the "tall" form as far as the supervisors were concerned, however. The apparent aim is to profit from the advantages of the "flat" form at the work level while steering clear of the dangers of allowing the supervisors too much leeway. Not that close supervision of supervisors seems the order of the day, but they are on a potentially-short organization tether.

Moreover, the 1948 reorganization also seems to reflect a lesson learned from the earlier attempt at change, for it suggests dual purposes. First, many of the 1948 changes make it easier for the individual to identify with the formal organization. Second, many of them reduce the reason for membership in in-

209

formal groups whose structure and goals oppose those of the formal organization. Indeed, the high turnover also may serve the purpose of keeping group cohesiveness relatively low.

Both purposes are suggested by the 1948 reorganization's treatment of the relatively capable copy pullers. The reorganization provided for wide job training and relatively rapid promotion. Both factors would encourage a relatively favorable attitude toward the formal organization, and informal groups would be likely to reflect this opinion, especially since the more capable and/or the more upwardly mobile would tend to rise to high informal status. The lack of promotions before the 1946 reorganization, in contrast, caused much discontent, and the promotions made following the 1946 reorganization probably passed over the informal leaders. Consequently, most individuals had open but a single avenue of advancement: gaining status in informal groups which, reasonably, would develop a norm of low output. The more capable and ambitious would probably take this route, for they would chafe most under the handling of promotions.

The 1948 reorganization, then, is a third alternative for inducing high output in the Copy-Pulling Section. Two other alternatives have been emphasized above: the O & M approach, and the approach using the potential for the control of behavior implicit in a small group with high cohesiveness. Only an as-yet-unperformed experiment will determine whether any substantial losses in productivity or employee satisfaction resulted from the approach of the 1948 reorganization, as contrasted with the use of a group with high cohesiveness to control the behavior of group members. Existing research suggests that such losses often could be expected. However, the 1948 approach avoids the possible resistance which a group with high cohesiveness could offer to the formal organization. Many administrators might prefer such a work unit.

The two reorganizations also imply substantially different behavioral consequences. This says much about the adaptability and perseverance of the O & M specialists who came to the Patent Office in 1948 with a set of recommendations quite different from those derived from the O & M theory applied in 1945–46. But this adaptability in practice would not have been necessary, had the underlying theory been more accurate.

210

10

O & M AND THE SMALL GROUP:
A SUMMARY

THE CHAPTERS ABOVE CONSTITUTE A TWO-PRONGED REDESCRIPTION of an O & M application to the Patent Office and indicate the complexity of the interaction of the "formal approach" and the "behavioral approach." They also suggest the great costs of the failure of the O & M theory to recognize this complexity.

In sum, these chapters reflect man's limited ability to coordinate the behavior of men in organizations. There is no need to underestimate the task; it is colossal. Thus the outcome of the Patent Office reorganization has no particular significance *in itself*. Any understanding of man—including O & M specialists—must make ample provision for man's limited but growing knowledge.

The fate of the 1946 reorganization of the Patent Office, however, has a broader significance than a contribution to the well-documented fact that man's knowledge is limited. The point is not that *a* reorganization attempt failed, but that *the O & M theory* led to that failure. Hence the analysis above, for, hopefully, this little book is a prologue to a comprehensive theory as well as an analysis of a deficient one. The purpose below is the outline of some of the major implications of the preceding analysis for reworking O & M theory.

SOME EMPIRICAL PROBLEMS

OF THE O & M THEORY

The explanation via small-group analysis of the reorganization of the Patent Office establishes the inadequacy of the theory which (more or less implicitly) guided the O & M specialists. This explanation spotlighted the limitations of four central properties of that theory. These propositions are:

1. that authority is a formal, one-way relation;
2. that authority is most effective under conditions of close supervision;
3. that for practical job-relevant purposes, man is essentially a physiological organism; and
4. that the three prior assumptions will be realized most closely under conditions of specialization and routinization.

These properties are not always empirically adequate. In cases, they will correspond closely enough to reality for many practical purposes. The review of small-group variables and their application to the Patent Office case, however, has served two purposes. First, it indicated some of the limits of the propositions. Second, it indicated how the propositions must be modified to increase their usefulness.

There is no particular reason for detailing the ways in which small-group analysis gave the lie to these propositions. The analysis above either made its point or it did not. The impact of this two-pronged analysis of O & M theory, however, may be summarized usefully. Three themes will highlight this summary. First, the bias of O & M theory will be reviewed, the purpose being to establish its inadequacies of method. Second, the self-fulfilling nature of the O & M theory will be illustrated. The emphasis will be upon what might be called the gambit of "claiming all successes." Third, one of the propositions of the O & M theory will be reviewed. This review will outline the limits of the applicability of the O & M theory.

1. Method:
Its Significant, if Understandable, Limits

On the level of methodology, in a nutshell, the O & M theory has two vital drawbacks. It does not reflect the method of the type of theory required (goal-based, empirical theory), and it fails to respect the limitations of the type of theory utilized (utopian theory). This is hardly a satisfactory combination, but it has had a tenacious hold on students. This general evaluation may be supported briefly. First, O & M theory does not reflect the careful development of concepts and operations necessary to describe the important "somethings" of the empirical world. Nor is there evidence of the development characteristic of empirical theory: the testing and retesting, the formulation and reformulation of concepts and operations, and the development of an increasingly comprehensive web of theory. Instead, O & M theory is in a state of being rather than in a state of developing.

This methodological posture is understandable, however. Four main explanatory factors contribute to this understanding. Primarily, most of the practitioners in the area—including F. W. Taylor—were (and are) engineers. This professional bias encouraged an emphasis upon the mechanical aspects of organization. Had these practitioners been sociologists or psychologists in the main, a similar overweighting of behavioral factors could have been expected. This bias in personnel and training, plus the often remarkable successes of the "formal approach" to organization, have left O & M theory with a substantial blind spot.

Moreover, "scientific management" fell victim to certain misconceptions of "science" prevalent during the time of the pioneering work of Taylor and others. It was reasonable that the enthusiasm for "scientific management" was expressed in terms of this misconception, but the price has been high.

The mechanistic interpretation of Newton's laws, to explain, was massively influential in shaping much of the effort devoted to understanding the environment within which man lives, especially in the period near the turn of the present century. The common extrapolation of Newton's insights, to suggest the nature of this influence briefly, held that the future behavior of the universe was completely predictable for all time, given the initial positions and velocities of all bodies at a certain time and the forces acting on these bodies. This mechanistic bias determined the kind of "somethings" which were thought to be important in describing the world. As David Bohm incisively pointed out in discussing the development of modern physics:

> . . . the basic elements out of which the world was as-

213

sumed to be constructed were effectively conceived of as mechanical parts, each of which has its place in a universal machine. . . . The nature of these parts is rigidly fixed and does not grow out of the context in which they are placed, nor does it change as a result of the actions of other parts.[1]

One need but change a few words to describe "scientific management." The mechanistic interpretation of reality clearly underlay the efforts toward the "one best mechanical way," or toward "standard times." The nature of the "parts" of "scientific management," to paraphrase Bohm, did not grow out of the context in which they were placed. Their nature was thought to be fixed and unchanging, whatever the context.

The influence of the Newtonian approach is understandable, for Newton's laws triggered a revolution in our understanding of the universe. "Scientific management," of course, also triggered its own revolution in the study of productive organization. There is a monumental difference, however. It soon became obvious in the physical sciences that Newton's laws would hold only in rather special cases. This point of view is only now gaining substantial currency among users of "scientific management."

There is a substantial irony in the influence of the Newtonian approach, however. Even near the turn of the century, just as the Newtonian approach was gaining some currency in the study of social organization, it was becoming increasingly clear that the approach was but a baby step toward a full comprehension of our environment. To make a very long story painfully short, the "objects" of Newton's laws underwent a dramatic transformation. They had to be considered as *in various "fields,"* which affected them differently. Otherwise it was not possible to account for many observed phenomena. The behavior of these "objects," it turned out, was not fixed as had been assumed. The new focus of interest, in sum, continued to be upon relations between objects, but only as they are influenced by the properties of the particular field in which they happen to exist at any moment. Changes in field properties would cause changes in the behavior of objects in the field.

This is not so otherworldly as it may sound. In terms of

[1] David Bohm, *Causality and Chance in Modern Physics* (New York: Harper Torchbooks, 1957), p. 38.

practical effect, "scientific management" had put its money on a horse which had already demonstrated that it could not stay with the field of phenomena it had to explain. The utopian orientation of "scientific management," in addition, prevented calling the bet off.

Of even more practical relevance for present purposes, small-group analysis is a field approach. The analysis above makes this point in manifold ways. In the small-group field in the Patent Office, the O & M theory had a limited applicability. Similarly, the behavior of individuals cannot be understood apart from understanding the particular "fields" within which they behave. The small group is one of the important "fields." Recall the changes in the behavior of the two children switched between groups with different atmospheres, or "field" properties. In contrast, the "formal approach" to organization tended to assume that man's properties were singular and fixed. Once these properties (such as speed of hand) were determined, it was assumed, that was that. There was little place for the recognition of the effect of the various psychological "fields" within which these properties would exist.[2] As a result, the "formal approach" to organization—like Newton's laws—applied only in very special cases.

A final practical consequence of the importance of a "field" approach also strikes close to home. As in the physical sciences, two things must happen: the importance of "field" properties must be recognized; and something must be done about exploiting that importance. This book attempts to contribute toward both of these ends. Small-group analysis goes part of the way in increasing the comprehensiveness of the O & M approach by recognizing one "field" and its properties which may influence O & M applications.

There are other substantial reasons for the utopian approach of traditional organization theory. Little work in the "behavioral approach" to organization was available in the developmental days

[2] Early workers were not insensitive to social influences. Taylor, for example, had personally felt group pressure on the job. He had "soldiered" on the job (that is, helped restrict output) as a young man. Moreover, he felt no guilt about doing so, a stark indicator of the magnitude of social influence, given Taylor's deeply-held views against soldiering. See Frederick W. Taylor, *Scientific Management*, especially p. 771. But such sensitivity was not developed to the point that the O & M theory was modified.

of traditional organization theory, for example. Thus the *early* orientation of organization theory is reasonable. The tendency has been, however, for the *early* orientation to become the *only* orientation. Most students have accepted the early lack of work on behavior in organizations as a kind of natural law that such work was either impossible or unnecessary.

There are, of course, well-known exceptions to this making a virtue of a lack of knowledge. Fayol, for example, never lost sight of the bias of the early work, even though it was not possible to do much about it via the building of a behavioral theory for organization. Thus he wrote, "If we could eliminate the human factor, it would be easy enough to build up an organization. . . . But we cannot build up an effective organization simply by dividing men into groups and assigning them functions."[3] Fayol's business success suggests that he was able to act effectively within the framework of his own ideas. But the impact of his insight upon research was long delayed and is still limited. Organization theory has tended to be what Fayol thought it ought not to be: that is, "simply . . . dividing men into groups and giving them functions."

Finally, a utopian approach is more obvious and less difficult. The development of propositions dealing with man's characteristics as they are assumed to be, in short, is infinitely easier than the isolation of man's characteristics as they are. Early work may be pardoned for taking the natural avenue of the utopian approach.

The utopian approach characteristic of classical mechanics and much other work aided and abetted this all-too-understandable tendency. Thus classical mechanics assumed the conservation of mechanical energy and such analytical conveniences as non-frictionless machines and non-extensible lines. The axiom of the physiological individual was in good company, although its use was not nearly as careful as the use of similarly utopian properties in other areas of endeavor.

This methodological evaluation is also supported by the O & M theory's attempt to have its methodological cake and to eat it as well. The theory attempts to avoid the complexities of empirical theory: it is based not upon what the empirical world is like, but upon how the empirical world *would be most simple.*

[3] Henri Fayol, *Administration Industrielle et Général* (Paris: Dunod, 1925), p. 83. Trans. R.T.G.

216

But, paradoxically, O & M theory purportedly provides a model for empirical counterparts at the same time that it is independent of the complexity of the empirical world.

Similarly, the O & M theory at once profits from the analytical convenience of utopian theory and at the same time fails to respect the limits of that type of theory. The reference is to the neglect of the empirical and normative checks which must be applied to the *use*, as opposed to the *development*, of any utopian model. But here O & M theory is a victim of its own confusion, for an empirical check on the theory would require a comprehensive empirical theory. And this, of course, is what utopian theory attempts to avoid!

2. The "Claim All Successes" Gambit

The common use of the gambit of "claiming all successes" also illustrates the desire of workers using the "formal approach" to have it all ways.

The Budget Bureau report dealing with the Patent Office reorganization, to explain, emphasized these effects in the inter-mediate-run productivity increase in the Copy-Pulling Section: series organization, specialization, social isolation, and various mechanical elements. This report also summarized a second reorganization which increased production in another federal agency. It noted that, although accurate production figures are not available, "it is estimated . . . that production has doubled under the new plan." But this reorganization contrasted sharply with the Patent Office episode. The increased production seems to have been more psychologically than physiologically based. This increase, it was explained, occurred because:

WORKER INTEREST AND SATISFACTION—*morale* in general—was enhanced in [agency X], by establishing *parallel teams* doing identical work. The *increased interest* apparently arose from the ability of the worker to relate what he does to *a completed product*, the development of *team spirit* and *friendly competition* among teams, the *greater subject-matter variety of work*, and the increase in promotional opportunities. . . .[4]

[4] *Production Planning and Control in Office Operations*, p. 47. Italics supplied.

217

This description of the work-process change is hardly consistent with the theory from which the Patent Office work-process changes were derived. The contrasts abound: parallel versus serial organization; job enlargement versus job reduction; the worker as a being with psychological needs whose accommodation can have substantial on-the-job benefits for the formal organization versus a physiological caricature of man; the emphasis upon team, or group, spirit versus the emphasis on the socially isolated individual; and "friendly competition" as opposed to the high-threat condition implied by the traditional theory of organization. These are no accidental differences. They strike at the heart of the propositions assumed in the utopian theory underlying the Patent Office reorganization.

But the challenge to reformulate the bases of traditional organization theory was spurned. Thus the Budget Bureau report credibly explained that reorganization must acknowledge "the conditions faced." But the "condition" cited as making the difference indicates the bias of existing theory: "The difference in solution was largely the result of the difference in work volume, as indicated by the relative sizes of the working force."[5] Parallel organization in the Patent Office would have resulted in teams too small to be efficient, went the report's explanation. But the almost 600 personnel in Agency X could be organized in parallel fashion. In contrast, small units can be very efficient, in terms of both productivity and employee satisfaction.

3. An O & M Proposition from Three Viewpoints: A Summary

The empirical inadequacy of the O & M theory also may be illustrated through a review of the evidence applicable to one of that theory's propositions. The proposition chosen for illustrative purposes is that authority is a formal, one-line relation. This concentration does not sacrifice effectiveness, for the difficulties with this proposition illustrate the difficulties with the others.

Primarily, the analysis above should demonstrate the existence

[5] *Ibid.*, p. 41.

of a "behavioral organization" which exists along with the "formal organization." The very existence of such a behavioral organization poses a challenge to the theoretical proposition that authority is a formal, one-line relation. This challenge affects both emphases of the proposition, the "formal" and the "one-line." The behavioral organization exercises significant control over its members. In doing so, it competes to varying degrees with the formal organization, and this control is emotional and social rather than designed and formal.

That is, the O & M theory provides for a one-way relation. This, whatever else, certainly simplifies matters. The stress on the "behavioral organization," in contrast, implies a cross-pressure condition.

This contrast of simplicity and complexity deserves further analysis. The control exercised by the behavioral organization might be called "influence," or "power," to differentiate it from the "legitimate authority" of the formal organization. But this distinction begins to blur, for influence often receives the sanction of legitimate authority. For example, delegation might sanction a relation which had in fact existed for some time. The monolithic proposition of authority as a formal, one-line relation obscures such significant byplay. The control of behavior in organizations, indeed, requires at least a fourfold approach. Figure 19 gives such a breakdown.

The O & M theory does not encompass the complexity of Figure 19. Category I alone is implied in the O & M theory. This is patently insufficient. Category II helps, for a work unit might prescribe the kind of clothes which are socially acceptable on the job, to illustrate. O & M theory does not provide for such control of behavior. Of course, the subject matter of control may be of no concern to the formal organization in many cases. But Category II also includes such control sequences as output restriction, in which the formal organization has a very substantial interest. However, Categories III and IV probably include the bulk of control sequences in organization. These categories include the subtle interaction of formal and behavioral factors which is a major part of what we call "organization" in our convenient, but unrevealing, shorthand.

But even the breakdown in Figure 19 is simplistic, for the "behavioral organization" is not a monolith. It may include a

I	II	III	IV
Formal Organization	Behavioral Organization	Behavioral Organization as it affects Formal Organization	Formal Organization as it affects Behavioral Organization
in areas which conflict or are non-overlapping		in areas of mutual adjustment	

FIGURE 19. *An Organization's Authority-Influence Patterns by Sources*

variety of levels of social organization. Consider the small group, personality, and culture. Any or all may control the behavior of individuals. Figure 19 would have to be far more complex to provide for the effects of these levels of social organization on behavior. The formal, one-line concept of authority, of course, neglects these levels of social organization.

The important effects on behavior in organizations deriving from these levels of social organization may be outlined briefly. Enough, first, has been written of the importance of the small group in the control of the behavior of its members, sometimes in areas of great interest to the formal organization. This analysis, if nothing else, should establish that neither a "formal" nor a "one-line" concept of authority is sufficient to describe empirical reality. The small group exercises behavioral, as opposed to formal, influence, and it provides an alternate authoritative source for individuals, who often must reconcile its demands with those of the formal organization. Authority, then, has no single face.

Personality differences also challenge the theoretical proposition that authority is a formal, one-line relation. These personality differences, moreover, undermine the prediction that organization efficiency will be highest under the condition of formal, one-line authority.

The point may be brought home squarely. Consider the "response repertoire" concept. Some people rank authoritarian behaviors high in their response repertoires. Such individuals would be most comfortable, over the long run, in a directive atmosphere. These individuals also might be efficient and satisfied workers under the formal, one-line conception of authority. But many people (and most of those studied thus far) are quite uncomfortable within this context of traditional organization theory. Their discomfort may be reflected in low productivity, dissatisfaction, or neurotic symptoms.

The proposition that authority is a formal, one-line relation also overlooks cultural differences. For our purposes, "culture" may be defined as "the total pattern of living developed by a group of human beings which is passed on from generation to generation." These cultural patterns are not necessarily consistent with the presumptions about how people will behave which are built into traditional organization theory. Culture, like the small group and personality, contributes to making life in organizations one of cross-pressures.

A homely example illustrates the point here. A work process in a shoe factory had been organized so that its component steps were arranged in ascending order of skill and pay. A reorganization—consistent with traditional organization theory—attempted to change this "vertical" organization to a "horizontal" one. That is, the new work process included a number of component steps of a low and similar order of skill. The proposition of authority as a formal, one-line relation requires the success of this attempt. The sweetening of the pot—by allowing the operators to retain their old rates on less skilled jobs—does not undercut this expectation.

The outcome: stubborn resistance. The reduced skill level of the jobs contributed to this result. But more important, apparently, the initial "vertical" organization coincided with the social structure of the community from which the workers were drawn. Thus workers of different nationalities performed each step in the "vertical" work process, and the status of each job coincided with the status of the nationality group in the community. These work units even recruited and trained members of their own nationality group when replacements were necessary. The "horizontal" organization, then, destroyed this congruence of rank within the organization and rank within the community.[6] Hence the resistance.

Cultural differences also were reflected less strikingly in the

[6] Lloyd W. Warner and J. O. Low, *The Social Structure of the Modern Factory* (New Haven: Yale, 1947), p. 81.

analysis above. In general, not all individuals would react negatively to the type of authority implied in traditional organization theory. The character of the cultures within which people mature would have much to do with the reactions of individuals to any style of authority. To explain, assume a general cultural training which ranks permissive behaviors high in the response repertoires of most members of a particular "society." O & M theory would not be very useful. Indeed, the persistent use of high threat-levels on individuals who rank permissive behaviors highly often will boomerang: the threat will not be tolerated meekly and—overtly or covertly, immediately or later—output will suffer.

The point is not academic. The common association of a permissive atmosphere with high output clearly reflects that most subjects in existing studies have experienced a cultural training which favors permissive behaviors. O & M theory, then, seems to buck substantial social forces.

4. Technique and Theory:
"The Case of the Inappropriate Good Morning"

The analysis of the empirical inadequacies of the formal approach to organization may seem to put Frederick W. Taylor in an unfavorable light. His work, of course, did have its limits. But these limits derive in most part from what Taylor and his followers did in the formal approach, and what they did was quite different from what Taylor said ought to be done.

In broadest outline, that is, the analysis above makes Taylor a good prophet, for he clearly recognized the distinctions between techniques (time-and-motion analysis and the like) and theory. The techniques in and of themselves were simply not up to the job of restructuring work processes. They were static tools; they required direction to give them life.

Taylor attempted to give life to his techniques in two ways. First, he emphasized the need for *value limits* on the use of his techniques. This point will be stressed in the next section. Here note only the importance of a set of values, an ethical theory, to guide the applications of neutral techniques. Illustratively, an effective grip on a knife is a technique. It makes some difference whether the grip is used to peel an apple or to slit a throat.

O & M techniques are similarly neutral. That is, the techniques may yield such information as: Job X is composed of the sub-operations $a_1, a_2 \ldots a_n$, which must be performed in a certain order. But the technique does not tell one how the suboperations should be organized. Should one worker perform each sub-operation? Or should one worker perform all of the subopera-tions? The choice of a pattern of organization, in part, will depend upon ethical considerations. Which pattern of organi-zation ought to be used to guide the behavior of workers? How will the pattern be enforced? These are some of the guiding ethical questions.

Taylor also attempted to give life to his techniques, second, by emphasizing the need for *empirical limits* on their use. Thus the choice of the pattern of organization, in part, will depend upon a theory of what leads to what under which conditions. Which pattern of organization is more effective under which conditions? This is the type of guiding research question which must be investigated. The analysis above, of course, attempted to present a partial empirical theory of the conditions under which O & M applications might be successful. Or, more pre-cisely, the analysis tried to outline those conditions under which O & M techniques failed because of the theory on which they were based.

Taylor reflected this concern for limiting empirical conditions in many ways. Thus he cited the need for the development of a "true science," by which he seems to have meant an empirical theory which listed the conditions for successful and unsuccess-ful applications. This is, of course, a large order to fill, but it is to Taylor's credit that he recognized the job to be done. It has not been done, however.

The O & M application reviewed above gave short shrift to these ethical and empirical limits which Taylor emphasized. The O & M theory did this neatly. That is, it made some assumptions about what things were really like (e.g., the axiom of the physiological individual). Moreover, the O & M theory implied that these assumptions about what things were really like also were statements of desirable states of affairs. Thus the empirical problem was handled as a rational matter, begging important value problems in the process. This seemed con-venient, but the procedure has a way of leading to awkward consequences, as in the reorganization of the Patent Office.

223

But we may seem to be building a castle of air, for the distinction between techniques and theory is often unrecognized. An illustration thus usefully further establishes the distinction, if it does not already exist in the reader's mind.

Consider "The Case of the Inappropriate 'Good Morning.' " The following "clinical report" outlines the facts of the case. The case is not hypothetical, although I cannot recall its source.

SYMPTOMS: Supervisor A experiences great difficulties with the employees in his work unit. The atmosphere fairly crackles with tension. Output suffers.

DIAGNOSIS: Supervisor A pays only disdainful attention to his workers. He is aloof from them, seems unfriendly.

REMEDY: Say "good morning" to the employees to establish more friendly relations, improve the atmosphere, and raise productivity.

EFFECTS: Resentment grows and productivity drops still further.

"The Case of the Inappropriate 'Good Morning' " reflects the failure of a technique which is not supported by an adequate theory. To explain, Supervisor A was willing to employ the technique, but he did not change his theory of the factors which encourage an atmosphere favorable to reasonable productivity. Supervisor A still felt his subordinates had no individuality, were unimportant save as "factors of production." His employees, at the same time, were anxious to demonstrate their individuality. They did so by hitting the supervisor where it hurt, that is, by raising the question of the supervisor's ability to lead his men.

Consequently, Supervisor A's use of the technique was a self-defeating one, for it more sharply reflected his disdain for his employees than when he had not used the technique. Thus Supervisor A would sometimes say "good morning" three or four times to the same person, thus proving what everyone had suspected. Like Pavlov's dog, Supervisor A said "good morning" unreflectively to anything that moved. This inspired little enthusiasm among the employees, who did not appreciate being treated like anything that moved.

The "good morning" technique, then, is neutral. The theory underlying its use gives it meaning. Supervisor A's theory made the technique a cause of further difficulty, rather than a remedy for an existing difficulty.

"The Case of the Inappropriate 'Good Morning'" has a moral which holds for O & M applications. O & M techniques must be based upon an adequate theory detailing where and when they will work, an empirical theory of what is related to what. Traditional organization theory—with all its simplicity— is an inadequate support for O & M techniques. Small-group analysis—with its complexity of cohesiveness, status, norms, and the rest—supplies some of the where-and-when to make O & M techniques "take" better.

5. Can a Utopian Theory Do the Job?

Of course, empirical factors may be considered irrelevant. An O & M man might say, "I know that authority is sometimes neither formal nor one-way. My theory tells *only how things should be if you want high effectiveness*." Such a claim deserves close attention, for the Patent Office "experimentation" establishes that—for at least a limited period—there are techniques available which permit the approximation of the condition of authority as formal and one-way. High output also was attained.

This position of the O & M man, then, must be evaluated carefully. Three factors will be stressed. First, the position is a very convenient one, for when an O & M application does not have the expected results, the ready apology is that the conditions were not favorable.

Second, the position tends to encourage the slighting of an important question: Will the "proper conditions" for a successful O & M application occur often enough to support the usefulness of the theory? Several considerations rule out an unqualified "Yes." Thus high threat—often necessary to create the "proper conditions" for an O & M application—probably cannot be sustained over the long run without substantial negative consequences, at least in such complex societies as ours. The Patent Office experience supports this position. Moreover, the risk implicit in high-threat techniques need not be chanced, for small-group theory permits greater specificity. And it often leads to results which are at least as favorable as those of O & M theory, without the same risk of long-run reaction.

225

Third, a final point clinches the argument against the position attributed above to the O & M man. Forget the nagging question of whether the O & M man can reasonably expect the conditions presupposed in traditional organization theory to exist often enough or long enough to make his efforts worth while. Let us consider only those cases in which the conditions presupposed by traditional organization theory *do exist*. If the O & M theory is to be supported, effectiveness must be high at least in such cases. If you cannot win with a stacked deck, in short, you really should not play the game.

Much evidence contradicts flatly the expectations derived from traditional organization theory, even under these extremely restrictive limits. Thus when the O & M propositions do describe the state of affairs in an organization (e.g., close supervision), effectiveness often is low. And when the propositions do not describe the state of affairs (e.g., general supervision), effectiveness often is high. The reader need only refer to much of Chapters 5 and 6 for supporting evidence. This evidence is quite embarrassing to a theory which presumes to detail the nature of the most efficient organization set-up.

SOME NORMATIVE PROBLEMS

OF ORGANIZATION THEORY

O & M applications also must respect value limits. These limits are a good deal more difficult to test than the empirical limits, and individuals do not always share similar values. Illustratively, you learn decisively about gravity (an element in an empirical theory) by assorted bumps and bruises. They vividly bring home what the body can do and what it cannot do, given the nature of the world. The determination of value limits is based upon no such easy pleasure-pain calculation. Indeed, the generality of opinion over the ages has always held that a final judgment about one's values must wait on the afterlife. But no matter. The problem of the things we want as moral beings, the things we value as ends, is a tough nut to crack. No wonder, then, that great differences often exist in values held by individuals.

But these value limits cannot be neglected, whatever the problems associated with them. Values underlie all behavior, whether we like it or not. Even if we chose to behave randomly, we have made a value choice. So we will make value choices, whether we like it or not, whether we acknowledge it or not. And these choices of values will affect our behavior. We can at least recognize this in thinking about our theories of organization, even if we cannot agree on what the value limits ought to be.

The story should be a familiar one. In sum, the propositions of the O & M theory must be evaluated normatively if the theory is used as a model for empirical counterparts. No theory of organization, indeed, can avoid this problem.[7] This holds equally for utopian theories and goal-based, empirical theories.

Of course, many attempts at avoidance have been made. Indeed, the cat is out of the bag when *a* theory of organization is mentioned, as is usually the case. In contrast, there is an endless variety of organization theories—goal-based, empirical theories—which can be developed from the same empirical data. For example, accept as empirical fact that social factors are important on the job. This does not settle the question of how such social factors are to be treated in an organization theory, for one theory might attempt to tie such social factors into the purposes of the formal organization, and another theory might attempt to eliminate the factors.

The critical element in organization theory, then, is the set of values which the various organization theories attempt to achieve. Empirical data do not and cannot provide such sets of values. The more comprehensive our empirical knowledge, however, the more effective we will become in attaining whatever normative goals it is that we set for ourselves.

"Efficiency" Is Not Enough

The all-too-convenient tendency in organization theory has been to fall back upon a narrow dollars-and-cents concept of efficiency. This is, of course, a value preference. Some students, however, have argued that this concept is a universal necessity and not a value at all. As one student noted, "All values but

[7] See my review of March and Simon, *Organizations*, in *Midwest Journal of Political Science*, III (November, 1959), 404–7.

efficiency are environmental."[8] By this he meant, apparently, that only a narrowly-based efficiency could underlie organization theory.

There is nothing universal or inevitable about such a concept of efficiency (or any other), however, although it has an obvious short-run appeal to some hirers of the efforts of men. For example, Japan is a heavily industrialized country with a high level of productivity. But an O & M man could hardly go into the Japanese counterpart of the Patent Office and promote the highest-producing copy pullers to supervisors. Promotion is based largely on age, even when it is necessary to redesign the duties of a position to suit a person of a certain age who is not capable. Pay, similarly, is based on a number of very complicated considerations which have little or nothing to do with productivity. The use of threat also would probably be limited, for the exertion and the exposure to overt threat might cause both the supervisor and his employees to "lose face" and perhaps in very extreme cases force them to redeem themselves in the eyes of their ancestors by ceremonial suicide.[9] *For their normative goals*—which include a high degree of respect for age—their system is very efficient.

Statements of the purported universality of narrow definitions of efficiency only reveal the culture-boundedness of traditional organization theory. "Efficiency" must always be understood as "efficiency for a specific set of goals." And these goal sets may range from least cost to maximum facilitation of friendly contact on the job.

As the treatment should make clear, in addition, O & M theory is not always most "efficient" even in terms of a least-cost concept of efficiency. Often other approaches encourage higher output and higher member satisfaction. This spotlights the question of normative choice, of course.

But, whether or not an alternative theory of organization provides similar results, the O & M theory requires a hard look at its normative implications. This question, for example, must be asked: Do we want people to think and act as if authority were a formal, one-line relation? In many cases, a "Yes" answer

[8] Luther Gulick, "Science, Values and Public Administration," in Gulick and Urwick, *Papers on the Science of Administration*, p. 192.
[9] James Abbeglen, *The Japanese Factory* (Glencoe, Ill.: Free Press, 1958).

may not be *directly* dangerous. But the crucial factor is still the *content* of authoritative pronouncements, not the mere fact that they have been given. That is, should *any* order be obeyed simply because it is given by a formal superior? This is a tough question. But it must be faced.

Two Notes

Two brief notes will conclude this summary. First, this analysis implies that the case report does not tell all that happened that was of significance. The lesson is patent: current social findings apply a continually increasing pressure for case writers to change both the theory and the concepts underlying their efforts. Thus far, this pressure has been capped (and sometimes with a vengeance, as I have had occasion to learn).

Progress is being made. For example, the Inter-University Case Program's Working Group on Research has recently taken some promising preliminary steps toward exploiting recent behavioral advances. As with other case programs, however, such exploitation is coming very slowly. Indeed, it is coming more slowly than the progress of work such as that in small-group analysis warrants. Perhaps this volume will provide some impetus toward the required exploitation.

Second, this analysis implies many opportunties for the wide use of small-group analysis in the study and practice of organization and management. The future holds special promise. But even as things stand today, the O & M practitioner or student of organization ought to be more prepared for the next Patent Office case which comes along.

This volume, then, may be characterized briefly. It is a review of substantial existing research, and it is a prologue to the more sophisticated research to come.

INDEX

PRINTED IN U.S.A.